Crime in England 1688–

Crime in England 1688–1815 covers the 'long' eighteenth century, a period which saw huge and far-reaching changes in criminal justice history. These changes included the introduction of transportation overseas as an alternative to the death penalty, the growth of the magistracy, the birth of professional policing, increasingly harsh sentencing of those who offended against property-owners and the rapid expansion of the popular press, which fuelled debate and interest in all matters criminal. Utilising both primary and secondary source material, this book discusses a number of topics such as punishment, detection of offenders, gender and the criminal justice system and crime in contemporaneous popular culture and literature.

This book is designed for both the criminal justice history/criminology undergraduate and the general reader, with a lively and immediately approachable style. The use of carefully selected case studies is designed to show how the study of criminal justice history can be used to illuminate modern-day criminological debate and discourse. It includes a brief review of past and current literature on the topic of crime in eighteenth-century England and Wales, and also emphasises why knowledge of the history of crime and criminal justice is important to present-day criminologists. Together with its companion volumes, it will provide an invaluable aid to students of both criminal justice history and criminology.

David J. Cox is currently employed at Wolverhampton University, specialising in Criminal Justice History and Policing History. Previously, David has worked at Keele and Plymouth Universities as a Research Associate/Fellow as well as being the former Editor of *The Blackcountryman*, the quarterly journal of the Black Country Society. He gained a PhD in Modern History from Lancaster University in 2006.

History of Crime in the UK and Ireland
Series editor: Professor Barry Godfrey
University of Liverpool, UK

Rarely do we get the opportunity to study criminal history across the British Isles, or across such a long time period. *History of Crime in the UK and Ireland* is a series which provides an opportunity to contrast experiences in various geographical regions and determine how these situations changed – with slow evolution or dramatic speed – and with what results. It brings together data, thought, opinion and new theories from an established group of scholars that draw upon a wide range of existing and new research. Using case studies, examples from contemporary media, biographical life studies and thoughts and ideas on new historical methods, the authors construct lively debates on crime and the law, policing, prosecution and punishment. Together, this series of books builds up a rich but accessible history of crime and its control in the British Isles.

1   Crime in England 1688–1815
   David J. Cox

Crime in England 1688–1815

David J. Cox

Routledge
Taylor & Francis Group

LONDON AND NEW YORK

First published 2014
by Routledge
2 Park Square, Milton Park, Abingdon, Oxfordshire OX14 4RN

and by Routledge
711 Third Avenue, New York, NY 10017

First issued in paperback 2015

Routledge is an imprint of the Taylor & Francis Group, an informa business

British Library Cataloguing in Publication Data
A catalogue record for this book is available from the British Library

Library of Congress Cataloging in Publication Data
Library of Congress Control Number: 2013949171

ISBN 13: 978-1-138-92238-9 (pbk)
ISBN 13: 978-0-415-50183-5 (hbk)

Typeset in Times New Roman
by Sunrise Setting Ltd, Paignton, UK

Dedicated to my father, Frank, and my late mother, May

Contents

Acknowledgements

This book is the result of many misspent hours in archives and record offices. I would therefore like to take this opportunity to thank all of the staff of the numerous repositories that I consulted during the researching of this book. I would particularly like to thank the staff at the National Archives, Kew, which over the past few years has begun to feel like a second home to me.

I also owe a huge debt of gratitude and appreciation to those historians and other experts whose research is frequently discussed and quoted in this book; without their often groundbreaking work in the field of policing and crime history this publication would not have been possible. Special thanks go to John Beattie and Clive Emsley, as well as to Tim Hitchcock, Robert Shoemaker and the many others that created both the *Old Bailey Proceedings Online* and *London Lives*.

I would also like to record my thanks to Barry Godfrey (series editor) and the team at Routledge, especially to Nicola Hartley, who has been very helpful and supportive.

Finally, tracing the details of crimes that took place over 200 years ago is, despite historians' best efforts, not an exact science. I have been as meticulous and methodical as possible in my research, but accept responsibility for any errors or omissions that may remain.

David J. Cox, March 2013

Abbreviations

BL	British Library
CUP	Cambridge University Press
IUP	Irish University Press
LL	*London Lives, 1690–1800*
MUP	Manchester University Press
OA	Ordinary's *Account*
OBP	*The Old Bailey Proceedings Online, 1674–1913*
OU	Open University
OUP	Oxford University Press
PP	Parliamentary Papers
PUP	Princeton University Press
TNA	The National Archives
VCH	Victoria County History
YUP	Yale University Press

Information panel 1

Criminal courts in eighteenth-century England

During the period covered by this book criminal cases were first brought before one or more justices of the peace (JP) or magistrates – the terms are interchangeable – at Petty Sessions courts, which were held as and when the need arose and which were usually convened at a local community venue such as a public house, or occasionally at a magistrate's home. For more serious cases, magistrates (who were all male – women were not allowed to sit as magistrates until 1919) could send the case up to Quarter Sessions, which, as their name implies, were held every quarter (January, April, July and October), usually in the county town. These were presided over by county magistrates and further differed from Petty Sessions in that presented cases were heard first before a Grand Jury (a body of influential propertied men who decided if a case should proceed to trial – a system that also applied to the higher court of Assizes and which was not abolished until 1933), and then before a jury of twelve selected men (it was not until 1919 that women were given limited rights to sit on juries).[1] In cases where the magistrates felt that they were unqualified to deal with the complex or serious nature of a crime (such as murder) defendants could be imprisoned for an often considerable period to await trial at the next County Assizes, which were presided over by State-appointed judges and which normally took place twice a year, usually in the county town, at Lent (March/April) and Trinity or Summer (July/August). London's equivalent to the Assizes was the Old Bailey. A third Assize court – the Winter Assizes – could also be held if warranted by pressure of number of cases waiting to be tried in any particular year. The system of Petty Sessions, Quarter Sessions and Assizes was finally swept away by the passing of the Courts Act 1971 (19 & 20 Eliz. II c.23), which replaced the old system with Magistrates' Courts (which deal with petty offences) and the Crown Court (which hears more serious criminal cases).

Note

1 Sex Disqualification (Removal) Act 1919 (9 & 10 Geo. V c.71).

Information panel 2

The pre-decimal currency system

Throughout the period under discussion in this book the pre-decimal system of currency was utilized. Prior to decimalization in 1971 the British currency system was based on the ancient and complex system known as L.S.D. (derived from the Latin *librae, solidi* and *denarii*), more commonly known as £ (pounds), s. (shillings) and d. (pence). £1 was made up of 240 pennies (because a pound in weight of silver originally made that number of silver pennies), twelve of which made a shilling. The penny itself was subdivided into farthings (four of which made a penny) or halfpennies (two of which made a penny). To further complicate the matter there were also other coins of various denominations, including half-crowns (worth 2 shillings and 6 pennies) and florins (worth 2 shillings). A guinea (a solid gold coin) had its worth officially set at £1 and one shilling (i.e. twenty-one shillings) between 1717 and 1816. Another coin, the solid gold sovereign, ostensibly worth £1, had been in circulation in the medieval period, but was withdrawn between 1604 and 1817.

It is extremely difficult, if not ultimately impossible, to accurately equate monetary values from historical periods to those of the present day, owing to the fluctuating relative costs of and demand for basic goods and foods (for example, staple foodstuffs such as bread have become much cheaper, while property prices have risen exponentially), but a multiplication of somewhere in the magnitude of between 100 and 150 can generally be made to eighteenth- and early nineteenth-century figures in order to roughly estimate their present-day values.[1]

Note

1 For a fascinating overview of inflation and relative purchasing power over the past millennium, see Peter Wilsher, *The Pound in Your Pocket 1870–1970* (London: Cassell, 1970). A very useful website for price comparisons between the eighteenth century and today can be found at www.nationalarchives.gov.uk/currency/. This site provides both a currency converter and a facility to see the relative buying power of a given amount of money in two periods.

1 Introduction

Historical and geographical scope

This volume of the series *History of Crime in the UK and Ireland* covers 1688–1815, a period often referred to as the 'long' eighteenth century.[1] It therefore spans events from the so-called 'Glorious Revolution' (which resulted in the enforced removal of James II and the accession of his Dutch son-in-law William III and daughter Mary II) to the triumph of the duke of Wellington's victory over Napoleon at the Battle of Waterloo. It concerns itself primarily with England, with occasional passing mention of Wales, which had formally become a part of the Kingdom of Great Britain in 1536 and which was largely governed on the same legal principles as England, although there remained a clear division with regard to language and culture.

Scotland was a separate kingdom at the start of the period; it was not until the Acts of Union 1707 (6 Anne c.11 and Anne c.7) that it was joined politically with England and Wales (although the crowns of Scotland and England had merged in 1603 following the accession of James VI of Scotland to the English throne, whereby he also became James I of England). Similarly, Ireland remained a separate political entity until the Acts of Union 1800 (39 & 40 Geo. III c.67 and 40 Geo. III c.38). Throughout the eighteenth century both Scotland and Ireland enjoyed very different legal and judicial systems, and therefore these two countries remain largely outside the scope of this volume.[2]

Rationale

The book is written with both the criminal justice history/criminology student and the interested general reader in mind. It assumes no prior specialized knowledge of criminal justice history or criminology and it concisely describes and investigates key concepts and issues within a historical framework. The volume is by both necessity and design an overview of criminal justice history of the period. Therefore, a comprehensive Bibliography is included for those readers who wish to carry out more detailed study into particular aspects featured in the book, and all acts of parliament have been fully referenced to enable those interested in pursuing the legal aspect of a particular subject or case study to do so.[3]

A timeline of relevant major events is also included (see Appendix) in order to enable the reader to further contextualize the developments in criminal justice history within the general history of England during the period. Although part of a series dealing with the criminal history of the United Kingdom and Ireland during the past three centuries, this book is also intended to be a stand-alone introduction to the study of English criminal justice history in the eighteenth century.

It is hoped that, after reading this book (along with its companion volumes), the reader who is interested in criminology/criminal justice history or is studying either subject at university or college will be better equipped to understand how the past has influenced the development of present-day criminological thought. Although it is a well-worn truism that history never repeats itself, nevertheless a knowledge of what happened in similar circumstances in the past can undoubtedly inform our understanding of the present; as the Roman orator Marcus Tullius Cicero (106–43 BC) memorably stated, 'to be ignorant of what occurred before one was born is to remain forever a child'.[4] What seem at first glance to be purely contemporaneous debates about the number of people undergoing sentence, the merits and drawbacks of incarceration as a punishment, the right not to be detained without charge, ever-increasing public and private surveillance, the role of the State in preventing terrorism and the costs of policing crime all have their origins in our common past, and this book will illustrate how many of these debates were first aired in the eighteenth century.

The period also saw many challenges and changes to the organization of authority in the nation state, together with the beginning of mass urbanization and manufacturing. The nature of what constituted crime and criminal behaviour and the ways in which perceived criminals were dealt with also changed markedly throughout the century. This volume describes these developments in detail, with several aspects being further highlighted by the use of carefully selected and researched case studies. It documents the use of new methods of punishment and incarceration in the period, with a movement from punishing the body to early forms of imprisonment (Bridewells, Houses of Correction, etc.), and also explores concepts such as the use of transportation of offenders to a foreign land as a perceived means of 'cost-effective' punishment, 'social crime' and the development of the 'Poor Law' and the concomitant division of the poor into the needy or the indolent. It also investigates and explains the dramatic rise in contemporary literature about 'troublesome' groups in society – sturdy beggars, disobedient apprentices, vagrants and highwaymen, to name but a few.

While present-day Britain is fortunate in possessing a reasonably robust and fair legislature and judiciary, together with largely democratically accountable police forces (although the extent of this accountability has been increasingly questioned in recent years, not least in the Metropolitan Police's mishandling of several high-profile situations and the behaviour of members of South Yorkshire Police in relation to the Hillsborough disaster), this has not always been the case.[5] This book shows that many of the constituents forming the bedrock of our present criminal justice system, including the right to defend oneself before a jury, the expectation of receiving a fair trial, the right to appeal after judgement, the existence of a professional, full-time and publicly funded accountable police force, the need for prosecutors to prove a defendant's guilt rather than a defendant prove his/her innocence, the reliance on judges and juries to be apolitical and impartial and, finally, the knowledge that the majority of offenders are sentenced to defined and finite terms of imprisonment within regulated prisons, are in fact all relatively modern constructs.[6] Many of our predecessors (especially if poor) simply could not depend on the majority of these rights.

Sources

This book uses a wide variety of primary and secondary sources in its investigation of the criminal justice history of early modern Britain. With regard to primary sources, it relies to a great extent on the bureaucratic nature of the English legal system; an enormous posthumous debt is owed by historians and researchers to the untold legions of clerks who meticulously recorded many aspects of their daily work for posterity (albeit often unwittingly). Surviving Assize records and Quarter Sessions records (including sessions books, order books and minute books), together with justices' notebooks and other records of the various lesser courts operating from the early modern period, have proved an invaluable mine of information to modern historians.[7] Many Petty and Quarter Sessions records have fortunately been deposited over the intervening years within county/city archives or record offices, while the National Archives hold a staggering amount of detail on Assize trials from the twelfth century through to the twentieth century, as well as a wealth of information on many other aspects of criminal justice history. The proceedings of the Old Bailey from 1674 to 1913 (more than 100,000 trials) have recently been made freely available online and this resource, together with its companion website *London Lives*, has transformed research capability with regard to the criminal history of the metropolis.[8]

From the mid-seventeenth century onward the rapid increase in the publication of popular reading material in the form of newspapers, broadsheets, trial pamphlets and propaganda (both pro- and anti-Government) has provided the modern historian with an additional set of useful primary resources.[9] A surprising amount of privately published material also survives and this archive gives the historian and criminologist a glimpse into the past that is often not afforded by official documents.

It must always be borne in mind, however, that the majority of the consulted primary sources were written or created by members of the ruling local or national elite, with only relatively few accounts surviving from other, lower, levels of society. The potential bias of such evidence clearly has to be considered when utilizing such sources. Documents cannot always simply be viewed at face value, therefore; the reader of such texts always has to consider how and why they were produced, the audience that they were intended for, and what explicit and implicit motives there were for their existence. This is perhaps especially relevant to the pamphlets and broadsheets that were printed throughout the period; many were written with a specific purpose (apart from considerations of circulation) in mind and contained implicit propaganda for or against a particular cause.

Official documents also need to undergo considerable objective scrutiny. The vast majority of the population during the period was either illiterate or semi-literate and therefore was not part of the intended audience of such documents; literacy rates are notoriously difficult to calculate, but the rate in provincial early eighteenth-century England is generally accepted as being between 10–20 per cent for males (the rate for females was much lower owing to lack of educational opportunities for women at the time). The ability to read and write thus remained very much the exception rather than the rule.[10] Official records are also prone to being extremely formulaic in nature and containing little if any subjective matter; it is therefore necessary to avoid introducing considerable conjecture into the study of such sparse prose.[11] Unfortunately, the drawing up of official documents during the eighteenth century did not extend to the compilation of any meaningful criminal statistics, at either a national or a local level. It was not until the very end of the period under discussion (1805) that potentially meaningful national statistics were compiled (with annual judicial and criminal statistics not being published on a regular basis until 1857), and their accuracy and usefulness have long been hotly debated.[12]

This is not to deny that valiant and worthwhile attempts have been made to provide some measure of crime rates in the early modern period. James Sharpe was in the vanguard of such work, compiling and analysing such data in 1984 (mainly dealing with the surviving records from the Palatinate of Chester 1580–1709), while John Beattie's masterly study of the judicial records of Surrey and Sussex from 1660 to 1800 is further proof that such work can successfully be undertaken (with both authors making the limitations and pitfalls of utilizing such sources clear to the reader).[13] Most such studies, however, have concentrated overwhelmingly on indictable crimes: that is, those more serious criminal offences that were heard before a judge and jury at either Quarter Sessions or Assizes (see Information Panel 1 for further details of the structure of the various courts).

Much less research has been focused on petty or summary offences within the period, although such offences accounted for the vast majority of criminal behaviour that appeared before the judiciary in England (and, indeed, throughout Europe: Weisser has stated that 'assault and larceny [both largely petty offences] accounted for upwards of 85 per cent of all ordinary crimes committed (and reported) in Europe during the pre-industrial era').[14] However, the situation is improving all the time and recent publications, such as Irene Watts' valuable work on Gloucestershire Petty Sessions from the last quarter of the eighteenth century and Paley and Griffin's work on justices' notebooks, have gone at least some way to filling this lacuna.[15]

Despite these caveats the study of crime in the early modern period remains a fruitful endeavour; although criminological quantitative analysis is perforce somewhat limited by the paucity of available statistics, qualitative research can often throw light onto the criminal behaviour of our forebears. Such study can illustrate the changes through time in the legal process – how crime was defined and how it was was policed, largely without the assistance of any professional police force – and demonstrate the essentially discretionary nature of criminal justice in early modern England and Wales. Knowledge of the history of crime and criminal justice is also important to present-day criminologists, as it can inform them of the historical antecedents of many current issues that exercise the mind of those responsible for the policing, detection and punishment of criminal behaviour, such as the purpose of prisons, the role of the State in reforming the criminal and the definition of crime.[16]

Within recent years a myriad of primary sources has been made available to the historian through digital media and the internet, the sheer volume, depth, breadth and seeming inexhaustibility of which can appear at first sight overwhelming to both the novice and the professional. However, careful searches of the more useful websites, such as the *Old Bailey Proceedings Online* and the comprehensive National Archives website, can often yield material of unsurpassed detail and interest. Similarly, the increasing availability of early modern printed material through sites such as *British Newspapers 1710–1950*, *British Library Newspapers Online* (including the seventeenth- and eighteenth-century Burney Collection of newspaper and pamphlets), *Find My Past* and the freely available *Project Gutenberg*, together with subscription sites such as *Ancestry*, have made the research historian's job indisputably easier (though there is the caveat that such exponential growth in the availability of historical information can make interpretation of the sources more complex, insofar as there are just so many previously unavailable records to research within often strictly proscribed time limits).[17]

With regard to secondary sources, although the work of a great many historians, sociologists and criminologists has been employed in the writing of this book, particular mention must be made here of John Beattie's groundbreaking work *Crime and the Courts in England 1660–1800*. This book, with its comprehensive account of the operation of the judicial courts of England, was one of the first to study the process of criminal justice in early modern England from the instigation of the prosecution of a suspect to the punishment of the tried offender. Since its publication in 1986 it has remained a benchmark for subsequent criminal justice historians of the early modern period. In a similar vein, James Sharpe's 1984 book *Crime in Early Modern England 1550–1750* was one of the first works to both attempt a synthesis of the study of crime in the early modern period and contextualize its findings within the wider socio-economic background.

In the quarter-century or more since these two books were first published, and increasingly in the two decades since I embarked upon an academic career, much has been written about crime in the early modern period, with a plethora of academic research into many of the themes covered in this book (although criminal justice historians have still tended to gravitate to the nineteenth century).[18]

However, with a few exceptions, many of the research findings have been published within either specialist journals or books with a specifically academic audience in mind, and attempts to disseminate this knowledge to either undergraduate students or the general reader have been limited. The objective of this book (along with its companion volumes) is therefore to go some way towards bridging this gap. It is an attempt to synthesize the findings of numerous other historians' research into a single volume, and therefore makes no claim to be a comprehensive study of the subject; rather, it is intended to provide an easily accessible distillation of past and current knowledge of the history of crime and punishment in the early modern period.

Structure

Rather than simply regurgitating a broad chronological narrative from the forced abdication of James II in late 1688 to the end of the Napoleonic wars following the Battle of Waterloo in June 1815, this book is thematic in structure, each chapter dealing with a particular aspect of criminal justice history from the period. The chapters' introductions present the themes and areas of discussion contained within the remainder of the chapter. The main body of the chapter then discusses each of the themes in turn, while several aspects are further explored by the use of case studies, which are integrated into the text and are intended to give the reader a flavour of how the themes discussed related to and impacted upon both offender and victim in real-life situations. Some of the case studies feature well-known criminals and events, while others are perhaps less familiar to the reader; they have all been generously referenced however, in order to provide anyone who is particularly interested in a specific case to investigate it further.

Chapter 2: The impact of historical developments on the criminal justice system

This chapter outlines how the turbulent societal, political and economic upheavals resulting from the dramatic decline of the Stuart monarchy and the subsequent Hanoverian accession relate to the criminal justice of the period, enabling the reader to contextualize criminal justice developments within the broader history of the period. Such developments include the beginnings of urbanization and proto-industrialization, the fear of foreign invasions and interventions and lingering religious intolerance and political uncertainty from the previous tumultuous century, which led to the criminalization of certain religious beliefs and political activities. All of these processes are shown to have a direct or indirect effect on many aspects of crime in the period under discussion, from the changing nature of what was considered to be criminal owing to the prevailing moral and religious forces in operation to increasing legislation against often vulnerable sectors of early modern society.

It also investigates the growing role of the State in centralizing responses to perceived criminality and criminals. This role included the changing of legal concepts of crime by means such as the increasing implementation of various Poor Laws, by which a considerable sector of society was in effect criminalized; the growth of a centralized state which expanded the role of local and national authorities in the criminal justice process and provided for the increased regulation of perceived criminal behaviour such as 'sturdy begging'; the shift in moral codes resulting from the growth of religious fundamentalism during the mid-seventeenth century; the roles of the various courts of the period, including the Assizes and the Old Bailey; and the fall and rise of specific types of local courts, including manorial courts, church courts and Petty Sessions.

Chapter 3: Crime, 'traditional' and 'new'

This chapter discusses how criminal acts were defined and regarded by contemporary society and deals with both 'traditional' and 'new' forms of crime. The early modern period was one of the most turbulent times in Britain's social, economic and political history, with new opportunities for offending, including property crime and 'white-collar' crime, and new offences, such as workplace misappropriation, and this is reflected both in the changing perceptions of crime and in the types of crime committed. This chapter defines the nature of perceived crime, including 'new' forms of crime such as 'social' crime, fiscal crime and the increasing criminalization of the poor. It gives a clear definition of the types of activities considered to be criminal during the period and also suggests reasons for the many changes in what became perceived as 'criminal' acts. Several case studies outline the types of crime committed and how they changed through the period – for example, there was an increased focus on the ever-growing urban poor, which led to the forcible removal of people to their parish of birth.

Chapter 4: Capturing the criminal

This chapter discusses developments in the reporting and detection of crime throughout the period. These include the role of the amateur and often under-funded parish constabulary; the problems arising from the lack of a professional or full-time police force (and the associated problems with the rise of 'professional' thieftakers from the early seventeenth century onward); the rise of the coroner's court; and the increasing use of surveillance and spying by governmental bodies. The role played by the local judiciary in the form of the magistracy is also debated with regard to the increasing control of the parish through the introduction and prosecution of regulatory offences. The eighteenth century was a time of increasing debate about the need for an effective and professional police force; competing voices concerning the demands of liberty, cost-saving and political necessity were heard for the first time during this period.

Chapter 5: Punishment

The many changes in the structure and implementation of the punishment of crime in the eighteenth century are discussed here. These include a slow decline in the administration of both corporal and capital punishment and the increase in spatial and social control of offenders or perceived offenders through physical detention and the restriction of personal geographical movement. The period under discussion witnessed the introduction of mass transportation to the newly colonized America and Australia, and the chapter discusses the significance of such fundamental changes in policy. Specific case studies illuminate the arguments and rationale of this new system of punishment.

Chapter 6: Gender and the criminal justice system

The role of gender is investigated within this chapter, detailing what parts females played as offenders, often in gender-specific offences such as prostitution, where they acted both alone and in collaboration with men (for example, in the 'art' of 'buttock and twang', whereby a prostitute (buttock) would distract the victim while her male accomplice (twang) divested the victim of his wallet, money and so on), and in what ways they were treated differently from male offenders in terms of court appearances and subsequent punishment. The position of women as victims is debated not merely as the unfortunate and unwilling recipients of male violence or sexual aggression but in other ways too, including their status within the legal system and their role in the prosecution of offenders. These are aspects rarely discussed in the relatively few previously published histories of crime in this period.[19] The almost complete absence and negation of women in all aspects of the criminal justice system, from the judiciary and the legislative through to the executive, is also discussed with regard to the effects that this had on both crime and criminal justice.

Chapter 7: Crime in contemporary literature and culture

This chapter discusses how crime was reflected and discussed within eighteenth-century culture and literature. It charts the growth of popular literature and imagery relating to crime and criminals, from Captain Alexander Smith's *A Complete History of the Lives and Robberies of the Most Notorious Highwaymen, Footpads, Shop-Lifts, and Cheats of Both Sexes, in and about London, Westminster, and all Parts of Great Britain, for above an Hundred Years Past, Continued to the Present Time* (first published 1713–14 and subsequently reprinted on a frequent basis) to the official sanctioning of the publication of the Ordinary of Newgate's accounts of the lives and deaths of infamous criminals who suffered the ultimate penalty.[20]

Newspapers often carried a tremendous amount of scurrilous, libellous and inaccurate 'facts' about cases and criminals, and the influence of the development of the printing press and a growing literacy rate, together with the production of trial pamphlets, popular ballads and similar readily available literature, is discussed. Case studies include the meteoric rise and fall of Jack Sheppard, a prolific escapee from gaol. The chapter also discusses the birth of criminological enquiry and the attempts made to rationalize crime and criminal behaviour by practitioners such as the novelist Henry Fielding, who was also for a time the Chief Magistrate at Bow Street Magistrates' Court, and the magistrate and reformer Patrick Colquhoun.

Chapter 8: Review and conclusion: beyond the eighteenth century

The final chapter draws together the strands of the previous chapters in order to review the period and discuss how attitudes to crimes and criminals changed during the century and a quarter covered by the book. Criminology and penology were both in an embryonic state during the period and influential thinkers such as Fielding, Colquhoun and, further afield, Cesare Beccaria, had long-reaching and profound effects on the ways in which crime and criminals were viewed. It also highlights the significant judicial and political changes that affected how criminal justice was dispensed and controlled and discusses the extent to which crime and attitudes to crime were distinctive in this period. The chapter then looks forward, by relating the findings of the book to present-day criminological debates and discussions such as the role of the State, the effectiveness of punishment, increased prison capacity and the associated debate around sentencing policies, the calls for a more nationally accountable police force and the need for increased and continuing separation of the judiciary from the executive.

In conclusion, I hope that readers gain as much satisfaction and enjoyment from reading the book as I did in researching and writing it; the eighteenth century saw the piecemeal development of many fascinating and enduring aspects of criminal justice, including the growth of the adversarial trial, the move from physical punishment to long-term incarceration and the birth of a professional detective force, a process that resulted in a heady and often exciting mélange of ideas and practices. Hopefully I have managed to capture just a little of this interest and excitement within the following pages.

Notes

1 To avoid tedious repetition, further references to the period covered by the book will be given simply as the eighteenth century.
2 For Ireland, Scotland and Wales, see the respective companion volumes in this series.
3 The format of acts of parliament is explained using the Murder Act 1752 (25 Geo. II c.37) as an example: the first figure is the regnal year, so 25 Geo. II means that the act was passed in the twenty-fifth year of the reign of George II. The nomenclature after the respective monarch refers to the chapter number, i.e. the number of that act in each particular year, so c.37 means that the act was the thirty-seventh passed in that year.
4 Cicero, *De Oratore* sec. 120: *Nescire autem quid ante quam natus sis acciderit, id est semper esse puerum.*
5 The creation of the Metropolitan Police in 1829 falls outside the remit of this book, but, as will be demonstrated below, the 'Met' was not the first professional police force in England.
6 In 2012 over 6,000 prisoners in Britain were serving Indeterminate Sentences for Public Protection (IPPs). This sentencing mechanism was declared illegal by the European Court of Human Rights and IPPs were abolished in December 2012. However, the abolition was not retrospective and the debate about what to do with those prisoners currently serving such sentences rumbles on and has not been resolved at the time of writing.
7 With regard to all primary sources quoted in the text, original spelling and punctuation has been retained (except where the original is unclear to a modern eye).

8 Tim Hitchcock *et al.*, *The Old Bailey Proceedings Online, 1674–1913* (www. oldbaileyonline.org) and Tim Hitchcock *et al.*, *London Lives, 1690–1800* (www. londonlives.org). Subsequent references to these websites are given as follows: OBP for *Old Bailey Proceedings Online* and LL for *London Lives, 1690–1800*.

9 Broadsheets (also known as broadsides) were hastily published and cheaply printed single sheets that reported the sensational events of the day, often concentrating on the deeds and fate of notorious criminals. They often included a crude woodcut illustration normally depicting the death of the 'ne'er-do-well'.

10 An interesting recent synthesis of interdisciplinary research into literacy in early modern England can be found in Geoff Baker and Ann McGruer (eds), *Readers, Audiences and Coteries in Early Modern England* (Newcastle-upon-Tyne: Cambridge Scholars, 2006). Literacy rates improved markedly throughout the period of the Industrial Revolution and current research suggests that around two-thirds of the English population were literate to varying degrees by the first decades of the nineteenth century. Contemporary statistics relating to convicts' literacy rates (quoted in the *Manchester Guardian*, 25 April 1838) support this hypothesis: convicts unable to read or write: 35.85 per cent; convicts able to read and write imperfectly: 52.08 per cent; convicts able to read and write well: 9.46 per cent; convicts who received superior instruction: 0.43 per cent; convicts of an unknown standard: 2.18 per cent.

11 For a detailed survey of extant criminal justice records for the first half of the period under discussion and the contexts in which they were created, see J. A. Sharpe, *Crime in Early Modern England 1550–1750* (London: Longman, 1984), pp. 21–40.

12 See Robert M. Morris, ' "Lies, Damned Lies and Criminal Statistics": Reinterpreting the Criminal Statistics in England and Wales', *Crime, Histoire & Sociétés* 5.1 (2001): 111–27, and Howard Taylor, 'Rationing Crime: The Political Economy of Criminal Statistics since the 1850s', *Economic History Review* 51.3 (1998): 569–90 for critical analyses of the use of such statistics. Such national statistics can be of use, however, when utilized sensitively in comparing national trends with local or provincial crime figures: see, for example, Barry Godfrey, David J. Cox and Stephen Farrall, *Criminal Lives: Family Life, Employment, and Offending* (Oxford: OUP, 2007) and Barry Godfrey, David J. Cox and Stephen Farrall, *Serious Offenders: A Historical Study of Habitual Offenders* (Oxford: OUP, 2010).

13 Sharpe, *Crime in Early Modern England 1550–1750*, and J. M. Beattie, *Crime and the Courts in England 1660–1800* (Oxford: OUP, 1986). Peter King has also contributed greatly to the debate with regard to the eighteenth and early nineteenth century – see for example, Peter King, *Crime and Law in England, 1750–1840: Remaking Justice from the Margins* (Cambridge: CUP, 2006).

14 Michael R. Weisser, *Crime and Punishment in Early Modern Europe* (Hassocks: Harvester Press, 1979), 21. Magistrates' courts, consisting of either voluntary or stipendiary (i.e. professional, legally trained) magistrates, deal with more than 97 per cent of all criminal offences in twenty-first-century Britain. For a general account of the history of the magistracy from its founding in the thirteenth century through to the present day, see David J. Cox and Barry Godfrey (eds), *Cinderellas & Packhorses: A History of the Shropshire Magistracy* (Almeley: Logaston Press, 2005).

15 Irene Wyatt (ed.), *Calendar of Summary Convictions at Petty Sessions 1781–1837* [Gloucestershire Record Series vol. 22] (Gloucester: Bristol and Gloucestershire Archaeological Society, 2008); Ruth Paley, *Justice in Eighteenth-century Hackney – The Justicing Notebook of Henry Norris and the Hackney Petty Sessions Book* (London: London Record Society, 1991) and Carl Griffin, 'Woodtaking and Customary Practice: William Hunt's Justice's Notebook 1744–49', *The Regional Historian* 13 (2005): 19–24. Justices' notebooks were kept by many magistrates and often record the verdicts and many other details of the cases that they heard. A small number of notebooks have been transcribed and published: see, for example, Elizabeth Crittall (ed.), *The Justicing Notebook of William Hunt 1744–1749* (Devizes: Wiltshire Record

Society, 1982) and Alan Frank Cirket (ed.), *Samuel Whitbread's Notebooks, 1810–11, 1813–14* (Ampthill: Publications of the Bedfordshire Historical Record Society 50, 1971). Recent research into the lower courts of London can be found in Drew D. Gray, *Crime, Prosecution and Social Relations: The Summary Courts of the City of London in the Late Eighteenth Century* (Basingstoke: Palgrave Macmillan, 2009). For research into petty offending within the worsted industry of northern England from the late eighteenth century onward, see Barry Godfrey and David J. Cox, *Policing the Factory: Theft, Private Policing and the Law in Modern England 1777–1968* (London: Bloomsbury Academic, 2013).

16 For examples of historical studies that also engage with modern-day criminological debates, see Godfrey *et al.*, *Serious Offenders* and Godfrey *et al.*, *Criminal Lives*.

17 Relevant web addresses for the sites: www.nationalarchives.gov.uk; www.findmypast. co.uk/search/newspapers; www.bl.uk; www.findmypast.co.uk; www.gutenberg.org; www.ancestry.co.uk.

18 For more recent forays into the criminal justice history of the early modern period, see Clive Emsley, *Crime and Society in England 1750–1900*, 3rd edn (London: Longman, 2005); Barry Godfrey and Paul Lawrence (eds), *Crime and Justice 1750–1950* (Cullompton: Willan, 2005); John Hostettler, *A History of Criminal Justice in England and Wales* (Hook: Waterside Press, 2009); John Rule, and Roger Wells, *Crime, Protest and Popular Politics in Southern England 1740–1850* (London: Hambledon Press, 1997). For an intriguing investigation into the historiography of crime in early modern Britain, see Anne-Marie Kilday and David Nash (eds), *Histories of Crime: 1600–2000* (Basingstoke: Palgrave Macmillan, 2010).

19 For studies of female criminality and the way in which the judicial system interacted with women, see Deirdre Palk, *Gender, Crime and Judicial Discretion 1780–1830* (Woodbridge: The Royal Historical Society/Boydell Press, 2006); and for an collection of essays on female criminals in Scotland see Yvonne Galloway Brown and Rona Ferguson (eds), *Twisted Sisters: Women, Crime and Deviance in Scotland Since 1400* (East Linton: Tuckwell Press, 2002).

20 The Ordinary of Newgate was the chaplain of Newgate Gaol, and as such had access to all the condemned men and women awaiting the death sentence. He had the valuable perquisite of the right to publish the life stories and confessions of those awaiting the scaffold; this right could earn him in excess of £200 per year in additional income. Although occasionally embellished with subjective comments from the Ordinary, such accounts are generally accepted to be fairly reliable – see P. Linebaugh, "The ordinary of Newgate and his account", in Cockburn, J. S. (ed.), *Crime in England 1550–1800* (London: Methuen, 1977), pp. 246–69.

2 The impact of historical developments on the criminal justice system

Introduction

> Oh, if thou knew, thou English man, in what wealth thou livest, and in how plentiful a Country, thou would seven times of the day fall flat on thy face before God and give him thanks, that thou wert born an English man.
>
> (John Aylmer, 1559)[1]

Although this book concentrates on the period 1688–1815 it is necessary to give a brief overview of the huge societal, political and economic upheavals of the previous century. At the time of Aylmer's intensely patriotic words England was fundamentally still a medieval and largely feudal society. The kingdom remained overwhelmingly rural in its demography; the vast majority of its c.2,500,000 occupants lived and worked in hamlets, villages and small townships, with few cities having populations in excess of 10,000 (London, as so often, was the exception, with a population approaching 200,000). Although Elizabeth I's father, Henry VIII (r. 1509–1547) had left the country in a stronger position on the international stage than many of his predecessors, religious differences and concerns over the activities of foreign powers (most notably France and Spain) continued to trouble his three surviving children: Edward VI [r. 1547–1553], Mary I [r. 1553–1558] and Elizabeth I [r. 1558–1603].

By the first quarter of the eighteenth century, and despite the tumultuous upheaval of the Civil Wars (1642–1651) and the ensuing Commonwealth Period (1651–1660) the population of England had more than doubled to over 5,000,000, and a significant proportion of this population was moving from the countryside into urban areas in a process that had been going on since at least the first half of the seventeenth century.[2] Britain had also taken its first tentative steps to becoming the world's first modern industrialized power. Abraham Darby I (1677–1717), born in what would later become the heart and powerhouse of industry, the 'Black Country' of the western midlands of England, had perfected the smelting of iron using coke rather than charcoal, which freed ironmakers from the need to situate their works near forests that could provide a ready supply of wood.[3] His close contemporary Thomas Newcomen (1663–1729) had installed the world's first commercial steam engine at the pit-head of a coalmine owned by

Lord Dudley in Tipton, Staffordshire, in 1712, thereby creating reliable motive power to drive the wheels of industry.[4]

The British Empire was also in embryonic development. America and several Caribbean islands were under the rule of the British Crown and bringing in huge wealth and prosperity to those who had a share in highly lucrative though morally repellent trades such as slavery and fur-trapping.[5] The absolute power of the monarch had been fought over and conceded by the time that William III and Mary II jointly ascended the throne, while the wealth and influence of the Church had declined as a result of the political and religious turmoil of the mid-seventeenth century, with the Catholic faith in particular being regarded with suspicion and distrust. The following brief study provides a telling example.

Case Study 1: Mary Aubry, Petty Treason, 1688

On 8 February 1688 a coroner examined the dismembered corpse of a man recently identified as Denis Hobry, an immigrant Frenchman of Castle Street, St Martin-in-the-Fields. He had been strangled by his own garter and subsequently dismembered, his limbless body being found in a dunghill and his head and limbs disposed of in two separate houses of office (public toilets).[6]

After the body parts had been discovered in their respective places in late January 1688 they were put on public display at St Giles-in-the-Fields' 'bone house' in the hope that someone could identify the victim.[7] The dead man was subsequently identified on 2 February by means of a unique mark on one of his hands. His wife, Mary (or Marie) Hobry (or Aubry – spellings differ widely in the contemporary records) was a French Catholic who practised as a midwife, and she was immediately arrested and charged on suspicion of his murder. Mary was accused of murdering her husband by means of strangulation while he was asleep on 27 January 1688 and subsequently dismembering his body on 30 January. Three other men, including her son by a previous marriage, John Desermo, were accused of aiding and abetting her by concealing the murder. The process of dismemberment of the corpse would in itself have been an anathema to Catholic views of the body as a sacramental object which required its disposal by an honourable and reverential method.[8]

This gruesome murder and dismemberment came at a time when England was awash with tales of plots to forcibly reinstate the Catholic religion following the accession of James II in 1685 and the failed Monmouth Rebellion, in which James' nephew the duke of Monmouth had led a Protestant uprising in order to remove the unpopular Catholic James from the throne of England.

James had converted to Catholicism in 1669 (being described by the earl of Lauderdale 'as very Papist as the Pope himself') and openly opposed anti-Catholic measures such as the Test Act 1673 (25 Car. II. c. 2), by which any individual entering public service had to take an oath in the Anglican manner, thereby excluding both Catholics and Jews.[9] In 1685 his father Charles II had controversially followed his son's example by converting to Catholicism on his death-bed. It has been estimated that, at the time, Catholicism was practised by around one-fiftieth of the English population, and there was increased hostility between Protestants and Catholics following the savage aftermath of the 'Bloody Assizes', in which the majority of the Monmouth Rebellion participants had been either sentenced to death or sent into servitude overseas following their defeat at the Battle of Sedgemoor on 6 July 1685.[10]

The murder also came within a few years of the 'Popish Plot', a fictitious conspiracy dreamt up by Titus Oates (a minor Anglican clergyman) in 1678, in which he stated that he had incontrovertible evidence that Catholics planned to murder Charles II and place his son James on the throne in his place. The 'plot' was later proved to be a figment of his fevered imagination and he was convicted of perjury in 1685, but by then almost three dozen individuals had been executed as the result of his ravings. Consequently, rumours concerning the murder and links with yet another Catholic plot ran rife.

Mary, like her murdered husband, spoke little English (she had to have an interpreter provided for her at her trial), and this further alienated her from the English public, who were generally suspicious of 'foreigners' and 'foreign' – especially Catholic – behaviour. The murder of one's husband at the time was a crime known as 'Petty Treason'. As a wife was deemed to be inferior to and the subject of her husband, such a murder was seen as a crime against the status quo, in the same way that the murder of a sovereign constituted High Treason. This analogy was reflected in the identical punishments for Petty and High Treason: death by burning at the stake.[11] This punishment, significantly, was also reserved for the offence of heresy, again a perceived serious assault on the status quo of the nation.

The murder, which in actuality appears to have been a straightforward case of a desperate wife murdering her violent and drunken husband, who had regularly beaten and sexually assaulted her, was therefore afforded much publicity and speculation ran rife.[12] Mary had been married to Denis for some four years and had two children by a previous marriage. He had apparently often been unfaithful and on more than one occasion had left her to return to France. She had endeavoured to obtain a legal separation through the church courts, but to no avail – possibly because she was Catholic. Sir Roger L'Estrange, an eminent Tory commentator, bemoaned the fact that 'the late Barbarous Murder of Denis Hobry (what with Malice, Prejudice, Credulity and Mistake) has put more Freaks and Crotchets into the Hearts and Minds of the Common People, than any Story of that size perhaps ever did in this World before'. Several pamphlets were hastily produced by both factions in order to, respectively, stir up anti-Catholic feeling or show that the murder was simply a desperate measure carried out by an abused woman and had no wider political or religious significance.[13]

Those holding the latter view were not entirely successful in their aims. In the year following the murder a pack of playing cards commemorating the events of the 'Glorious Revolution' was produced; in it, Mary was depicted on the Queen of Clubs and the 'one' and 'two' of Spades, which showed her crime and punishment. The three cards were respectively entitled 'The Midwife cutting her husband to Pieces', 'The Popish Midwife putting his quarters in the privy' and 'The Popish Midwife burning'. As Vanessa McMahon has stated, 'Marie's role in these cares was as a representation of the nefarious nature of Catholics, foreigners and women.'[14]

Notwithstanding the various outpourings of anti- and pro-Catholic sentiment unwittingly instigated by Mary as the result of her actions, she was brought before the law on 22 February 1688 at the Old Bailey (now the Central Criminal Court). She pleaded guilty and a true bill was found against her on a charge of Petty Treason, after a trial heard before a jury of 'half aliens' comprised of six native Englishmen and six French ex-patriots.[15] She was consequently sentenced to death by burning, and on 2 March 1688 she was taken to Leicester Fields (modern-day Leicester Square) and met her end, being

> set upon a stool prepared for that purpose; and a rope being fastened through a hole of the post, or stake, and the noose of it put over her neck; the stool being taken away, she hung there for near the space of a quarter of an hour, in which time, the bavins and faggots were piled about her.[16]

In general, religious intolerance faded throughout the eighteenth century, the growth of more rationalist views during the Enlightenment (*c.*1650–1800) and the increasing separation of Church and State both helping to quell the fires of bigotry and suspicion. The power of the church courts (often referred to as 'bawdy courts') also declined during our period. These courts had for centuries been the main sources of jurisdiction over spiritual and religious matters, including incest, adultery and scolding, but they also heard cases involving what we would now consider to be secular civil law, such as probate, libel and matrimonial disputes.[17] By the end of our period their jurisdiction over such areas had been largely subsumed by the State – as Paul Langford states, 'generations of politicians had learned to treat religion as a matter of private conviction and public indifference'.[18] Between 1787 and 1860 a number of Acts Of Parliament collectively known as The Ecclesiastical Courts Acts stripped the church courts of much of their power and influence.[19]

Concomitantly there was also a steep decline in prosecutions for witchcraft; throughout the latter half of the seventeenth century there had been a move from absolute belief in witchcraft as a demonic threat to society to a more rational scepticism of misguided superstition.[20] Witchcraft had formally become a felony punishable by death under an Act Of Parliament of 1542 (33 Hen. VIII c.8). In 1604 an 'Act against Conjuration, Witchcraft and dealing with evil and wicked spirits' (2 Ja. I c.12) was passed that removed the sentence of burning at the stake for witchcraft offences (except for cases that also involved Petty Treason). Minor witchcraft offences were made punishable by sentence of up to one year in prison. This Act was in turn repealed by the Witchcraft Act 1735 (9 Geo. 2 c.5), which replaced offences of witchcraft with offences involving the pretence of witchcraft; in essence, the offences became those of vagrancy and obtaining money or goods by false pretences, rather than the actual practice of witchcraft.[21]

These legislative changes are reflected in the Old Bailey Proceedings; from 1674 to 1815 only a handful of proceedings are recorded in which women were accused of witchcraft (and the majority of these were discharged for want of evidence). However, 'cunning' behaviour could still lead to criminal prosecution, usually under the guise of fraud against a credulous individual or group, as witnessed by the following case study.

Case Study 2: Mary Poole, grand larceny, 1699

On 12 January 1698 Mary Poole, described as a 'gypsy of the Parish of St Giles-in-the-Fields', knocked at the door of Powis Hall and offered to tell the fortune of the person who opened the door to her, one Richard Walburton, in exchange for crossing her palm with silver.[22] Upon receiving sixpence from Walburton, Poole informed him that some of his servants were conspiring against him. She then instructed him that she would come back within the hour, return the sixpence and provide the means by which he could rectify the situation. The prosecution stated at her trial at the Old Bailey on 13 December 1699 that 'with much Perswasions of her Canting Dialect' he agreed to this and he also agreed to gather all his money together in order to prevent it from falling into the hands of the servants.[23] Poole duly returned as promised and gave the sixpence back to Walburton. She then asked to see any gold that he had, and he showed it to her. Poole then:

> showed him some Juggling Tricks, till she had Juggled away his Money; Then she wanted to be gone; and told him, that some People that lived there formerly had hid some Treasure in such a place under the Earth, and if he would go, he should immediately find it.[24]

Walburton (who seems to have been an incredibly gullible individual) then hastened upon his wild goose chase for the hidden treasure, only to find upon his return that Poole had disappeared, along with £7 10s. of his money.

Poole seems to have been something of a well-known character in the area, as another witness stated that 'a while back' she had cheated him out of some money by means of sleight of hand, 'which put him in such a Consternation, that he had not power to cry out or stop her, but let her go away with the Money'.[25] Yet another witness stated that while he was riding between Gravesend and Rochester he met and argued with Poole, who he stated had insulted him. He:

> turned back and gave her a Cut with his Whip, and Rode away as fast as he could, but had not gone Forty yards from her, but his Horse fell down, and she overtook him; with that he said, he thought she was a Witch, and had bewitched him and his Horse.[26]

Other witnesses appeared for the prosecution stating that they had been duped by Poole, and she presented little or no defence to the charge. She was subsequently found guilty of grand larceny and sentenced to be branded on the hand.[27]

Fear of the other could also play a part in suspecting an individual of witchcraft. Jane Kent was accused of causing a child's death by bewitchment in 1682 and one of the witnesses stated on oath that 'she had a Teat on her back, and unusual Holes behind her ears'.[28] Kent was found not guilty and discharged after it had been proved that she 'had lived honestly, and was a great pains-taker, and that she went to Church'.[29]

The 'gentrification' of law and order

The eighteenth century also saw the beginning of the 'gentrification' of law and order; that is to say, a move from law and order being maintained by more collective means, such as the use of 'hue and cry' and 'rough music' within individual parishes, in which all levels of society took an active role, to its maintenance and execution by 'the great and the good' of the county – men of fairly substantial wealth and local influence – and this also had a direct impact upon how crimes were viewed and dealt with.[30] The respective demises of 'hue and cry' and 'rough music' will be dealt with more thoroughly in Chapter 5, but, briefly, 'hue and cry' was a means dating back to at least the Norman Conquest (and probably originating in Saxon law) by which the victim of a crime could raise the neighbourhood in pursuit of the suspected offender. It was, therefore, very much an example of communal policing; as Sir Thomas Smith remarked in 1580, the hue and cry meant that 'everie Englishman is a sergeant to take the theefe'.[31] Similarly, 'rough music', also known by many other local names, such as 'riding the stang' (Scotland), the 'Skimmington horse' (south-west England) or the 'Ceffyl Pren' (Welsh for wooden horse), was another communal means of punishing suspected wrongdoers, this time by ritual humiliation and shaming. Victims of rough music would be paraded through the streets being insulted and subjected to various indignities. Such punishment was often reserved for those suspected of moral or civil impropriety, such as slander or adultery, rather than of more serious criminal offences.[32]

However, by the beginning of our period such communal punishments had largely disappeared, being replaced by more formal methods of justice. In terms of less serious crimes magistrates were increasingly influential. Roger Swift has stated that:

> It has been estimated that by 1689, the year of the 'Glorious Revolution', around eighty Commissions of the Peace were in operation in the counties of England and Wales, with a collective complement of some 3,000 magistrates.[33]

The duties of a magistrate had increased gradually from the mid-sixteenth century, especially in the field of Poor Relief, but during the 'long eighteenth century', from the 'Glorious Revolution' of 1688 to the fall of Napoleon in 1815, the role of the magistracy of England underwent several fundamental changes that resulted in a gradual but inexorable increase in workload. It has been remarked that during the eighteenth century 'in England everything drifted into the hands of the justices of the peace'.[34] This may be somewhat overstating the situation, but the eighteenth century undoubtedly saw a transfer of power from both the Crown and local communities to county and borough officials. The absolute power of the monarch had, of course, been violently and abruptly ended with the beheading of King Charles I on the balcony of the Banqueting House, Whitehall, on 30 January 1649. Although the monarchy had been restored in 1660 with the accession of King Charles II it was as part of a constitutionalist rather than an absolutist system; never again would the monarch be able either in theory or in practice to rule against the will of Parliament.

At the same time other forms of jurisprudence and social control had lost much of their former powers in the tumultuous seventeenth century. Manorial courts and parish vestries had often become little more than honorific bodies or simply a good excuse for an annual formal dinner, while church courts had declined in both their number and influence (see Chapter 3).

In addition, the business of the county was increasingly being conducted more formally and behind closed doors. The setting of the county rates and similar decisions during Quarter Sessions were, by now, not publicly witnessed, and there was also a downward delegation of both administrative affairs and summary justice from Quarter Sessions to Petty Sessions. The latter were not formally recognized until 1828, but certainly occurred from the sixteenth century: David C. Cox states that 'Petty sessions seem to have originated with the Licensing Act 1552 (5 & 6 Ed. VI, c. 25), which required ale-sellers to be licensed once a year by any two J.P.s.'[35] With regard to criminal cases, as David Phillips has stated, 'legislation in the 18th century also greatly increased magistrates' jurisdiction for summary convictions'.[36]

Before 1732 the appointment of magistrates had been subject to consideration by Assize judges prior to their names being put forward to a nationally appointed Commission.[37] In an attempt to prevent Assize judges possibly exerting undue influence on the choice of candidates the law was changed, while the property qualification for magistrates was increased at the same time to £100. It has been suggested that the removal of the right to appoint magistrates from the hands of the Assize judges 'gave the Lords Lieutenant, in whom the right of nomination now vested, a free hand [. . .] inevitably personal, social, and political prejudices sometimes prevailed'.[38]

From 1689 one of the criteria for becoming a Justice of the Peace was based on a financial qualification of holding land worth a minimum of £20 per year. By 1744 this had increased to a minimum of £100 per year, with the land having to be within the county on whose Commission of Peace the justice wished to be recorded. These qualifications clearly ruled out the vast majority of men, who held no land and thus had no opportunity to serve their community in this way (women were not admitted as magistrates in England until 1919).[39]

It has been calculated that, during the eighteenth and early nineteenth centuries, 'less than 3 per cent of the adult male population were rich enough to be legally entitled to act as justices of the peace'.[40] The system thus ensured that it was only men of local importance and financial influence, rather than merit, who were appointed as magistrates. This, combined with the view expressed by some historians that the Commissioners who were ultimately responsible for appointing such magistrates were 'almost entirely confined to the class which dubbed itself in social terms "the County"', would suggest that the magistrates had little in common with the majority of defendants who passed before them.[41] It is therefore not unreasonable for historians to make claims such as 'in a country like England where notions of democracy have been closely connected to traditions of local government, criminal justice policy has also been significantly shaped by the relationship between the local and central state'.[42]

Marc du Bombelles, a French diplomat (who was possibly also on a mission of industrial espionage), toured through the English midlands in 1784 and, in his diary, voiced the criticism of many:

> Several owners of land or merely a house in each county acquire greater authority than the local lord of the manor when they are honoured by being made justices of the peace and this honour is awarded too easily, seeing the importance of their functions, by the lords lieutenant of the counties. The lords lieutenant make this nomination out of politeness for those of their neighbours and acquaintances whom they wish to honour. There are justices of the peace who have this title but do not exercise the functions for which they have sworn an oath.[43]

The position was often regarded by such men as little more than a 'confirmation of their local prestige', and many were content for their names to be included in the Commission of the Peace without taking the necessary further steps to an executive role within the county.[44] Similarly, of those potential magistrates who did take the necessary oaths, by no means all considered themselves beholden to appear at the Quarter Sessions. In 1701 Richard Gough (1635–1723), author of *Gough's Antiquities of Myddle*, wrote of an anonymous Shropshire magistrate: 'I cannot tell whether he knew where the bench was where the [*Quarter*] sessions was kept, for I never saw him there.'[45]

It has been suggested that only about 40 per cent of those eligible to join the Commission of the Peace actually put their names forward, while, among those who did, the necessary degree of conscientiousness was not always present. On 3 July 1793 W. Upton, a magistrates' clerk at Hatton Garden Police Office, wrote to the Home Department stating that, prior to the introduction of stipendiary magistrates, 'had a canine animal brought a shilling in his mouth with a label for specifying his complaint, a Warrant was readily granted'.[46] Admittedly this referred specifically to the situation in London, but there was undoubtedly a widespread problem in recruiting enough men of the right calibre and dedication to the ranks of the unpaid magistracy.

By contrast, many of those who did serve as magistrates seem to have come to regard it as an almost hereditary position; for example, G. C. Baugh records that William Cludde of Orleton (d. 1765) was a Shropshire magistrate for over forty years, his son Edward was a magistrate from the 1750s until his death, his son-in-law Edward Pemberton was a leading magistrate and Chairman of the Bench from 1785–97 and his nephew Thomas Pemberton and grandson Edward Cludde both continued what had clearly become a family tradition.[47]

Not only was it difficult on occasion to recruit enough magistrates, it was also extremely hard to punish a Justice of the Peace for misbehaviour. From 1736 only the senior judges of the King's Bench had 'the power to review magisterial behaviour and also to punish it criminally', and it was very rare for these powers to be called into use.[48]

From the beginning of our period newly appointed magistrates had to swear oaths of allegiance to the monarch, the Protestant faith and the office of Justice of the Peace and then authorize these oaths by taking out a writ of *dedimus potestatem* (literally 'we have given the power'). Such a series of oaths survives from 1738, in which John Bright, Esquire, commenced by swearing the following in front of Maurice Pugh and Thomas Moore on his appointment as a Justice of the Peace for Shropshire: 'I do hereby promise and swear that I will be faithful and bear true allegiance to his Majesty King George so help me God'. The oaths continued with Bright's hand remaining on the Bible and, after swearing to 'abhor, detest and abjure' Catholicism (memories of the reign of Catholic King James II were still fresh in people's minds), he was instructed that:

> Ye shall swear that as Justice of the Peace in the county of Salop in all arti-cled in the King's Commission to you directed ye shall do equal right to the poor and to the rich after your cunning wit and power, and after the Law and customs of this Realm and Statutes thereof made; and ye shall not be at counsel with any person in any quarrel hanging afore you; and that ye hold your Sessions after the form of Statutes thereof made; and that fines [which] shall happen to be made and all forfeitures which shall fall before you, ye shall truly cause to be entered without any concealment or embezzle-ment and truly send them to the King's Exchequer; ye shall not look for gifts or other cause, but well and truly ye shall do your office as Justice of the Peace in that behalf; and that ye take nothing for your office of Justice of the Peace to be done but of the King's fees accustomed and cost limited by the Statutes; and ye shall not direct or cause to be directed any warrant by you to the parties but ye shall direct them to the Bailiffs of the said county of Salop or other of the King's Officers or Ministers or other indif-ferent persons to do exactly thereof, so God you help and by the contents of this book.[49]

Despite the perceived need for such admonitions, however, many magistrates did take their duties seriously and acted in what they considered to be a responsible manner. The entry in the burial register for Edward Pemberton of Wrockwardine, Shropshire, who died in December 1800 aged seventy-three, reads:

> An able & upright Magistrate, a man greatly esteemed & beloved, not only in his own Village, but through the whole Neighbourhood. He was accompa-nied to his grave by many sincere mourners & his loss will be long lamented

in a Parish, whose regularity & peace were, in a great measure, preserved, by his excellent example & benevolent exertions.[50]

And even these conscientious magistrates seemingly had little to guide them in their duties until the Reverend Richard Burns, vicar of Orton in Westmorland, published *Justice of the Peace and Parish Officer*, a handbook that attempted to deal with all the situations that a magistrate or parish officer might expect to encounter. This book was phenomenally successful, running through thirty editions from 1755 to 1845. Burns died in 1785, but various subsequent editors updated the book and by the time of its twenty-third edition in 1820 it ran to five volumes with a total of almost 4,000 pages.[51] It covered in alphabetical order almost every imaginable aspect of the law, with details of genuine cases to illustrate particularly difficult areas. Other books giving procedural and legal notes were available to magistrates, such as *The Magistrate's Assistant*, published in 1784 and probably by Samuel Glasse, a county magistrate for Oxfordshire.

The zeal and self-importance of some magistrates, however, could occasionally land them in considerable difficulties, as the following case study reveals.

Case Study 3: Samuel Gillam JP, murder, 1768[52]

In 1762 John Wilkes, MP for Aylesbury, established the *North Briton*, a Radical newspaper that carried several unfavourable articles regarding the behaviour of George III and his *de facto* prime minister John Stuart, the 3rd earl of Bute.[53] After the publication of one such article in June 1763 Wilkes was arrested for seditious libel, but was discharged shortly afterwards following a ruling by the Lord Chief Justice that, as an MP with Parliamentary privilege, Wilkes could not be arrested on such a charge. This ruling outraged both the king and Wilkes' Tory opponents, and in November 1763 Parliament voted to amend the law in order to allow the arrest of MPs on libel charges. However, before Wilkes could be detained he was smuggled out of the country to Paris by friends.

In 1768 Wilkes (who, as a result of his actions, had by now become a popular champion of liberty for many people) returned to England and, after an inconclusive court appearance in which he was released without charge, he stood for, and was returned as, Radical MP for Middlesex. However, on 27 April he was served with a writ of *capias utlagatum* (a document commanding the arrest of an outlaw), arrested and detained in the King's Bench prison, Southwark. For several days in early May 1768 large crowds (various contemporary witnesses put the number at anything between 1,000 and 20,000) gathered at the adjacent St George's Field, chanting "Wilkes and Liberty!" and other perceived inflammatory sentiments. On 10 May 1768, the date of the State Opening of Parliament, large crowds once again gathered in the expectation that Wilkes, as a duly elected MP, would be released from prison in order to take his seat in the House of Commons. However, this did not happen and tensions remained high.

Present in St George's Field was a 53-year-old magistrate for the county of Surrey, Samuel Gillam, who was sworn in as a Rotherhithe magistrate on

6 January 1763.[54] Mr Gillam was one of a handful of magistrates who had been sent for by the keeper of the King's Bench prison, who was fearful of the prison being stormed by the crowd in an attempt to forcibly release Wilkes. A detachment of Scots Guards (3rd Regiment of Foot) arrived at around 10 a.m. to relieve troops who had been previously stationed outside the prison. Shortly after the arrival of the replacement troops the Riot Act, which had been enacted in 1715 as an attempt to deal with unruly and riotous crowds, was read by a magistrate in an attempt to disperse the crowd:

> Whereas of late many rebellious riots and tumults have been in divers parts of this kingdom, to the disturbance of the public peace, and the endangering of his Majesty's person and government, and the same are yet continued and fomented by persons disaffected to his Majesty [. . .] be it enacted [. . .] that if any persons to the number of twelve or more, being unlawfully, riotously, and tumultuously assembled together, to the disturbance of the public peace, at any time after the last day of July in the year of our Lord one thousand seven hundred and fifteen, and being required or commanded by any one or more justice or justices of the peace, or by the sheriff of the county, or his under-sheriff, or by the mayor, bailiff or bailiffs, or other head-officer, or justice of the peace of any city or town corporate, where such assembly shall be, by proclamation to be made in the King's name, in the form herein after directed, to disperse themselves, and peaceably to depart to their habitations, or to their lawful business, shall, to the number of twelve or more (notwithstanding such proclamation made) unlawfully, riotously, and tumultuously remain or continue together by the space of one hour after such command or request made by proclamation, that then such continuing together to the number of twelve or more, after such command or request made by proclamation, shall be adjudged felony without benefit of clergy, and the offenders therein shall be adjudged felons, and shall suffer death as in a case of felony without benefit of clergy [. . .] Our Sovereign Lord the King chargeth and commandeth all persons, being assembled, immediately to disperse themselves, and peaceably depart to their habitations, or to their lawful business, upon the pains contained in the Act made in the first year of King George the First for preventing tumults and riotous assemblies. God Save The King![55]

Strictly speaking, the Riot Act 1715 allowed groups of a dozen or more people up to an hour to disperse, but at least some of the Scots Guards seem to have been keen to expedite the dispersal of the crowd and started to prod members of the recalcitrant crowd with their bayonets. One man was chased through the field and stabbed in the shoulder. From this point on the situation rapidly deteriorated and several people were seriously injured or killed.[56]

In the early afternoon of the same day Mr Gillam was again present outside the King's Bench prison with another JP. Both men were pelted with stones and other objects after an attempt to remove an 'inflammatory' paper that had been pasted to the walls of the prison. Mr Gillam apparently made several attempts to persuade the crowd to disperse, but, upon this failing, he read the Riot Act on at least two occasions. A witness to the events stated that Mr Gillam then shouted:

> 'For God's sake, good people go away, if I see any more stones throwed I will order the guards to fire': while he was so saying a stone came and hit him over the head, about the temple, it caused him to reel three or four yards backwards; and when he recovered himself, or soon after, I heard him say, 'fire'; the soldiers were then in two rows, they fell back a few paces into four rows, and then fired.[57]

William Redburn, a journeyman weaver living at High Street, Mile End, was subsequently hit in the back of the thigh by a musket ball. He was, according to his friend John Taylor, not part of the noisy crowd, but was on his way to Westminster with a friend and had stopped to watch the unfolding events.[58] Taylor stated that when the soldiers started to shoot Redburn turned to him, saying ' "Taylor, let us go"; we came out of the causeway into the road, our backs were towards the soldiers.' During his cross-examination he further stated that:

Taylor: We turned our backs, and in that time he received a ball.

Q: Do you mean he received the wound the instant he returned back?

Taylor: I cannot say the exact time, because a great many people were running; when he stopped he told me he was wounded; I looked down, and saw the blood upon his stocking.

Q: Where was he wounded?

Taylor: In the hind-part of the thigh.

Q: Was he running or walking, or was it at the time he was turning?

Taylor: At the time he was running I believe, but I cannot justly say, I did not know it till the time he stopped; I had not power to help him along, though a great many did; he went to a surgeon in Blackman-street.

Q: Did you see the wound examined?

Taylor: The surgeon probed it, it went in behind and came out before; I was told the ball was found in his breeches, but I did not see it.[59]

William Redburn was tended by a surgeon but died of his injuries three days later. Gillam was subsequently arrested for ordering the troops to open fire and thereby directly causing the death of Redburn. On 6 July a Grand Jury of the county of Middlesex brought a True Bill against Gillam and he was ordered to trial at the Old Bailey.

> Samuel Gilliam, Esquire was indicted, together with a certain person to the jurors unknown, for the wilful murder of William Redburn; for that the certain person to the jurors unknown, with a musket loaded with gunpowder

and a leaden bullet, on the 10th of May, on and against the said William Redburn, feloniously, wilfully, and of malice aforethought, well knowing the musket being so charged, did discharge and shoot off, by the force of the gunpowder, him the said Redburn, in and upon the hind-part near the middle of the thigh, did strike and penetrate, giving to him one mortal wound, the breadth half an inch, and depth one inch, of which mortal wound, as well in the parish of St. George the Martyr, Southwark, as in the parish of St. Dunstan, Stepney, by which means the said William Redburn, from the 10th of May, did languish till the 13th of the same, and then died; and that the said Samuel Gillam, Esq.; feloniously, wilfully, and of malice aforethought, was present, aiding, helping, abetting, comforting, and maintaining him the said person unknown, to do and commit the said murder.[60]

In the evidence for the prosecution James Darbyshire, a bookseller who was near Gillam during the events, made the following statement:

Mr. Gillam told me he had orders from the ministry to fire upon the people, and that there must be some men killed, and that it was better to kill five and twenty to day than have an hundred to kill to-morrow; this was in the field opposite the marshal's house.[61]

He repeatedly stated that Gillam had said this in the presence of other witnesses, but was unable to provide any names. Other witnesses also stated that they had heard Gillam enquire as to the manner of the firing of the muskets of the soldiers, saying:

"I hope there is no mischief done"; this was a very short time after the firing; the commanding officer said, "You may depend upon it there is no mischief done, because we always fire in the air".[62]

The amount of contradictory evidence given by numerous witnesses continued for some time, but this eventually proved too much for the prosecutor Serjeant John Glyn, who concluded the prosecution evidence by stating:

I call no more witnesses, your Lordships will never find me acting a part against humanity and candour; I am not now pressing this gentleman's conviction; I opined the law, that where it was absolutely necessary for suppressing a riotous mob, there the magistrate is justified; the application thereof from facts is the whole question with respect to me, I shall say not a word more about it.[63]

After this statement the jury declined to hear the defence and Gillam was immediately acquitted without a stain on his character; indeed, the presiding judge, Henry Gould, remarked that magistrates were 'obliged to take every possible method to suppress riots, which are, of all other things, the most disgraceful, as well as the most dangerous infractions, upon the laws of the community'. His sentiments were echoed by the Lord Chief Baron, who remarked that:

> If any mob continued together an hour after [the Riot Act] was read, they had nobody but themselves to blame for disagreeable consequences [and] that if in cases of this nature, where the laws were related, an innocent person should even suffer, it was to be lamented as a misfortune, and not imputed to the magistrate as a crime.[64]

The dismissal of the case and the words of both the judge and the Lord Chief Baron sparked much controversy, as did the other deaths among the protesters at the hands of the troops. Contemporary debate (both pro- and anti-establishment) raged in the form of publications such as *A Collection of Pieces relative to the inhuman massacre in St George's Fields on 10th May 1768*, in which the anonymous author railed against the government's and king's apparent approbation of the behaviour of the troops.[65] In the collection was included a letter dated 11 May 1768 from William Barrington, Secretary of State for War, in which Barrington stated:

> I have great pleasure in informing you, that his majesty highly approves of the conduct of both the officers and men [. . .] Employing the troops on so disagreeable a service always gives me pain, but the circumstances of the times make it necessary. [. . .] I beg you will be pleased to assure them, that every possible regard shall be shewn to them; their zeal and good behaviour on this occasion deserve it.

Opponents of the actions of the magistrates and troops were clear that the government was determined to maintain order no matter what the cost to the individual's rights. John Wilkes and his supporters lobbied hard for a Parliamentary enquiry into the events of the St George's Fields riots, but without success.

The unfortunate events described above are by no means unique in English history. Several other 'riots' resulted in the death and serious injury of innocent bystanders, most famously the 'Peterloo Massacre' of August 1819, in which at least fifteen people were killed and several hundred seriously wounded following a cavalry charge by the Manchester and Salford Yeomanry.[66] The use of troops to control unruly behaviour continued despite the Peterloo Massacre: for example, in Wolverhampton in May 1835 several people were seriously injured (including a young lad who had to have his leg amputated following a musket ball injury) by a cavalry charge of the King's Dragoons during disturbances resulting from a Parliamentary by-election. This cavalry charge, instigated by a local magistrate, again resulted in a Parliamentary enquiry, which not only cleared the Dragoons of any wrong-doing but also presented them with commemorative trinkets for their brave action.[67]

Serious criminal offences that magistrates felt unable to deal with would be transferred to the county Assizes to be heard before a judge and jury.[68] The full majesty and power of the law was undoubtedly present at the twice-yearly Assizes, which, for many reasons, including fascination with some of the more serious and scandalous trials, often attracted considerable interest from all sections of society. It has been argued that this majesty and power was directed towards the maintenance of the prevailing social order and that proceedings were heavily biased in favour of wealthy property owners, whose interests were closely mirrored by the interests of those who administered and made the law. However, other scholars argue that this interpretation is erroneous and the power and authority of the law may instead be seen as confirming the impartiality and sense of fair play innate in the English system of criminal justice.[69]

Douglas Hay has stated that:

> The antics surrounding the twice-yearly visits of the high-court judges had considerable psychic force. They were accorded far greater importance by contemporaries than by most historians [. . .], the assizes were a formidable spectacle in a country town, the most visible and elaborate manifestation of state power to be seen in the countryside, apart from the presence of a regiment.[70]

Although the spectacle of the Assizes as described by Hay was undoubtedly considerable at times, this view has been strenuously challenged by V. A. C. Gatrell, who, quoting from a Royal Commission of 1836, suggests that 'an assize day was more like a market-day than a solemn moment of state', with:

> the witnesses, totally unacquainted with, and equally uncertain of the hour when, and the place where, they are required to be in attendance, are first dragged into court through a crowd of persons [. . .], to be sworn to the evidence to be given by them upon the bill of indictment before the grand jury; from thence they are taken back, through the crowd [. . .] to await their being called on the bill [. . .] but at what hour, or even on what day, they know not.[71]

Moreover, an anonymous and undated source suggests that the proceedings of the Assizes were not always successful in arousing feelings of awe and fear:

Countryman: What mummery is this, 'tis fit only for guisers!
Townsman: No mummery Sir, 'tis the Stafford Assizes.[72]

In fact, many engravings and cartoons of the day show that those who had nothing to fear from them often regarded the Assizes as little more than an excuse for memorable days out. The Assizes were undoubtedly regarded by many in the upper echelons as something of a social gathering, the judges often being fêted and courted during their time on the circuit. For example, records show that for the Stafford Lent Assizes of 1813 the account for the two judges' lodgings amounted to the considerable sum of £45.[73] Such bills normally fell mainly to the

High Sheriff of the county and often represented a 'considerable financial burden which included entertaining the Assize judges and providing dinner for the justice'.[74] The salary of a judge was also considerable; *puisne* (less senior) judges earned £1,500 p.a. by 1714, rising to £2,000 p.a. in 1759, £2,400 p.a. in 1779, £3,000 p.a. in 1799 and £4,000 p.a. in 1809.[75]

Such sums were a far cry from the wages of most of those tried (and, indeed, from the wages of the majority who attended the Assizes).[76] However, the considerable remuneration received by judges was not necessarily concomitant with their expertise: V. A. C. Gatrell in particular is scathingly critical of the system by which judges – whom he refers to as 'furred homicides, sable bigots' – were appointed,[77] and also disabuses 'any notion we may have that the [. . .] judges of the era were men of intellectual or legal distinction', castigating Assize judges such as Baron Graham, who 'owed his elevation to toadying to the Prince [Regent]'.[78] It is certainly true that Graham held the unenviable record of being the judge who sentenced more people to death during his period of office than anyone else. In any case, the Assize judges, whether capable or not, remained throughout our period a 'small and relatively well-known élite', with only twenty-nine being appointed in the period 1790–1820.[79]

Because of their State-imbued power and authority, judges were also regarded with fear and suspicion by many of the non-elite population. Of course, as Duman has remarked, perceptions, favourable or otherwise, can be dependent on one's lot in life:

> Certainly the judges, as seen from below, would have appeared very differently from the way they do to [modern historians]. In place of their education and professional achievements, their large fortunes and fine houses, one would find other accoutrements – the black cap, the gallows and gibbet [. . .]. The assize judges were often the most immediate and accessible representatives of the ruling classes in the provinces, and were perceived as persecutors of the poor and defenders of the interests of the rich and powerful.[80]

Juries were, of course, not always above exercising prejudice and self-interest. Petty jurors served for the whole of the Assize sessions, with twelve men, all of whom had to fulfil a property qualification, being selected from the pool for each trial. The balance of self-interest and the desire to partake in a fair and objective trial on the part of the jurors has been the subject of much debate, most notably between Douglas Hay (together with acolytes such as Peter Linebaugh) and John Langbein.[81] In *Albion's Fatal Tree* Hay meticulously attempts to link the holding of property to the increasing demonstration of self-interest and self-preservation that he sees as holding sway in the late eighteenth and early nineteenth century, stating that 'once property had been officially deified, it became the measure of all things. Even human life was weighed in the scales of wealth and status.'[82] Hay argued that the ruling classes successfully managed to extend what he calls the 'communal moral sanction' to a criminal law that was mainly concerned with upholding an unequal division of property. To this end Peter Linebaugh suggests that 'the jury was composed of a small, propertied portion of the population whose interests were more closely allied with those of the most élite class than with those of the working class that supplied the majority of offenders'.[83]

Linebaugh's quotation, above, is from an article that springs to the defence of Hay after John Langbein issued a strenuous riposte to *Albion's Fatal Tree* in 1983 in which he challenged all of Hay's fundamental views.[84] In a powerfully argued case Langbein suggested that 'the criminal law and its procedure existed to serve and protect the interests of the people who suffered as victims of crime, people who were overwhelmingly non-élite'.[85] It is certainly true that, as we shall see in Chapter 5, juries often exercised considerable discretion as to the value of goods stolen in order to lessen the sanction against an offender.

The debate concerning the uses of and reasoning behind the criminal justice system continues, but it is clear that in many ways the judicial system was implicitly (and sometimes overtly) biased against the unpropertied and usually uneducated defendant. One of the most notable of these was the complete absence of women from the picture: judges, magistrates, court officials, lawyers, barristers, coroners and jurors were, without exception, male. The only appearances that women make are as either defendants or witnesses. Their absence from the criminal justice system in general must be a major consideration in regarding the wider picture.

To present-day eyes the judicial system of the eighteenth and early nineteenth century seems extremely biased against the defendant. Apart from the implicit gender partiality represented by all-male judges and juries (whose members were all propertied individuals and therefore further unrepresentative of the population as a whole), until the nineteenth century there was also little legal representation available to the ordinary defendant in a criminal trial, especially outside of London. While both prosecuting and defending counsel could call and cross-examine witnesses, defence counsel was prohibited until 1836 from summing up and it was not until the passing of the Criminal Evidence Act 1898 (61 & 62 Vict. c.36) that defendants were allowed to give evidence on oath.

Until the nineteenth century there was also little legal representation available to the ordinary defendant in a criminal trial, especially outside of the metropolitan area. A 'dock' or 'guinea' brief – i.e. a barrister from a bank available for employment usually for the fee of one guinea – who migrated round the country with the Assizes in order to further his professional experience could be employed, but these were often of limited effectiveness. Until 1815 all barristers had a duty to ride the circuit of Assizes;[86] such barristers would not have earned much money in comparison to their civil law counterparts and it would be understandable, therefore if they did not always give of their best for their employer, whom they often did not meet until just before the trial. The prevalence of barristers in criminal courts was to blossom spectacularly through the first half of the nineteenth century: *Law Review* figures show that in 1809 there were only 456 practising barristers, compared with over 3,000 by 1846.[87]

Prosecuting crime

Throughout the whole of the eighteenth century and the majority of the nineteenth century there was no system of public prosecution. It was the sole responsibility of the victim (or his/her friends or relatives in the case of incapacitation or death) to instigate the prosecution of suspects. The campaigning legal reformer Patrick Colquhoun had mooted the creation of an office of Crown Prosecutor in a series of suggestions to the 1798 Finance Committee, but his proposal was not acted upon and it was not until 1880 that a government-appointed Public Prosecutor took up his office, following the passing of the Prosecution of Offences Act 1879 (42 & 43 Vict. c.22).[88]

Although some magistrates did go beyond the call of their duties in investigating crimes, the vast majority played no part in criminal investigation beyond hearing the statements of the victim and arranging for the parish constable to search for suspects.[89] Certain costs were refunded to the victim or their representatives following a successful prosecution, but, as John Beattie has remarked, 'it seems reasonable to assume that poor men must have had to be moved very strongly to bring a prosecution against someone who had assaulted them or stolen from them'.[90]

Consequently, a popular course for those who could afford it was to belong to a private prosecution society, funded by subscription. These were known as Associations for the Prosecution of Felons, and were usually comprised of members from either a single county or borough. The earliest known such Association dates back to 1693, but by the end of the eighteenth century they had multiplied throughout the country. The *Wolverhampton Chronicle* of 6 January 1813, for instance, contains typical advertisements for more than half-a-dozen such Associations in the immediate area around the town, many containing preambles such as that of the Tettenhall Association: 'Whereas several burglaries, felonies, grand and petit larcenies have frequently of late been committed [. . .] and the Offenders have escaped Justice with impunity, for want of proper Pursuit'.[91]

In their study of American vigilantism Craig B. Little and Christopher P. Sheffield provide an interesting comparison between English and American eighteenth- and nineteenth-century ideas of how to deal with the problems of law–enforcement. They argue that in both countries it was the failure of the executive to implement the legislation that led to the respective creation of vigilante societies and Associations for the Prosecution of Felons: 'neither the concept of the law nor its content were in question – only problems surrounding the effectiveness of the law's enforcement'.[92] David Eastwood suggests that these problems were dealt with to at least some extent by the creation of such Associations, which he regards as 'the most significant components in a programme to deter crime in later Hanoverian England without abandoning traditional forms of communal policing'.[93] However, in reality they often had little effect on serious crime. Very few murders appear to have been prosecuted by such Associations and, because of the relatively high subscription costs, they were not seen as an attractive or a viable alternative by the majority of the local community, who often suffered disproportionately from crime but were largely unable to pursue suspects owing to the prohibitive cost of private prosecution.[94] Although often well-heeled, even Associations of the Prosecution of Felons were not willing to authorize blank cheques. In his research into the Dursley Association for the Prosecution of Felons (founded in 1773) Bryan Jerrard notes that:

> One expense that was not allowed after 1820 was the employment of any officer from Bow Street or any other police office, probably because of the high charges that the Bow Street 'Runner', Vickery, made to the Earl of Berkeley when his gamekeeper was shot in 1816.[95]

Conclusion

We have seen from the above brief overview how various social, economic and political developments of the previous century impacted upon events of the eighteenth century. This chapter has also demonstrated the importance of contextualizing the social, economic and political turmoil of the eighteenth century, which played a key part in the development of the English criminal justice system. The move from an overwhelmingly rural to an increasingly urban and industrialized economy had grave consequences for many people with regard to the paucity and cost of staple foods, leading to much popular discontent and perceived 'criminal' behaviour, together with increasingly harsh treatment of those regarded as the 'undeserving' or indigent poor. There was also a distinct move from communal and informal justice to a more bureaucratic and 'gentrified' system in which magistrates (always male, always members of the influential and propertied classes) assumed more and more responsibility for the effective government of their boroughs and counties and the criminal justice system was put on a more official footing.

The decline of spiritual and kingly authority and the establishment of a secular State, presided over by a Parliamentary oligarchy rather than an absolute monarch, together with the proto-industrialization and urbanization resulting from the nascent Industrial Revolution, all influenced the ways in which our criminal justice system developed, and, as we shall see in the next chapter, also played a significant role in defining and creating both criminal behaviour and new forms of crime.

Notes

1 An Harborowe for Faithfull and Trewe Subjects Against the Late Blowne Blaste (Strasbourg 1559), quoted in Hindle, Steve, *The State and Social Change in Early Modern England, c.1550–1640* (London: Macmillan, 2000), p. 38. John Aylmer became bishop of London in 1576 and was a well-known commentator on religious and political affairs.
2 See Weisser, *Crime and Punishment*, p. 12, for the demographic shift by 1640; he suggests that only 15 per cent of the rural population of that time were living in the same village as their parents.

3 Abraham Darby I was born in Woodsetton, near Sedgley, Staffordshire, close to the Worcestershire town of Dudley. The area around Dudley subsequently became known as the 'Black Country', a polycentric area of small settlements on the western fringes of what is now the West Midlands. First referred to as such in the early nineteenth century, it gained its name from the prevalence of heavily polluting activities such as chainmaking and metalworking. It owed its rapid growth to the ready availability of staples of heavy industry, including coal, fireclay and limestone. In 1843 the first report of the Midland Mining Commission (*Midland Mining Commission: First Report South Staffordshire (508)* [London: HMSO, 1843]) referred to the area as 'an interminable village, composed of cottages and very ordinary houses [. . .] These houses, for the most part, are not arranged in continuous streets, but are interspersed with blazing furnaces, heaps of burning coal in process of coking, piles of iron-stone, calcining forges, pit-banks and engine chimneys.' (quoted in M. W. Greenslade and D. G. Stuart, *A History of Staffordshire*, 2nd edn (Chichester: Phillimore, 1998), p. 19. For further details concerning the heritage and history of the Black Country, see www. blackcountrysociety.co.uk.

4 Although Abraham Darby I was undoubtedly the first man to use iron smelted using coke on a long-term commercial basis there is evidence that Dud Dudley, an illegitimate son of Lord Dudley and a fellow native of Sedgley, Staffordshire, obtained a patent for the process of producing iron using coal from King James, granted on 22 February 1620, almost a century before Darby's process was to burst upon the industrial world – see D. Dudley, *Metallum Martis: or Iron made with Pit-Coale, Sea-Coale, &c. And with the same Fuell to Melt and Fine Imperfect Mettals, And Refine perfect Mettals* (London: Dud Dudley, 1665). With regard to Newcomen's steam engine, a magnificent full-size working replica can be seen at the Black Country Living Museum in Dudley (www.bclm.co.uk), very near the site of the original. Newcomen's engine provided the basis from which James Watt pioneered major improvements, enabling Britain to utilize and exploit her enormous mineral wealth.

5 British involvement with slavery on a large scale began in 1562, when John Hawkins captured some 400 persons in Sierra Leone and sold them into slavery in the West Indies. It is impossible to accurately quantify the number of men, women and children taken from Africa and sold as slaves, but current estimates suggest in excess of 11 million people (www.bbc.co.uk/worldservice/africa/features/storyofafrica/9chapter6.shtml). The fur trade in North America became a British concern in 1763, when 'New France' (the area of North America colonized by France) was captured and all trading rights and privileges were ceded to the British. The British Empire continued to expand throughout the subsequent years until the outbreak of World War I.

6 Public toilets (also known variously as houses of office, houses of easement or, more vulgarly, bog-houses) were often provided in larger towns and cities by private speculators; human waste in the form of both excrement and urine had considerable value owing to its use in industrial processes such as the fulling of cloth, the tanning of leather, the manufacture of gunpowder and dyeing. It was not until the passing of the Public Health Act 1848 (11 & 12 Vict. c.63) that every dwelling in Britain was required by statute to have access to a sanitary facility, be it an earth-closet, an ash-pit or a privy. For details of a case where a house of office was erected illegally, see David J. Cox, *Foul Deeds & Suspicious Deaths in Shrewsbury and around Shropshire* (Barnsley: Wharncliffe, 2008), pp. 17–24.

7 St Giles-in-the-Fields' burying ground was a popular burial site with Roman Catholics. Enlarged in 1628, by the late seventeenth century it had become notoriously overcrowded, a state of affairs that continued throughout the next century and a half. A scandalized reporter in 1838 remarked: 'What a horrid place is Saint Giles's church yard! It is full of coffins, up to the surface. Coffins are broken up before they are decayed, and bodies are removed to the "bone house" before they are sufficiently decayed to make their removal decent' (*Weekly Despatch* 30 September 1838).

8   The Roman Catholic Church consequently forbade cremation as a funerary rite (with certain exceptions) until 1963.

9   Earl of Lauderdale quoted in J. P. Kenyon, *The Stuart: A Study in English Kingship* (London: Fontana, 1970), p. 144.

10 Religious statistic quoted from T. B. Macaulay, *The History of England from the Accession of James the Second in Five Volumes*, Vol. II [originally printed 1848] (New York: Cosimo, 1999), p. 185. The Monmouth Rebellion was a failed uprising in the west of England led by the Protestant duke of Monmouth, Charles II's illegitimate son. For further details of the Monmouth Rebellion and its aftermath, one of the best general accounts remains P. Earle, *Monmouth's Rebels: The Road to Sedgemoor 1685* (London: Weidenfeld & Nicholson, 1977).

11 In contrast, the murder of a wife by a husband was not seen as Petty Treason, but simply 'wilful murder'.

12 It appears that Mary's husband had forced her to take part in various sexual activities (probably including anal intercourse) against her will, leading to bodily injury. She could not have chosen to prosecute her husband for rape, however, as at the time no husband could be accused of such a crime: 'the husband cannot be guilty of a rape committed by himself upon his lawful wife, for by their mutual matrimonial consent and contract the wife hath given up herself in this kind unto her husband, which she cannot retract' (Sir Matthew Hale, *History of the Pleas of the Crown*, 2 volumes (London: Payne, 1736), vol. 1, ch. 58, p. 629).

13 See P. Fumerton *et al.* (eds), *Ballads and Broadsides in Britain, 1500–1800* (Farnham: Ashgate, 2010), p. 170, for a list of such publications, several of which had such lurid titles as *A Warning Piece to all Married Men and Women. Being the full confessions of Mary Hobry, the French midwife who murdered her Husband on 27ᵗʰ January*. For a transcript of the original trial, see OBP t16880222–24. For other accounts of the case, see Frances E. Dolan, 'Hobry, Mary (*d.* 1688)', *Oxford Dictionary of National Biography* (Oxford: OUP, 2004) [www.oxforddnb.com/view/article/68003]; and Vanessa McMahon, *Murder in Shakespeare's England* (London: Hambledon & London, 2004), pp. 67–78; for details of other Petty Treason cases, see Kirsten T. Saxon, *Narratives of Women and Murder in England* (Farnham: Ashgate, 2009); Randall Martin (ed.), *Women and Murder in Early Modern News Pamphlets and Broadside Ballads, 1573–1697* (Farnham: Ashgate, 2005), which contains the full text of *A Warning Piece to all Married Men and Women. Being the full confessions of Mary Hobry, the French midwife who murdered her Husband on 27ᵗʰ January*.

14 McMahon, *Murder in Shakespeare's England*, p. 76.

15 OBP t16880222–24. This use of foreign-born jurors appears to have been relatively unusual; the OBP contains only a handful of other trials in which this option was offered to the accused, but it was certainly a recognized legal precept. In one of the trials (OBP t17431012–16) the proceedings record that the defendant was informed that he had the right to insist on half the jury being aliens. Such juries were known as a *Jury de medietate linguae* (jury of the half-tongued). For further details on the history of the *Jury de medietate linguae*, see M. Constable, *The Law of the Other: The Mixed Jury and Changing Conceptions of Citizenship, Law and Knowledge* (Chicago: University of Chicago Press, 1994), pp. 112–23.

16 *An Account of the Manner, Behaviour and Execution of Mary Aubry* (London: D. Mallett, 1688), p. 2. Bavins were faggots (twigs of wood tied together) around three feet in length and two feet in circumference.

17 Church court cases for the Diocesan Courts of the Archbishopric of York from 1300 to 1858 have recently been made available online by the Borthwick Institute for Archives at the University of York at www.york.ac.uk/library/borthwick/projects-exhibitions/church-court-records/. For accounts of the work of church courts in the sixteenth and early seventeenth centuries, see M. Ingram, *Church Courts, Sex and Marriage in England, 1570–1640* (Cambridge: CUP, 1990) and Susan Doran and Christopher

Durston, *Princes, Pastors and People: The Church and Religion in England, 1500–1700*, 2nd edn (London: Routledge, 2003). For further information concerning such courts in the eighteenth and early nineteenth centuries, see P. Hair (ed.), *Before the Bawdy Court: Selections from Church Court and Other Records Relating to the Correction of Moral Offences in England, Scotland and New England, 1300–1800* (New York: Barnes & Noble, 1972).

18 P. Langford, *Public Life and Propertied Englishmen 1689–1798* (Oxford: OUP, 1991), p. 586.

19 The individual acts covered by this blanket phrase included: Ecclesiastical Suits Act 1787 (27 Geo. III c.44), Ecclesiastical Courts Act 1813 (53 Geo. III c.127), Ecclesiastical Courts Act 1829 (10 Geo. IV c.53), Privy Council Appeals Act 1832 (2 & 3 Will 4 c.92, Ecclesiastical Courts (Contempt) Act 1832 (3 & 4 Will 4 c.93), Ecclesiastical Courts Act 1840 (3 & 4 Vict. c.93), Ecclesiastical Courts Act 1844 (7 & 8 Vict. c.68), Ecclesiastical Jurisdiction Act 1847 (10 & 11 Vict. c.98), Ecclesiastical Courts Act 1854 (17 & 18 Vict. c.47), Ecclesiastical Courts Act 1855 (18 & 19 Vict. c.41), Ecclesiastical Jurisdiction Act 1858 (21 & 22 Vict. c.50) and Ecclesiastical Courts Jurisdiction Act 1860 (23 & 24 Vict. c.32).

20 The most thorough (and readable) survey of the decline in witchcraft in the early modern period remains Keith Thomas's outstanding study combining history and anthropology, first published in 1971 – see K. Thomas, *Religion and the Decline of Magic: Studies in Popular Belief in Sixteenth and Seventeenth Century England* (Harmondsworth: Penguin 2003). For an account of witchcraft from the mid-eighteenth century onwards, see O. Davies, *Witchcraft, Magic and Culture 1736–1951* (Manchester: MUP, 1999).

21 This act was repealed in 1951, being replaced by the Fraudulent Mediums Act (14 and 15 Geo.VI c.33).

22 OBP t16991213a-2. Walburton may well have been the butler or another senior man-servant at the house, as the Powis Hall referred to in the OBP was probably Powis House, a grand town mansion house built in the 1680s for William Herbert, the 2nd marquis of Powis. The house subsequently became the French Embassy and burned to the ground in 1713, an event that the novelist Jonathan Swift memorably put down to the 'carelessness of [the ambassador's] rascally French servants' – see letter dated 26 January 1713 in T. Sheridan (ed.), *The Works of the Rev. Dr Jonathan Swift in 17 volumes*, Vol. 15 (London: Bathurst *et al.*, 1784), p. 383.

23 OBP t16991213a-2.

24 OBP t16991213a-2.

25 OBP t16991213a-2.

26 OBP t16820601a-11.

27 OBP s16991213–1.

28 OBP t16820601a-11.

29 OBP t16820601a-11.

30 The ways in which the executive branch of our criminal justice system developed, such as the birth of professional police forces and the demise of 'hue and cry' and 'rough music', are examined in detail in Chapter 5.

31 Quoted in Philip Rawlings, *Policing: A Short History* (Cullompton: Willan, 2002), p. 31.

32 Another name for such shaming was 'Charivari', and this word survived in the title of the satirical magazine *Punch or the London Charivari*, founded in 1841.

33 R. Swift, 'The English Magistracy Past and Present', in Cox, D. J., and Godfrey, B. (eds), *Cinderellas & Packhorses: A History of the Shropshire Magistracy* (Almeley: Logaston Press, 2005), pp. 1–12: p. 5.

34 J. L. Hammond and Barbara Hammond, *The Village Labourer 1760–1832: A Study in the Government of England before the Reform Bill*, 4th edn, 2 volumes (London: Guild Books, 1948), Vol. I, p. 13.

35 David C. Cox, 'Shropshire Justices of the Peace before the 18th century', in Cox, David J., and Godfrey, B. (eds), *Cinderellas & Packhorses: A History of the Shropshire Magistracy* (Almeley: Logaston Press, 2005), pp. 13–22: p. 22.

36 Douglas Hay, 'Dread of the Crown Office: The English Magistracy and Kings Bench 1740–1800', in Landau, N. (ed.), *Law, Crime and English Society 1660–1800* (Cambridge: CUP, 2002), pp. 19–45: p. 20.

37 Bertram Osborne, *Justices of the Peace 1361–1848: A History of the Justices of the Peace for the Counties of England* (Shaftesbury: The Sedgehill Press, 1960), p. 164.

38 Osborne, *Justices of the Peace*, p. 164. The post of Lord Lieutenant dates from the 1540s and the holder of the title was originally expected to organize and be in charge of the county militia or yeomanry when under threat of invasion. However, by the eighteenth century their duties had become largely ceremonial; they were the personal representative of the monarch within their county. One of their remaining functions was to nominate the appointment of individuals as magistrates.

39 Mrs Ada Summers, Mayor of Stalybridge, was sworn in as an ex-officio magistrate on 31 December 1919, following the passing of the Sex Disqualification (Removal) Act 1919 (9 & 10 Geo. 5 c.71). It is sometimes claimed that this distinction belonged to Miss Emily Cecilia Duncan, who was Chairman of the West Ham Board of Guardians and who became a Justice of the Peace on 26 May 1913, but Miss Duncan was permitted by the Lord Chancellor to act as an ex-officio magistrate only within strictly proscribed limits: she was permitted to officiate as such only in lunacy matters in the workhouse infirmary – see *The Times* 27 May 1913.

40 Douglas Hay, 'Crime and Justice in Eighteenth and Nineteenth Century England', in *Crime and Justice: an annual review of research* 2 (1980): 45–84: p. 46.

41 Osborne, *Justices of the Peace*, p. 164.

42 Philip Rawlings, *Crime and Power: A History of Criminal Justice* (London: Longman, 1999), p. 175.

43 Joseph Hunt (ed.), 'Bombelles in Britain: The Diary kept by a French Diplomat during a Visit to Midlands England 1784', trans. L. E. Page (unpublished material, 2000), pp. 33–34.

44 Beattie, *Crime and the Courts*, p. 59.

45 Quoted in D. C. Cox, 'County Government 1603–1714', in Baugh, G. C. (ed.), *Victoria County History: Shropshire*, volume III (Oxford: OUP for the Institute of Historical Research, 1979), pp. 90–114: p. 95.

46 TNA Home Office Records HO 42/26, f.28.

47 G. C. Baugh, 'County Government 1714–1834', in Baugh, G. C. ed., *Victoria County History of Shropshire*, Vol. III (Oxford: OUP for the Institute of Historical Research, 1979), pp. 115–14: p. 117.

48 Hay, 'Dread of the Crown Office', p. 19.

49 Shropshire Archives 3053/4/3 Oath Subscribed by John Bright Esq. Before Maurice Pugh and Thomas Moore, on appointment as Justice of the Peace 1738. Salop is an historic alternative name for Shropshire.

50 Entry in Wrockwardine Parish Register quoted in Shropshire Archives 665/5969, notes on letter sent by FS to Mrs. Pennington, Ashburnham Place, near Battle, Sussex, 20 March 1801.

51 Richard Burns, *Justice of the Peace and Parish Officer*, 23rd edn, ed. George Chetwynd, 5 volumes (London: Longman *et al.*, 1820).

52 Much of the defence evidence for this trial can be found in *Rex v Samuel GILLAM one of HM justices of the peace for Surrey: Old Bailey sessions, July 1768*, TNA TS 11/920.

53 'Radical' here refers to a political view that the electoral system was in need of radical reform, as originally espoused by Whig parliamentarian Charles James Fox in 1797. The term 'Prime Minister' was contended throughout the eighteenth and nineteenth centuries; the Prime Minister was appointed by the monarch and not parliament and

therefore the office was not statutorily created, remaining an honorary appellation until the twentieth century.

54 Return of Writs: Surrey – oath of Samuel Gillam JP, TNA C202/151/1.

55 Preamble to the Riot Act 1715 (1 Geo. 1 c.5).

56 At least six people appear to have been killed (at least one of them female) and over a dozen were seriously wounded during the day's events, but exact numbers are difficult to ascertain owing to the variance of contemporary evidence. The anonymous author of *A Collection of Pieces relative to the inhuman massacre in St George's Fields on 10th May 1768* lists six dead and four seriously wounded and gives their names and details of their injuries (p. 101).

57 Constable Richard Nicholl's evidence, OBP t17680706–58.

58 John Taylor's evidence, OBP t17680706–58.

59 John Taylor's evidence, OBP t17680706–58.

60 OBP t17680706–58. The Grand Jury consisted of between twelve and twenty-four propertied and influential men (none of whom had legal training) who sat at the opening of each Quarter Sessions or Assizes in order to decide which criminal indictments should be proceeded with. If at least twelve of them thought that the prima facie evidence suggested sufficient grounds for prosecution the words 'A True Bill' were written on the back of the original indictment; if not, the bill was thrown out with the words 'not a True Bill' or 'Ignoramus' ('to be ignored') written on it. Grand Juries effectively ceased functioning in 1933 and were abolished by the Criminal Justice Act 1948 (11 & 12 Geo. VI c.58).

61 OBP t17680706–58.

62 Constable Robert Allen's evidence OBP t17680706–58.

63 John Glyn was a Wilkite (i.e. a supporter of John Wilkes) and had been a Serjeant-at-Law since 1763. Serjeants-at-Law were an elite order of barristers that dated back to at least the early fourteenth century. For further details see H. W. Woolrych, *Lives of Eminent Serjeants-at-Law of the English Bar*, 2 volumes (London: W. Allen, 1869, reprinted Law Book Exchange, 2002). For a detailed survey of the English adversarial legal system, see J. H. Langbein, *The Origins of Adversarial Criminal Trial* (Oxford: OUP, 2003).

64 OBP t17680706–58.

65 Anon., *A Collection of Pieces relative to the inhuman massacre in St George's Fields on 10th May 1768* (London: n.p., 1768). For a further example of the debates raised by the events, see Anon., *Remarks on the Riot Act with application to certain recent and alarming facts* (London: G. Kearsly, 1768).

66 See R. Reid, *The Peterloo Massacre* (London: Heinemann, 1989) for a detailed account of this incident.

67 See David J. Cox, '"The wolves let loose at Wolverhampton": a study of the South Staffordshire Election Riots, May 1835', *Law, Crime and History* 1.2 (2011): 1–31 (available online at www.pbs.plymouth.ac.uk/solon/journal.htm).

68 Assizes had been created in 1166 by Henry II when he established the principle of trial by jury.

69 See Douglas Hay, 'Property, Authority and the Criminal Law', in Hay, D. *et al.*, *Albion's Fatal Tree: Crime and Society in Eighteenth-Century England* (London: Allen Lane, 1975), 17–64, and John Langbein, 'Albion's Fatal Flaws', *Past and Present* 98 (1983): 96–120, for the heated debate concerning the early nineteenth-century judicial system.

70 Hay, 'Property, Authority and the Criminal Law', p. 27.

71 V. A. C. Gatrell, *The Hanging Tree: Execution and the English People 1770–1868* (Oxford: OUP, 1996), p. 533. Gatrell's exploration of the role of capital punishment remains one of the most thought-provoking and influential books on the subject. Unusually, he makes no pretence of objectivity in his approach, instead providing the reader with a highly subjective but compelling argument.

72 Hay, 'Property, Authority and the Criminal Law', p. 27.

73 TNA T. 90/169 Sheriffs' Cravings etc. 1807–1813.

74 Thomas Skyrme, *History of the Justices of the Peace*, 2nd edn (Chichester: Barry Rose Publishers, 1994), p. 468.

75 J. Sainty, *The Judges of England 1272–1990* (London: Selden Soc. Supp. Series X, 1993), quoted in D. Lemmings, *Professors of the Law: Barristers and English Legal Culture in the Eighteenth Century* (Oxford: OUP, 2000), p. 275. Lemmings points out that, although these salaries were extremely high, several high-flying barristers in the late eighteenth century declined the opportunity to become judges because it would have involved a considerable drop in their salary (p. 276).

76 Gatrell, *The Hanging Tree*, p. 505.

77 Ibid., p. 497.

78 Ibid., pp. 502–503.

79 D. Duman, *The Judicial Bench in England 1727–1875: the Reshaping of a Professional Elite* (London: Royal Historical Society, 1982), p. 2.

80 Ibid., pp. 99–100.

81 Douglas Hay *et al.*, *Albion's Fatal Tree: Crime and Society in Eighteenth-Century England* (London: Allen Lane, 1975); Peter Linebaugh, 'A Reply to Professor Langbein', in Weiss, R. P. (ed.), *Social History of Crime, Policing and Punishment* (Aldershot: Ashgate, 1999), pp. 55–88; Langbein, '*Albion's* Fatal Flaws', pp. 96–120.

82 Hay, 'Property, Authority and the Criminal Law', p. 19.

83 Linebaugh, 'A Reply to Professor Langbein', p. 59.

84 Langbein, '*Albion's* Fatal Flaws', pp. 96–120.

85 Ibid., p. 97.

86 Duman, *The Judicial Bench*, p. 2.

87 Hostettler, *A History of Criminal Justice*, p. 45. John Langbein's work on the rise of the criminal barrister sheds considerable light on the role of the barrister during the latter part of our period – see John Langbein, 'Criminal Trials before the Lawyers', *University of Chicago Law Review* 45.2 (1978): 263–316; and John Langbein, 'Shaping the Eighteenth-Century Criminal Trial: A View from the Ryder Sources', *University of Chicago Law Review* 50.1 (1983): 1–136.

88 *Reports from Committees of the House of Commons vol. XIII Finance Reports XXIII to XXXVI 1803, containing Twenty-eighth Report from the Select Committee on Finance: Police, including Convict Establishments 1798* (London: House of Commons, 1803), p. 355. Patrick Colquhoun's attempts at reform are further discussed below in Chapter 7.

89 For a fascinating account of the detective efforts of one magistrate, see John Styles, 'An Eighteenth Century Magistrate as Detective: Samuel Lister of Little Horton', *Bradford Antiquary* New Series XLVII (1982): 98–117.

90 Beattie, *Crime and the Courts*, p. 47.

91 Some research into the activities of particular Associations was carried out in the early twentieth century, while much more detailed recent research has been carried out by David Philips and R. P. Hastings – see G. P. Mander, 'The Wolverhampton "Association"', *The Wolverhampton Antiquary* 11.1 (1934): 60–63; David Philips, 'Good Men to Associate and Bad Men to Conspire: Associations for the Prosecution of Felons in England 1760–1860', in Hay, D., and Snyder, F. (eds), *Policy and Prosecution in Britain, 1750–1850* (Oxford: Clarendon, 1989), pp. 113–70, and R. P. Hastings, 'Private Law-Enforcement Associations', *The Local Historian* 14.4 (1980): 226–31. David Friedman of the University of Chicago Law School has penned an interesting piece on the role of such associations and their preventive value in his article 'Making Sense of English Law Enforcement in the Eighteenth Century', *The University of Chicago Law School Roundtable* 2.2 (1995): 475–505.

92 Craig B. Little and Christopher P. Sheffield, 'Frontiers of Criminal Justice: English Private Prosecution Societies and American Vigilantism in the Eighteenth and Nineteenth centuries', *American Sociological Review* 48 (1983): 796–808, p. 798.

93 D. Eastwood, *Government and Community in the English Provinces 1700–1870* (Basingstoke: Macmillan, 1997) p. 140.

94 Eastwood, *Government and Community*, p. 140. Many of these Associations appear to have quickly degenerated into little more than an excuse for an annual social event in the form of a grand dinner and by the middle of the nineteenth century most had disappeared altogether. The *Crewe Chronicle* of 20 October 1877 details the business of a rare active survivor: it reported on the activities of the Crewe and Church Coppenhall Association for the Prosecution of Felons (Cheshire) for that year, stating that eighteen cases were brought before the Association. Of these, sixteen paid a small fine, and two were sent from the Association to the magistrates' court, suggesting that the crimes dealt with were minor misdemeanours rather than felonies.

95 Bryan Jerrard, 'Early Policing in Gloucestershire', *Transactions of the Bristol and Gloucestershire Archaeological Society for 1992* C (1993): 221–40, pp. 229–30. Research has shown that the Bow Street 'Runners' were very rarely utilized by poorer members of society owing to the often considerable cost of employing them – see David J. Cox, *A Certain Share of Low Cunning: A History of the Bow Street Runners 1792–1839* (London: Routledge, 2012), pp. 78–80.

3   Crime, 'traditional' and 'new'

Introduction

This chapter discusses how criminal acts were defined and regarded by contemporary society and deals with both the increasing criminalization of 'traditional' wrongdoing and the introduction of 'new' forms of crime resulting from economic and technical developments. As noted above, the period under discussion was particularly turbulent, and this was reflected in the changing perceptions of crime and in the types of crime committed. Here will be discussed the changing perceptions of what constituted criminal behaviour, including 'new' forms of crime such as 'social' crime and financial crime, and the increasing criminalization of the poor. A clear definition of the types of activities considered to be criminal during the period will be attempted and also reasons for the many changes in what were perceived as 'criminal' acts suggested. Several case studies, again, act as exemplars.

Urbanization and poverty

England throughout the seventeenth century was becoming an increasingly urbanized society. By the end of the Elizabethan period some 20 per cent of the population were living in towns or other urban settlements. Increased pressure came to bear on food production as the overall population grew but fewer people were employed in agriculture, as many of the previously rural workforce were now employed in more profitable and less seasonal urban-based activities such as glassmaking, nailmaking and lacemaking. There were various attempts to improve agricultural productivity, but some of these, such as the enclosure of communally organized field systems, proved highly unpopular and generated what was seen by the authorities as increased criminal behaviour. These social changes resulted in a growing number of both rural and urban poor, who often lacked the means to maintain themselves and were thereby forced to either throw themselves upon the mercy and charity of others more fortunate or to obtain the basic necessities of subsistence by criminal means.

Contemporary society was not blind to the problems that increased urbanization and population growth brought – even before the accession of Elizabeth I there had been attempts to regulate and control the movement and behaviour of the population. The parish, although originally created as an ecclesiastical unit – the area served by a particular church – had by Tudor times become the fundamental unit of local government and civil administration. As such, parish vestries (the body of influential ratepayers responsible for maintaining the interests of the parish) became increasingly concerned with the problems posed by the peripatetic poor. As early as 1494 the Vagrants and Vagabonds Act (11 Henry VII c.2) stipulated that:

> Vagabonds, idle and suspected persons shall be set in the stocks for three days and three nights and have none other sustenance but bread and water and then shall be put out of Town. Every beggar suitable to work shall resort to the Hundred where he last dwelled, is best known, or was born and there remain upon the pain aforesaid.[1]

In 1538 a system of recording births, marriages and deaths within parish registers, kept in locked chests within the parish church, was begun. This was designed to ensure that each of the 15,000 parishes in England and Wales should know where and when every person was born, lived and died. Further legislation to control the movement of beggars and vagabonds was enacted in 1547, when 'sturdy beggars' – that is, people who were deemed capable of work but who refused it – were liable to be branded or placed in short-term enslavement.[2] The same Act did make some concession to those that were considered to be the 'impotent' or unwilling poor, those who were unable to work illness, injury or old age: financial relief was to be offered and basic habitation provided.

During the reign of Elizabeth I further legislation attempted to deal with the problem of the indigent poor. By 1601 a series of laws had both categorized the poor into 'deserving' (those who were made poor through no fault of their own, including the elderly and the infirm) and 'undeserving' ('sturdy' beggars, itinerant workmen and criminals) and introduced a compulsory poor law tax, workhouses and the post of Overseer of the Poor. The Poor Law Act 1601 (43 Eliz. I c.2) consolidated several previous acts and remained the benchmark for dealing with the poor until 1834.

As a result of these measures the poor became reliant not on individual charity but on a proto-welfare state based on parish of birth; one could claim poor relief only in one's own parish. This had the effect of criminalizing many itinerant workers, who regularly tramped the country looking for casual labour. The preamble of the 1572 Poor Law Act (14 Eliz. I c.5) stated that:

> Whereas all parts of this Realm of England and Wales be presently with rogues, vagabonds and sturdy beggars exceedingly pestered, by means whereof daily happens in the same Realm horrible murders, thefts, and other great outrages, to the high displeasure of Almighty God, and to the great annoy of the commonweal . . .

Punishments for those found guilty of being a rogue and vagabond were harsh; anyone found guilty of begging or vagrancy:

> Shall upon their apprehension be brought before one of the Justices of the Peace or Mayor and be presently committed to the common gaol, there to remain without bail or mainprise until the next Sessions of the Peace [. . .] at which Sesssions [. . .] if such person or persons be duly convicted of his or her roguish or vagabond trade of life, either by inquest of office, or by the testimony of two honest and credible witnesses upon their oaths, that then immediately he or she shall be adjudged to be grievously whipped and burnt through the gristle of the right ear with a hot iron, manifesting his or her roguish kind of life.

Throughout the seventeenth and eighteenth centuries the persistent problem of 'the poor' remained, and in predominantly agricultural counties the problem was often exacerbated by the seasonal nature of much of the available work. Magistrates were responsible for much of the administration of the Poor Laws and issued directives to the various Overseers of the Poor in the parishes in which they held jurisdiction. On 14 April 1741 Thomas Jones, a Shropshire magistrate, issued the following judicial decision to the Overseers of the Poor in the parish of Cardington:

> Whereas Louis Edwards, a poor person of your parish came before me this day and made oath that he is not able to subsist himself and family for want of work [in] your said parish, I do therefore hereby order you, the said officers, to pay unto the said Edwards the sum of two shillings every week until such time as you shall put him to work and that you find his wife hemp or flax to spin according to the instructions in you nomination warranty or until you shall come before me and show cause to the contrary; and hereof fail ye not. Given under my hand and seal this 14th day of April 1741.[3]

The ill-fated Speenhamland System of poor relief was also developed by the magistracy. The system (by which local winter wages of agricultural labourers were supplemented by the parish poor-rate, the amount of supplementation being tied to the price of bread and the number of dependants of each labourer) is generally believed to have been instigated in 1795 by a group of magistrates in Speenhamland, Berkshire. The system spread rapidly through much of southern England and Wales (roughly south of a line drawn from Gloucester to Hull) and led to much abuse by employers (many of them magistrates), who were quick to realize that they could cut wages in the knowledge that the parish would, theoretically, make up the resultant shortfall. Such were heavily criticized from many quarters; the MP for Shrewsbury, Robert Aglionby Slaney, stated in February 1831 that:

> I was induced to turn my Attention to what I conceive to be an Abuse of the Practice of the Law in the Southern Districts of England, which appeared to me to have the Effect of lowering the Condition of the Labourers, and

lessening the natural Value of their Labour; besides being greatly injurious to them in every Way, it also appeared to me that it was extremely injurious to the Interests of Landed Gentlemen residing in those Districts, for it seemed much dearer to maintain the Poor in the Way they were maintained in some of the Southern Districts of England, than to adopt the better Practice of the North, where Men were well paid. There are Three or Four Abuses which prevail in the Southern Districts of England. In the first place, they pay the Rents of able-bodied Persons out of the Poor's Rate; secondly, an Allowance for the Children (I am always speaking with reference to able-bodied Persons); thirdly, making up the Wages out of the Poor's Rate. This System was adopted in several of the Southern Districts. The Wages were made up to the Number of a Family, according to a fixed and invariable Scale, varying only with the Price of Wheat; in others without a Scale, but still upon the same bad Principle.[4]

Such criticisms grew inexorably throughout the early decades of the nineteenth century and led eventually to the introduction of the New Poor Law in 1834.

Proto-urbanization

The growth of towns had several impacts upon crime during the period: high population densities in urban areas were associated with a concentration of property or goods that could prove a temptation to others. The urban economy was more monetary in nature, rather than relying on a system of bartering for goods and services as in rural areas, and therefore coin was present in larger amounts; and, finally, as some towns and cities grew to a considerable size, their social make-up was characterized by a level of anonymity that had been previously unknown in smaller communities, where strangers would be immediately noticed and often commented upon. The rapid expansion of many towns also caused problems with food supply, as described below.

Case Study 4: 'Bread and Butter Riots', 1766

In September 1766 the *Annual Register* (a yearly compendium of memorable events) remarked:

> There having being many riots, and much mischief done, in different parts of England, in consequence of the rising of the poor; who have been driven to desperation and madness, by the exorbitant prices of all manner of provisions; we shall, without descending to minute particulars, or a strict regard as to the order of time, in which they happened, give a short abstract of these disturbances.[5]

It went on to describe over thirty popular uprisings throughout England (with a concentration in the western Midlands) caused by a combination of factors related to the price and availability of foodstuffs. Such uprisings were not a new phenomenon in England, but they became increasingly common during the latter half of the eighteenth century owing to ever-increasing costs of staple foods. The average price of wheat had remained relatively stable during the first half of the century, averaging 34s. 11d. per quarter-hundredweight for the period 1713–1764, but in 1765 it rose to 55s. per quarter-hundredweight, reaching an individual peak of 128s. per quarter-hundredweight in 1800.[6] Research suggests that 'in late eighteenth-century Staffordshire about ten percent of families were unable to buy sufficient bread, rising to about forty percent in years when prices were high'.[7] There were several particularly bad harvests, with the years 1800–1801 being notable for their shortages, but 1812 had the highest average quarter of wheat prices (126s. 6d.) between the years 1792 and 1818, compared to average prices of less than 70s. fifteen years previously.[8]

The harvest of 1766 was a particularly poor one and the number of popular uprisings dramatically increased: 'something like sixty incidents were reported in the press in a dozen weeks'.[9] These uprisings were almost unfailingly described as 'riots', but this term is perhaps not appropriate for all of the demonstrations and activities witnessed throughout the country in this year. The term 'riot' suggests an out-of-control mob, intent on pointless destruction, whereas contemporary sources such as the *Annual Register* or the *Gentleman's Magazine* were at pains to remark that, although goods were seized by force, personal violence was not usually employed. Self-control, rather than brute intimidation, often characterized such demonstrations. E. P. Thompson, in his classic work *The Making of the English Working Class*, quotes a contemporary report concerning an incident in 1766 at Honiton in Devon in which 'lace-workers seized corn on the premises of the farmers, took it to market themselves, sold it, and returned the money and even the sacks back to the farmers'.[10] Similarly, in other areas both the participants and many observers often regarded the uprisings as a justifiable method of righting a perceived wrong, rather than as mindless destructive rioting. Other methods, too, were employed by those unhappy at the price of staple food: for example, anonymous posters were put up in prominent places, exemplified by one posted in Portsmouth signed by 'Old English' and stating in doggerel:

> To the Farmer, Miller and Baker,
> These three you see.
> Each of you take your choice
> The greatest rogue shall have the greatest hoist.[11]

It is interesting to note that in many of these uprisings (commonly known as 'bread and butter riots') the active participants usually belonged to the proto-urban working class and were not agricultural workers or rural inhabitants. This would tend to support the view that 'food riots in Britain were in the main the direct collective actions of town artisans and proto-industrial and industrial, that is non-agricultural, workers'.[12] The rapidly industrializing Black Country was no exception to this trend; in 1795, 1800 and 1810 the main body of 'rioters' was comprised of colliers. *Hue & Cry* (forerunner of *The Police Gazette*) stated on 16 June 1810 that:

> Some disposition to riot, under the pretence of the high price of provisions shewed itself among the very lowest of the people of Birmingham and Wolverhampton, and the Colliers in the vicinity of Stourbridge a few days back; but [it] was immediately suppressed by the prompt but humane interference of the Magistrates with other civil assistance, and the appearance of some Military parties.[13]

There was no doubt that the disturbances did occasionally take a violent and abusive turn; threatening letters such as the one reproduced below were sent to farmers and millers, often containing graphic and specific details of what could be expected if they were suspected of profiteering:

> Winter Nights is not past therefore your person shall not go home alive – or if you chance to escape the hand that guides this pen, a lighted Match will do eaqual execution. Your family I know not But the whole shall be inveloped in flames, your Carkase if any such should be found will be given to the Dogs if it Contains any Moisture for the Annimals to devour it.[14]

Local magistrates, aware of the tide of public opinion, often ensured that farmers and millers sold wheat and other staple foods at a reasonable rate during periods of shortage. The *Annual Register* informed its readers that 'at Kidderminster [in Worcestershire] the populace obliged the farmers to sell their wheat at 5s a bushel', while at Stourbridge (Worcestershire) 'they lowered the price of butter, meat, and wheat'.[15] Similarly, at Halesowen (until 1844 a detached part of Shropshire) 'they rose, and forced the people to sell cheese at two-pence halfpenny, and flower [*sic*] for 5s. They destroyed two dressing-mills before they dispersed.'[16]

Despite the semi-official attempts by local magistrates to forestall such incidents by putting pressure on farmers and millers, the government of the day was not prepared to stand idly by and let matters worsen into open revolt. Letters were sent to chief magistrates in each town where rioting had occurred requiring the names of known offenders as evidence for special Commissions that were set up to prosecute the rioters. Repression could often be swift and final – research by John Bohstedt has established that at least eight individuals (including one defender of property) were shot during the disturbances of 1766.[17]

However, the government also took some positive steps to alleviate the problem. One of the main bones of contention between the rioters and the authorities was the export of grain to the Continent, which continued even in times of poor harvests. An order to prohibit the export of corn, grain, meal, malt, flour, bread, biscuit and starch was made on 26 September 1766 and further measures soon afterwards licensed the importation of duty-free grain from America and the Continent.

This had a beneficial short-term effect, but 'bread and butter' uprisings, together with other demonstrations about the high price of staple foods, continued sporadically throughout the eighteenth and early nineteenth centuries (especially after the introduction of the Corn Laws (which limited the import of foreign grain, thereby increasing the price of domestic corn), and many more threatening letters were sent to magistrates and farmers. Thomas Biggs, a wealthy Stourbridge magistrate, received the following anonymous note in early September 1812:

> Mr. Bigges,
>
> Sir
>
> We right to let you no if you do not a medetley see that the bread is made cheper you may and all your nebern [neighbouring] farmers expect all your houses rickes barns all fiered and bournd down to the ground. You are a gestes [justice] and see all your felley cretyrs starved to death. Pray see for som alterreshon in a mounth or you shall see what shall be the matter.[18]

The Corn Laws and agitation for their repeal ensured that public unrest over staple food prices remained a threat to the social, political and economic *status quo* until the late 1840s.[19]

The rise of the propertied and the criminalization of customary perquisites

Private wealth and property had become an increasingly important sign of afflu-ence and respectability. Those who had amassed it (by whatever means) were increasingly unwilling to forfeit even a small part of it and were willing to expend considerable time and effort to regain it if lost. That the legal definitions of crime were very much a construct of the ruling social and cultural milieu is thus demonstrated by the reform of the criminal codes and penalties from a concen-tration on crimes against the person to a concentration on crimes against prop-erty: the eighteenth and early nineteenth centuries saw an inexorable rise in propertied interests and the codification of statute law against property theft and misappropriation, to the extent that it has been claimed that 'Parliament became for practical purposes the servant of propertied society after 1688.'[20]

The Industrial Revolution provided the basis for a further revolution in societal responses to property acquisition and larceny, with manufacturers and employers in the newly emergent factories and large commercial concerns becoming increas-ingly concerned about the continuation of what had formerly been seen as cus-tomary perquisites, such as the taking of wood chips from dockyards or the gathering-up of 'waste' textile materials in the booming textile mills of northern England. Frank McLynn suggests that the attitude of employers towards perks of the job had continually hardened throughout the preceding century, stating that 'in the woollen trade alone, eleven new embezzlement statutes were passed from 1725 to 1800'.[21] Indeed, the scale of workplace appropriation appears to have been 'rife' and of almost 'epidemic' proportions in the manufacturing industries of the nineteenth century.[22] Watchmen in factories, ironworks and other manufacturing concerns, whose job required them to apprehend 'embezzlers', admitted that they missed hundreds of workplace thefts for every one that they detected.[23] In the textile districts magistrates complained that the problem was out of control:

> In the town and neighbourhood whence I write, the principal employment of the labouring classes is that of weaving, in which misery and vice abounds to a greater extent than among any other class of operatives, but one of its demoralizing effects is seen in the training of weavers from their earliest childhood through all their subsequent career, in the various practices of embezzling the raw material [. . .] Their dealings in embezzlement, in every variety of form, destructive alike to the morals of the operative and the property of the respectable manufacturer, were never more rife than at present, and considerable activity is being shown in detecting offenders, making seizures, etc.[24]

In the late eighteenth century an increasing number of laws were drafted in order to try and prevent this misappropriation, most notably in the woollen and worsted industries. Godfrey and Cox have recently stated with regard to the punitive laws passed against the appropriation of worsted and associated materials that:

> Although a number of anti-appropriation acts were passed in the eighteenth century, just three acts, one passed in 1749 (22 Geo. II c.27) and two in 1777 (17 Geo. III c.11 and 17 Geo. III c.56) – collectively known as The Worsted Acts – changed the character of the fight against workplace appropriation [. . .] From 1749 the law acted against the 'theft' of manufactured goods, or goods in the process of being manufactured, whether they were taken from the street directly outside the factory, from the warehouse, or from inside the premises where the goods were made. Workers were essentially subject to the same laws of larceny inside the workplace as they were on the streets.[25]

The 1749 Act was a crucial development in that it altered the relationship between working people and the law in at least two key areas. First, it extended the scope of legal action against employees by allowing the prosecution of domestic workers who had failed to return the materials given out to them within twenty-one days (later reduced in 1777 to eight days by 17 Geo. III c.56). The 1749 Act was designed to enable the prosecution of those workers who were believed to have sold the materials entrusted to them to other parties where no real evidence existed other than the absence of the material itself, but it also struck hard at those workers who had pawned materials but who could not afford to redeem them. Second, the Act extended the power of surveillance into hitherto private areas. It permitted the houses and outbuildings of suspects to be searched by a policeman, accompanied by other interested parties. Of course, the issuing of a search warrant had previously allowed law agencies to enter and search a suspect's house, but now the victim or their agent was allowed to accompany the legal officers. Any suspicious goods that were found were confiscated by the authorities and could then be claimed by the owner. Alternatively, proof of purchase could be given by the accused within twenty-one days. If, however, the goods remained unclaimed by any party which could prove ownership the goods were publicly sold, the profits going to the parish.

The Worsted Acts passed in 1777 continued this process by further increasing the punishments for workplace appropriation, but they also refined the techniques of prosecuting the law in significant ways: the law forbade the embezzling of worsted waste or finished cloth, or the selling and/or buying of the same; it also made it illegal for workers to take a job in a false name, to be employed by more than one master, to wilfully damage their work, to leave their work uncompleted for eight days or to be found carrying suspicious goods after sunset.

Most importantly, the Act also established an employer-organized policing and prosecution agency financed in its operations by Yorkshire, Cheshire and Lancashire manufacturers from the rebate which they received relative to the amount of duty they had paid on soap used in the manufacturing process (from 1712 a heavy tax on soap had been introduced, continuing in various guises until 1853, and worsted manufacturers were able to claim a rebate on at least some of this tax). This agency was known as the Worsted Inspectorate and was invested with sweeping powers, including those of search and entry of suspects' houses and acting as both witness and prosecutor at trials involving worsted misappropriation.[26]

It was not just urban centres in which proprietorial interests were increasingly jealously guarded; from the late seventeenth century onward poaching and the taking of game from rural estates became the subject of severe and draconian punishment. Poaching became a major concern to the landed gentry throughout the period under discussion; it was seen as an attack both on their physical possessions and on their perceived social status. As a result, strenuous and often costly efforts were made to control or eradicate the activities of both opportunistic individuals and organized groups of poachers.[27]

The first line of defence in game preservation was the gamekeeper, who by this period played an important part in local law enforcement with regard to the Game Laws first codified in 1671 by 'An Act for the better preservation of the Game, and for securing warrens not inclosed, and the severall Fishings of this Realme' (22 & 23 Car. II c. 25), by which 'all lords of manors or other royalties not under the degree of esquire may from henceforth by writings under their hands and seals authorize one or more gamekeeper or gamekeepers within their respective manors or royalties'.[28] Peter King has argued that 'with their extensive rights to search labourers' cottages for game or poaching equipment the gamekeepers represented a powerful form of private policing'; they were 'given power to search houses for guns, bows or sporting dogs (in houses less than £100 freehold, £150 leasehold for 99 years or less, excepting houses of heirs apparent of squires and others of a 'higher degree')'.[29] P. B. Munsche has gone further, arguing that:

> The gamekeeper, in short, was a policeman. Indeed, aside from excise officers, he was the closest thing to a professional law-enforcement official to be found in rural England before the middle of the nineteenth century.[30]

While this claim is questionable given that the somewhat limited aims of a game-keeper extended only to protecting the property of his master rather than safe-guarding the commonweal, there were certainly a considerable number of gamekeepers throughout Britain in the late eighteenth and early nineteenth centuries. After the introduction of Game Licences in 1784, which required 'every person qualified in respect of property to kill game' to register his name and abode with and pay fees to the Clerk of the Peace and to register every appointment of a gamekeeper, the figure approached 4,000.[31]

In 1723 an Act (9 Geo. 1 c.22) 'for the more effectual punishing wicked and evil disposed Persons going armed in Disguise and doing Injuries and Violence to the Persons and Properties of His Majesty's Subject, and for the more speedy bringing the Offenders to Justice' became statute law following a series of daring poaching raids by two groups of men known respectively as the 'Waltham Blacks' and the 'Windsor Blacks', who blackened their faces in order to escape detection. The resultant Act, known as the Waltham Black Act, introduced the death penalty without the benefit of clergy for over fifty offences, including that of deer-stealing:

That after the first Day of June, 1723, whatever Persons, arm'd with offensive Weapons, and having their Faces black'd, or otherwise disguis'd, shall appear in any Forest, Park, or Grounds inclos'd with any Wall or Fence wherein Deer are usually kept, or any Warren where Hares or Conies are kept, or in any Highway, Heath or Down, or unlawfully hunt, kill, or steal any red or fallow Deer, or rob any Warren, or steal Fish out of any Pond, or maliciously break down the Head of any Fish-pond, or kill or wound Cattle, or set Fire to any House or Out-house, or Stack of Hay or Corn, or cut down, or otherwise destroy Trees planted for Shelter or Profit, or shall maliciously shoot at any Person, or send a Letter demanding Money, or other valuable Things, or shall rescue any Person in Custody of an Officer; for such an Offence, or by Gift or Promise procure any one to join with them, shall be deem'd guilty of Felony, without Benefit of Clergy, and shall sister Death as Felons so convicted.[32]

As the following case shows, the results for unsuccessful poachers could be devastating.

Case Study 5: William Johnson, poaching and murder, 1733

On 5 December 1733 William Johnson (aka Johnston), who was thirty years old and formerly a cooper who had served out his apprenticeship, appeared at the Old Bailey on one charge of deer-stealing and another of wilful murder.[33] He was accused of having illegally entered the fenced grounds of Bush Hill Park and killed one red deer and one fallow deer with dogs. Bush Hill Park was at the time a 438-acre estate belonging to Sir Jeremy Vanacker Sambrooke. Sir Jeremy was an influential and wealthy man, a baronet and MP for Bedford said to have been worth £12,000 a year.[34]

George Brice, one of Sir Jeremy's gamekeepers, stated that on the morning of 13 June he had reviewed the herd and found a number of deer missing. He inspected the fence surrounding the estate and found that two of the fence pales had been broken down. He made enquiries and detained Joseph Burgess, who appears to have turned King's Evidence and appeared for the prosecution at the trial.[35] Burgess stated that he had met Johnson in a public house and complimented him on his three dogs. After a few beers Johnson invited him to come with another acquaintance to 'see the dogs run'. Burgess accompanied Johnson and the other man, Robert Hill, to the boundary of Bush Hill Park, where Johnson broke down the fence and unleashed the dogs. A short while later Burgess and Hill came out of the park with two dead deer: one fallow, one red. Burgess then went back in and returned with a live fawn.

The parish constable, Andrew Hood, and his assistant, William Burley, were engaged by Brice and arrested Johnson some months later on 26 October in Bucklersbury, City of London.[36] The constables managed to pull Johnson from his horse and disarm him of two pistols in his pocket, but they were then apparently assaulted by Thomas Turner, an acquaintance of Johnson's, and in the mêlée Johnson recovered his pistols and ran for it.[37] A mob of men followed after him shouting 'Stop, thief!', including a resident of Dowgate, James Taaman, who tried to grab hold of Johnson, but who was then shot at by Johnson as he made one more grab at his coat.[38] Taaman received a pistol ball in the neck which shattered several of his vertebrae and died the next day from his injuries. Johnson was caught shortly after the shooting. In the Old Bailey's Ordinary's *Account*, Johnson claimed that he had fired the pistol in self-defence:

> [He] confest that he kill'd him, but without any Design; for he alleg'd, that as he persu'd him, he Burnt him in the Neck with a red-hot Iron, and he held out the Pistol to push him back, or give him a blow.[39]

The same account gave a potted biography of Johnson, stating that he was:

> Of reputable Parents in the Country, who gave him good Education at School, and put him to a Cooper in Town, to which he serv'd out his Time, and He liv'd by his Business for sometime; but being of an unsettl'd Disposition, he could not be confin'd, but frequented himself to bad Company, particularly of Deer-Stealers, which prov'd the occasion of all his Misfortunes. He for several Years past made it his chief Business to go in the Country, and robb'd Gentlemen's Parks of Deer. [He also] own'd, that he was very much guilty of Deer-stealing, and that he sold the Deer in Town, and sometimes kept it for his own Use; but excepting in trifling Things he never was a Thief.

Johnson obviously considered that deer-stealing from the wealthy was more a form of redistribution of goods than theft, but his actions in attempting to evade capture suggest that he was also fully aware of the consequences of his activities: that he was likely to be sentenced to death under the Waltham Black Act. Despite his claim that the gun went off by accident, at his confession before the death sentence was carried out on 19 December 1733 he 'confess'd himself Penitent, declar'd his Faith in Christ, and that he dy'd in Peace with all Mankind'.[40]

By the beginning of the nineteenth century organized poaching was widely considered (especially by its victims and its victims' employees) to be on the increase; David Jones remarks that 'in the second quarter of the century poaching was widely regarded as one of the fastest growing crimes in Britain' and, consequently, throughout the first decades of the century, anti-poaching laws became increasingly severe.[41] Lord Ellenborough's Act 1803 (43 Geo. III c.53) imposed an automatic death penalty if armed poachers resisted lawful arrest (including arrest by a gamekeeper) and in 1817 the penalty for unarmed night-time poaching was raised to seven years' transportation.[42]

Poaching and other acquisitorial activities such as workplace appropriation and smuggling have often been referred to by many modern historians as 'social crimes' – a term first coined by Eric Hobsbawm in the late 1950s, although, as John Lea remarks, 'the concept of social crime [. . .] is quite broad and at times even opaque'.[43] This type of crime has, however, been defined succinctly by James Sharpe:

> Crime, according to the classic formulation of this concept, can be regarded as 'social' when it represents a 'conscious, almost a political, challenge to the prevailing social and political order and its values'. It occurs when there exist conflicting sets of official and unofficial interpretations of the legal system, when acts of law-breaking contain clear elements of social protest, or when such acts are firmly connected to the development of social and political unrest.[44]

The authorities in the eighteenth century undoubtedly cracked down on property offences, including activities such as workplace appropriation, poaching and demonstrations of popular unrest. The rapid changes resulting from the burgeoning Industrial Revolution – from rural to urban society, from agricultural subsistence to proto-mass production – undoubtedly led to changes in attitudes to 'social crimes' such as poaching, smuggling, plundering and gleaning – such behaviour was increasingly no longer to be tolerated by those in positions of authority.

Increasing legislation against property and tax offences

These changes in the attitudes of those in power to such crimes were reflected in increasing legislation and stiffer penalties for those caught breaching the newly rewritten 'rules of the game'. There are, of course, numerous caveats to be aware of with regard to the attribution of specific offences to the category of 'social crime'. The activities of the notorious Hawkhurst Gang (see below), are unlikely to be simply attributable to poor individuals carrying out an illegal activity for their immediate social and economic need; rather, the gang can legitimately be seen as an early example of an organized criminal franchise, given the sheer number of those involved and the quantities of goods illicitly smuggled.[45]

Case Study 6: John Cook, smuggling, 1747

The *London Gazette* of 17 April 1747 carried the following public notice:

> At the Court at St James, the 16th day of April 1747
>
> Whereas John Cook, of Hawkhurst in the County of Kent, Labourer; Robert Mapesden [. . .]; Thomas Fuller [. . .]; Daniel Bunce, commonly called or known by the Name of Great Daniel, of or near Sittingbourn in the said County of Kent, Labourer; and Robert Bunce, commonly called or known by the Name of Half-Coat Robin [. . .] were upon the twenty-sixth day of March last, charged by Information of a credible Person upon Oath, by him subscribed before Thomas Burdus, Esquire, one of his Majesty's Justices of the Peace for the County of Middlesex, with having been guilty, upon the Eleventh Day of February last, of being, together with divers other Persons, armed with Fire Arms, or other offensive Weapons, and so armed being assembled at a Place called Folkstone Warren [. . .] in the County of Kent, in order to be aiding and assisting in the Running, Landing and Carrying away uncustomed Goods [. . .] – His Majesty doth [. . .] require and command, That the said John Cook [et al. . .] do surrender himself and themselves, within the Space of Forty Days after the first Publication of this Order in the London Gazette, to the Lord Chief Justice, or one other of his Majesty's Justices of the Court of King's Bench, or to one of his Majesty's Justices of the Peace.

The above order was published in two successive editions of the *London Gazette*, the government's official newspaper, and was also sent to the sheriff of the county in which the offence had taken place, to be proclaimed:[46]

> Between the Hours of ten in the Morning, and two in the Afternoon, in the Market-Places, upon the respective Market-Days, of two Market-Towns in the same County, near to the Place where such Offence shall have been committed; and a true Copy of such Order, shall be affixed upon some publick Place, in such Market-Towns; and in case such Offender or Offenders, shall not surrender himself or themselves, pursuant to such Order of His Majesty, or escaping after such Surrender, shall from the Day appointed for his or their Surrender, as aforesaid, be adjudged, deemed, and taken to be convicted and attainted of Felony, and shall suffer Death (as in Cases of a Person convicted and attainted, by Verdict and Judgment, of Felony) without Benefit of Clergy.

These proceedings had been brought about as a result of an Act of 1746 (often referred to as the Smuggling Act), in which it was enacted:

> That if any Persons shall go, to the Number of three, with Firearms or other offensive Weapons; shall from, and after the 24th Day of July 1746, be assembled in order to the assisting in carrying away uncustomed Goods, or Goods liable to pay any Duties; every Person so offending, being thereof

lawfully convicted, shall be adjudged guilty of Felony, and shall suffer Death without Benefit of Clergy.[47]

It was further enacted that anyone who turned in a '*Gazetted*' smuggler would receive a £500 reward. Any smuggler who killed a Customs or Revenue officer would be hanged and then gibbeted, while unresolved offences would incur fines on the county in which they took place, thereby providing an incentive for the county officials to exert themselves in catching perpetrators.[48]

John Cook, the first individual named in the above proclamation in the *London Gazette*, was a 28-year-old labourer born in Hastings to an agricultural day-labourer and his wife. He apparently received no formal education and followed in his father's footsteps until he turned to smuggling and became involved with the notorious Hawkhurst Gang. This highly organized gang of smugglers, which contemporaries reckoned to consist of up to 500 individuals, had spread terror and fear among both Revenue officers and members of the public for a number of years in the early 1740s with their audacious exploits:

> The Smugglers about Hawkhurst are so numerous, that upon founding a Horn they can assemble four or five hundred desperate Fellows; they are reckoned the most flagitious Crew of all that Set of People. Some Time ago a Gang of them met another belonging to Folkstone at Wingham-Street in East Kent, and robb'd them of their Horses, and broke open several Houses in the Country, call'd for what Drink they pleas'd at the Inns, and threatening to Shoot or Murder such as had the Impudence to ask any Money for their Liquor.[49]

The gang was also notorious for their cruel treatment of both captured informants and Revenue officers; the Ordinary at Newgate reported that Cook informed him that:

> They were scarce to be restrained by any Ties of Society, but those of their own Illegitimate, or to be persuaded to have any Regard to Men, or Things, but would have every thing their own way, unless he interposed to prevent Disorders, which he frequently did. Especially if an Officer has at any time fallen into their Hands, his Treatment was sure to be very barbarous; such as threatening with Pistols, and other offensive Weapons, being put in Fear of his Life, if not made away with.[50]

Indeed, in December 1744 Cook had personally been witness to this barbarity; three of four Customs officers who had been employed to round up the gang were themselves captured by the gang. One of the officers was let go, but the other two were horrifically tortured until:

> the unhappy Men begg'd they would knock them on the Head to put them out of their Miseries; but these barbarous Wretches told them, it was time enough to think of Death when they had gone through all their Exercise that they had

for them to suffer before they would permit them to go to the Devil. They then kindled a Fire between the two Trees, which almost scorched them to Death, and continued them in this Agony for some Hours, till the Wretches were wearied with torturing them; they then released them from the Trees, and carried them quite speechless and almost dead, on Board one of their Ships, from whence they never returned.[51]

On 15 July 1746 John Cook appeared at the Old Bailey charged with:

unlawfully and feloniously assembling themselves together, on the Eleventh of February last, at the Parish of Folkstone, in the County of Kent; being then and there armed with, and carrying Firearms, and other offensive Weapons, in order to be aiding and assisting, in the clandestine running, landing, and carrying away uncustomed Goods, and Goods liable to pay Duties, which had not been paid or secured; against the Statute.[52]

The evidence against Cook was overwhelming, and he was found guilty and sentenced to death despite the evidence of John Bolton, a Revenue officer, who stated with reference to the events of December 1744 that:

I was carried away in the Year 1744 by a Gang of Smugglers down to Hawkhurst; and we were carried down to the Place were the Prisoner at that Time lived, and he did prevent a great deal of Mischief that would have been done. I believe he was the chief Instrument of saving our Lives at that Time.[53]

Cook held out hope of a reprieve from his death sentence until the very end; the Ordinary remarked that:

Till he was told the Warrant to order his Execution was come down, he entertain'd great Hopes of Mercy, thinking what the Person (who is, or was an Officer) admitted by the Court to speak in his behalf, when upon his Trial, had given in Evidence, and upon Oath, wou'd have had some Weight towards mitigating the Rigout of his Sentence. But, were Circumstances ever so favourable, as I observed to him, the notorious Riots and Disorders which have been committed, seem to leave very little Room for Mercy to be extended to any Smuggler; especially such as have been advertised in the publick Papers, as common Disturbers of the Peace of their Country.[54]

The Ordinary was proved correct in his observations and John Cook was hanged at Tyburn on Wednesday 29 July 1747.

The Ordinary of Newgate observed in his account of the life and death of John Cook that:

Men, who follow this unlawful Practice of Smuggling, have long been under a strong Prepossesion, that the Crime for which they were condemned was not so heinous in the Sight of God, as the Punishment was severe by the

Laws of Men; and I am afraid, not only the unhappy Criminals themselves, but many well-meaning though unthinking Men labour under this fatal Mistake. The common People of England in general fancy that there is nothing in it, but cheating the King of a small Part of his Revenue; and that there is no Harm done to the Community in general, or to the Properties of particular Persons.[55]

He then provided a detailed account of his views on smuggling, concluding that:

Thus it is plain, that Smuggling is a Crime of the most dangerous Nature, both against the Community and private Persons, and as such subject to the Divine Displeasure, as much as any other Felony. It is not only a Sin as destructive to Society, and contrary to human Laws enacted for the Peace, Protection, and Subsistance of the State, but is a Sin against the literal Precepts, as well as the Meaning and Intent of Christianity: We are commanded Obedience to Government for Conscience sake; we are commanded to pay Tribute to whom Tribute is due.[56]

As the Ordinary of Newgate suggested, smuggling was one of those crimes that seemed to many people to be without a victim and was therefore perceived as a relatively trivial offence, merely a matter of economic survival and self-preservation, its overwhelming characteristic being what Lea has termed 'positive popular sanction', as opposed to political, economic or social protest.[57] For its perpetrators it had been a 'traditional' means of supplementing income for centuries, but the scale of governmental and official response in the eighteenth century was unprecedented, with increasingly severe laws legislating against its continuance.

The plundering of wrecks and the appropriation of salvageable goods was another 'traditional' activity which increasingly also came under the spotlight of the authorities during the eighteenth century, as is illustrated below.

Case Study 7: Plundering of the Adamant, 1815

On 5 December 1815 the *Morning Post* carried a report of the shipwreck of the *Adamant*, from Malta:

The brig, Adamant, Woodcock, Master, from Malta, with wine, came on shore under Seaford Cliff at five o'clock this morning [3 December]; she was got off by the boats from hence and Seaford, but a gale coming on she sunk about three-quarters of a mile before she reached the Pier-head. The Captain, crew and all who assisted her, are place under quarantine. Part of the ship is expected to be got at, at low water, but it is much feared this will prove a total loss of both ship and cargo. All the crew are safe.[58]

The *Adamant* was previously a Royal Navy vessel, *HMS Thrasher*, and as such was intrinsically valuable for her copper-bottomed hull. She had foundered in bad weather off the Sussex coast near Newhaven while carrying a considerable amount of cargo, which was underwritten by the insurers, Lloyd's of London, for £100,000. Such a large insurance figure was not unique – the *Scaleby Castle*, sailing from Bombay to London in 1801, was insured for a total of £148,700, while J.J. Angerstein, chairman of Lloyd's, estimated that private underwriters covered risks worth £140 million in 1809 alone.[59]

News of the wreck spread rapidly throughout the locality. *The Times* reported that 'the cargo and vessel were besieged by the inhabitants for miles round the country, and considered fair game for plunder'.[60] It was further reported that members of the local military force, rather than attempting to prevent the plundering, decided to help themselves; *The Times* reported that five soldiers 'joined in the general scramble for plunder', 'tapped a pipe of wine and carried away the wine in bushels'.[61]

Lloyd's were understandably perturbed by the illegal behaviour of the locals and therefore 'determined to endeavour to stop the system of plundering wrecks, and to make an example of the ringleaders'.[62] Consequently, two experienced Bow Street Principal Officers, along with Lloyd's representative Mr J.B. Stone, were directly employed by the Committee of Underwriters at Lloyd's to prevent the continuance of the plundering and to recover what stolen cargo they could.[63] They subsequently visited over 200 properties in the area. *The Times* reported that, on being told that they had carried out an illegal activity:

> the owners and occupiers [. . .] appeared astonished that they should be considered to have done wrong, considering it an undisputed and ancient right of the inhabitants near the spot where a wreck takes place, to appropriate whatever of the cargo and vessel they could save from the sea.[64]

It is unclear what part, if any, the sailors from the *Adamant* took in the salvage/plundering operation (the *Caledonian Mercury* of 11 December 1815 reported that the crew had by this time been released from quarantine), but they would certainly have had a vested interest in recovering goods, as Rainer Behre's research has suggested that 'only if the ship was salvaged could the sailors claim their wages'.[65] Participants in the activity of plundering argued that they were merely continuing ancient customs and rights of salvage, rather than consciously engaging in an illegal activity.

Among numerous finds the Officers recovered herring barrels stuffed with opium from the cellar of the Pelham Arms in Seaford near Newhaven and apprehended a marine stores dealer who was carrying a sack full of copper sheathing from the ship's keel. *The Times* reported that 'the part of the cargo of the wreck, principally saved by the officers, consisted of nutgalls [used for dyeing], quicksilver, goat skins, otto of roses [rose-water], yellow birch for making carpet brooms, and a variety of other articles'.[66] Contemporary newspaper reports make it clear that Lloyd's of London were as anxious to prevent the continuance of such behaviour as to reclaim the stolen goods and property, and the case also illustrates that plundering on such a large scale went on for many days, if not weeks – the cargo must have been considerable, as the Principal Officers managed to catch several perpetrators 'in the act' despite having arrived several days after the ship foundered.

Lloyd's of London evolved from the 1680s coffee house of Edward Lloyd as an insurance company specializing in the underwriting of shipping and by the early nineteenth century had become one of the leading private companies in England. The company employed insurance agents throughout the country, but these agents often complained when investigating cases of plundering that they did not receive sufficient help from local law-enforcement authorities. The agents on occasion attempted to prevent plundering by appearing at the wreck site in person and appealing directly to the plunderers; on one occasion in 1838 on the Wirral peninsula it was reported that: 'when a Lloyd's agent tried to stop them plundering [. . .] the wreckers replied: 'We are not taking anything. I suppose every man has a right to take what is here, one as much another.'[67]

The plundering of the *Adamant* was on such a scale that Lloyd's wanted to create a fear of retribution among the perpetrators of such an offence. Consequently, they employed the services of Bow Street, the use and reputation of which appears to have at least partially fulfilled the insurers' wishes; after it was made known that anyone found in possession of plundered goods would face prosecution and a severe punishment much of the 'booty' was subsequently handed in to the Bow Street Officers. The inhabitants involved in the plundering were clearly intimidated by the presence of the Principal Officers and the strenuous efforts of the insurance company. There was obviously a conflict of identities with regard to class and locale, with local affairs interfered in by people hired from London at the behest of the insurers. Prior to the proliferation of insurance companies and the creation of the London Police Offices, with their groups of professional, full-time police officers, there was no one, apart from the local parish constable, to enforce the law in such a situation. The parish constable may well have been reluctant to try to prevent such a popular activity, especially as he lived in the local community and had to face the consequences of his actions.

The act of plundering, although considered by many of those who participated in it to be nothing more than taking sensible advantage of someone else's unfortunate situation, as is illustrated by this case, had in fact been illegal for a considerable time. An Act passed in 1753 'for enforcing the laws against persons who shall steal or detain shipwrecked goods; and for the relief of persons suffering losses thereby' contained the following preamble:

> Whereas notwithstanding the good and salutary laws now in being against plundering and destroying vessels in distress, and against taking away shipwrecked, lost or stranded goods, many wicked enormities have been committed, to the disgrace of the nation, and to the grievous damage of merchants and mariners of our own and other countries.[68]

This was clearly an attempt to strengthen existing laws on plundering, the legal penalties for which were extremely harsh: death without benefit of clergy, whil petty larceny was punishable by six months' imprisonment. JPs were to issue search warrants and assaults on JPs or officers of the law were punishable by seven years' transportation. The Act does not differentiate between plundering and wrecking, although these activities could be quite separate; the deliberate wrecking of ships by luring them on to rocks by means of false signals often had far more serious consequences with regard to loss of life than did removing property from a ship that had been wrecked accidentally.[69]

Such breaches of these regulations were by no means confined to the Newhaven area; contemporary sources carry numerous accounts of plundering. In a letter circulated to his subordinates in January 1817 the bishop of St David's exhorted them to preach against:

> The cruel and unchristianlike enormity of plundering wrecks; and that, for the future, they will preach to them on this subject once a quarter, or at least twice a year [. . .] the practice is wholly repugnant to every principle, spiritual and practical, of the benevolent religion they profess.[70]

The burgeoning Industrial Revolution and the rapid growth of financial services (on which so much of Britain's prosperity was to rely in the following century) also provided individuals with many new opportunities for enterprising criminal activity, as following case study shows.

Case Study 8: William Phillips senior and junior, coining, 1815–18

Following the creation of the Bank of England in 1694 and the Bank of Scotland a year later the success of the burgeoning financial industry led to a flourishing of provincial banks throughout Britain, each of which produced their own currency.[71] This provided a hithero unrivalled opportunity for forgers and counterfeiters. Forgery in the form of counterfeiting also increased dramatically in the years following the decision to suspend payment in gold by the Bank of England in 1797; the Bank simply did not possess enough gold to honour its pledge to redeem its paper notes. The subsequent paper notes issued in lieu by the Bank proved irresistible to forgers, causing a caustic anonymous correspondent in 1809 to suggest that every time a forgery was discovered a Bank of England director should be publicly hanged. This measure, contended the writer, would rapidly improve note design and quality of printing.[72]

Strenuous efforts were made by the Bank of England and its Scottish counterpart to detect and apprehend forgers. Freshfields (solicitors acting for the Bank of England) employed several investigators on at least a semi-permanent basis, one of the best known being Thomas Glover, who is referred to in correspondence from West Country sources concerning widespread rumours of forgeries.[73] Such investigations could often result in high costs.[74] Randall McGowen estimates that in 1820 alone the Bank of England spent over £50,000 on the prosecution and investigation of forgery.[75]

Two examples will suffice to indicate the often considerable costs involved in such investigations. First, in 1779 a forgery investigation carried out by two

Bank of Scotland employees is recorded as reaching a total cost of £56 16s. 7d. Successful prosecution of the case cost a total of £128 17s. 11d., justice coming at a high price in this instance.[76] Second, an investigation of a forgery case at Cockermouth in 1812 carried out on behalf of Freshfields cost the Bank over £93 for the services of their investigator Mr Christian and his deputy.[77]

The Royal Mint, as the body charged with producing and standardizing much of the coin of the realm, also carried out prosecutions for coining. Coinage was in desperately short supply owing to the demands of the Army and Navy payroll, a situation the government had attempted to rectify in 1804, when on 8 March of that year the Privy Council requested blank dollars of Spanish silver to be stamped by Matthew Boulton of Birmingham and circulated at 5s. By 11 May 1804 dollars were being stamped at the Soho Mint in Handsworth. The *Manchester Guardian* of 12 May 1804 reported that:

> the new coinage of crown pieces from Dollars is now going on with all possible dispatch, at Mr Boulton's manufactory, the Soho, near Birmingham. Within these few days three waggons loaded with dollars were sent from the Bank, under a proper escort, to that place, each waggon contains about seven tons weight.

The 'proper escort' seems to have been a contingent of Bow Street Principal Officers, presumably accompanied by armed guards; Fitzgerald reports that two particular officers, John Vickery and Stephen Lavender, were often used for such purposes.[78] Similarly, in 1812 the *Morning Chronicle* of 18 August reported that Harry Adkins (another Bow Street Principal Officer) had conveyed the huge sum of £33,000 in overstamped dollars (well over £3 million in today's terms) to Portsmouth in order to supply the Army Pay officers with cash with which to pay the army.

From 1811 to 1813 the Bank of England made further attempts to alleviate the problem by introducing Bank of England tokens in denominations of 1s. and 3s. 6d. These tokens had a face value greater than that of their metal content, with a total amounting to almost £2 million. Unfortunately, the scarcity of small denominations of coin continued to worsen during the Napoleonic Wars. In 1815 Britain's national debt stood at over £800 million and the shortage of coin, combined with a general economic turndown due to the return of some half a million demobbed soldiers and sailors, led to many people taking serious risks in order to return a quick profit – the penalty for forgery and counterfeiting was death.

On 29 July 1818 Joseph Smith, a 41-year-old farmer from Halesowen, together with William Phillips senior, a 50-year-old steel toymaker from Birmingham, and his son, William Phillips junior, a 20-year-old shoemaker, appeared at Shrewsbury Assizes charged with High Treason by dint of 'counterfeiting the current coin of the realm'.[79]

As much of the evidence in the trial was circumstantial in nature, Sir William Owen, counsel to the Royal Mint, refused to pay the considerable prosecution expenses and expressed a wish that the trial not proceed. This view was heavily criticized by both the Grand Jury and the trial judge, who stated that the trial expenses would be met from the County Rate, and the trial then went ahead.

Joseph Smith resided at Uffmoor House, on the outskirts of Halesowen. He turned King's Evidence at the trial and stated that a few years ago two people named Bradley and Newnham asked to rent an upper room and cellar in his farmhouse. He agreed, and the two men then installed a nine-foot-long iron machine into the cellar, which he since knew to be a press for the production of counterfeit coins. Bradley and Newnham continued with their activities in the cellar for about a year until Newnham died in September 1816. At Christmas 1816 Bradley removed all his goods from Smith's farmhouse with the exception of the press. The following September William Phillips senior visited Smith, stating that he was a friend of Bradley (who had since been transported to Australia for felony), and he negotiated terms for continuing to use the press in the cellar.[80]

Phillips senior and junior used the press from the following April. The cellar's window was blocked up except for a small ventilation hole. Smith visited the press in operation on one occasion and stated at the trial that the operation was very quick, with the forged items being struck in a matter of seconds. The existence of the press appears to have leaked out, as Joseph Smith's son testified that he had been given a message from Phillips senior that 'a screw was loose': in other words, the game was up and Phillips intended to relocate the press. Smith panicked and instructed his son to bury the flywheel in a field on 7 May 1818.

Smith's and Phillips' fears were justified, as Chief Constable Joseph Grainger of the Halesowen parish constabulary paid a visit to the farm on 9 May 1818 as the result of a tip-off. Ostensibly he searched the farm for some lost poultry, but soon discovered the press, together with some unstruck blanks, several forged bank tokens and other forged coins. Chief Constable Grainger took Smith into custody and then arrested the Phillips at their home in Birmingham.[81]

Smith voluntarily confessed all at a pre-trial hearing in front of Halesowen magistrates on 15 May 1818. At the subsequent Assizes he strongly denied knowing that there was a reward offered upon successful conviction of the other prisoners; he also refuted the claim that he sought to escape punishment by turning King's Evidence. *The Times* of 8 August 1818 carried the following statement by Smith:

> I first gave information to Mr Woodcock [one of the Halesowen magistrates] on the 9th May last: I voluntarily confessed to him; I do not know, upon my honour (at this expression of witness there was an involuntary laugh in the Court), upon my word, upon my oath, that there is a reward for convicting the prisoners; I do not know that I shall be free from punishment by giving evidence to convict the prisoners; but I have been told by the elder prisoner [Phillips senior], and before I have heard such a thing said in my own country. I told the magistrate I would confess, before I knew I should be free for so doing.

An expert witness in the shape of a Shrewsbury silversmith was called to the witness stand to give evidence as to the nature of the forged items found at the Uffmoor press. He opined that the forged coins were illegally stamped, but that they were not in a finished condition – it appears that they were not milled around the edge, which they would need to have been in order to pass for coin of the realm.[82] He further deposed that the forged items would also have needed to be resilvered after being stamped in the press.

In his summing-up the judge cautioned the jury that they must not reach a verdict solely on Smith's evidence, as two men's lives depended upon their decision. He also stressed the judiciousness of the prosecution in basing its case on the operation of the die, as the unfinished forgeries found at the scene could not have sustained a prosecution on their own as they were in an unfinished state. Neither could the trial have been founded on the possession of the machine, as it remained unclear which of the Phillips owned it. However, the *Chester Chronicle* reported that 'the Jury consulted for a few minutes, when they returned a verdict of GUILTY against both prisoners'.[83]

However, Phillips senior and junior appear to have been extremely fortunate in that the judge, Mr Justice Holroyd, clearly had doubts as to the legal validity of the verdict, stating that 'the evidence might possibly not be sufficient to support the indictment' of High Treason, and conscientiously he respited the verdict.[84] The case was therefore placed before the 'Twelve Judges', a body comprising the most senior Law Lords in the House of Lords that was consulted on cases in which the legality of the verdict was questionable.[85]

Surviving records as to the eventual fate that befell Phillips senior and junior are conflicting; the Calendar of Prisoners for the Summer Assizes of 1818 (a printed record of those suspects appearing before Assize judges) states that judgement in their case was indeed respited and that they were not sentenced to death, but rather to sentences of seven years' transportation to Australia. However, the *Chester Chronicle* of 18 December 1818 carried the following report:

> The point reserved by Mr Justice Holroyd at the trial of William Phillips the elder, and William Phillips the younger, who were found guilty at Shrewsbury Assizes, of having in their possession a die on which was the impression of a shilling, having been referred to the Twelve Judges, his Royal Highness the Prince Regent has, in consequence of their report thereon, granted the prisoners a free pardon.

Joseph Smith appears to have learned the error of his ways; he is not mentioned in any subsequent criminal records and in the 1851 census he is recorded as still living at Uffmoor House farm with his family, farming 110 acres and employing three agricultural labourers and one domestic servant.

Counterfeiting and forgery of coins and notes of the realm continued to be a serious problem, but from 1817 counterfeiters found it increasingly difficult to forge used coins as in that year the Royal Mint recalled all official silver coinage and issued new coins that were more difficult to copy.

Conclusion

It has been demonstrated in this chapter that throughout the eighteenth century there was a considerable hardening of attitudes towards property offences and this was reflected both in increased legislation against such behaviour and a concomitant introduction of stiffer penalties for those caught breaking the newly written laws.

The increased policing of such crimes – including the creation of the National Coast Guard in 1821, the use of Bow Street and Revenue Officers in smuggling cases, and the increasingly severe Game Laws, together with the plethora of new legislation aiming to stamp out property crimes – was the result of what Stanley Cohen and Andrew Scull have referred to in *Social Control and the State* as a period 'when the whole apparatus of the State dealing with the criminal law, police and punishment underwent a revolution as substantial as the Industrial Revolution that Britain was experiencing at the same time'.[86]

This 'revolution' also had significant consequences in the executive branch of criminal justice involved in the detection and capture of criminals, and it is this aspect to which our attention turns in the following chapter.

Notes

1 A hundred was an administrative area created in the tenth century normally consisting of a number of parishes.
2 1Edw. VI. c. 3.
3 Shropshire Archives P54/L/12/8 Notice to the Overseers of the Poor at Cardington, 1741.
4 *Journal of the House of Lords: volume 63: 1830–1831*, 'Appendix: Poor Laws: 18 February 1831'.
5 *Annual Register*, vol. 9 (1766) p. 137.
6 George Rudé, *The Crowd in History* (London: Serif, 1995), p. 37.
7 John Rule, *Albion's People: English Society, 1714–1815* (London: Macmillan, 1992), p. 11.
8 John Rule, 'Food Riots in England 1792–1818', in Quinault, R. and Stevenson, J. (ed.), *Popular Protest and Public Order: Six Studies in British History 1790–1920* (London: Allen and Unwin, 1974), pp. 37–74: p. 35.
9 George Rudé, *The Crowd in History: A Study of Popular Disturbances in France and England 1730–1848* (London: Serif, 1995), p. 37. These uprisings were concentrated largely in the Midlands of England. For a comprehensive list of riots in 1766 see www. web.utk.edu/~bohstedt/files/RCV_1766–1767.pdf.
10 E. P. Thompson, *The Making of the English Working Class* (Harmondsworth: Penguin, 1991), p. 69.
11 Rule, 'Food Riots in England', p. 54.
12 A. Charlesworth (ed.), *An Atlas of Rural Protest in Britain 1548–1900* (London: Croom Helm, 1983), p. 63.
13 See Chapter 7 for further details of the creation of what became known as the *Hue & Cry and Police Gazette*.
14 *Hue & Cry*, 16 June 1810.
15 *Annual Register*, vol. 9 (1766), p. 137.
16 *Annual Register*, vol. 9 (1766), p. 137.
17 Reports of the death of eight rioters near Kidderminster appeared in several letters published in contemporary newspapers, but recent research has cast doubt on the

validity of the claim – see J. Bohstedt, *The Politics of Provisions: Food Riots, Moral Economy and Market Transition in England c.1550–1850* (Farnham: Ashgate, 2010), p. 158. For the definite fatalities, see www.web.utk.edu/~bohstedt/files/RCV_1766–1767.pdf.

18 *Hue and Cry*, 6 February 1813.

19 The Corn Laws were introduced by the Importation Act 1815 (55 Geo. 3 c.26) and repealed by the Importation Act 1846 (9 & 10 Vict. c.22). For details of food disturbances from the sixteenth to the eighteenth century, see R. B. Outhwaite, *Dearth, Public Policy and Social Disturbance in England, 1550–1800* (Cambridge: CUP, 1995). For further details of rural food riots during the eighteenth century, see Rudé, *The Crowd in History*, pp. 33–46, and for wider social unrest during the period see Rule and Wells, *Crime, Protest and Popular Politics*.

20 Langford, P., *Public Life and the Propertied Englishman 1689–1798* (Oxford: Clarendon Press, 1994), p. 586. For the role of women in riots, see 'The Woman Rioter or the Riotous Woman', in O. Hufton, *The Prospect Before Her: A History of Women in Western Europe volume one 1500–1800* (London: HarperCollins, 1995), pp. 458–86.

21 Frank McLynn, *Crime and Punishment in Eighteenth-century England* (London: Routledge, 1989), p. 302.

22 A. Randall, 'Peculiar Perquisites and Pernicious Practices. Embezzlement in the West of England Woollen Industry, c.1750–1840', *International Review of Social History* 35 (1992): 193–219, p. 193; R. Soderlund, '"For the Protection of Manufacturer's Property": Policing the Workplace in the Yorkshire Worsted Industry in the Age of Liberal Capitalism, 1810–45' (paper given to the annual meeting of the North American Labour History Conference 1993).

23 D. J. V. Jones, *Crime in Nineteenth Century Wales* (Cardiff: University of Wales Press, 1992): p. 124.

24 *Justice of the Peace* 1843: p. 1243. For a detailed examination of workplace appropriation in the late eighteenth and early nineteenth century, see Godfrey and Cox.

25 Godfrey and Cox, *Policing the Factory*, p. 9.

26 The Worsted Inspectorate continued in much modified form until 1968.

27 The preservation of game and attempts to prevent poaching were not exclusive to the eighteenth century; several laws preventing the taking of game from royal and feudal estates dated back to the early medieval period, but the Game Law of 1671 was the first attempt to provide a coherent and codified law against the practice. For a detailed examination of game and anti-poaching laws in the eighteenth and early nineteenth centuries see P. Munsche, *Gentlemen and Poachers: the English Game Laws 1671–1831* (Cambridge: CUP, 1981).

28 22 & 23 Car. II c.25.

29 Peter King, *Crime, Justice, and Discretion in England 1740–1820* (Oxford: OUP, 2000), p. 64, and J. F. Stephen, *A History of the Criminal Law of England*, 3 volumes (London: Macmillan, 1883), vol. 3, p. 280.

30 P. B. Munsche, 'The Gamekeeper and English Rural Society', *Journal of British Studies* XX.2 (1981): 82–105, p. 83.

31 Game Certificates Act 1784 (24 Geo. III c.43).

32 Benefit of clergy was a legal fiction dating back to the Middle Ages by which anyone who could read or recite a Psalm from the Bible (normally Psalm 51: *Miserere mei, Deus, secundum misericordia tuam* [O God, have mercy upon me according to your heartfelt mercifulness], which thereby came to be known colloquially as the 'Neck Verse') could claim to be tried by an ecclesiastical court rather than by secular, royally appointed judges. By claiming the status of a cleric offenders could be sentenced under spiritual rather than temporal law, which replaced the secular death penalty for felonies with the lesser punishment of branding (usually on the left thumb). In 1706 the reading test was abolished and all perpetrators of offences that could receive

benefit of clergy were allowed it. The system of benefit of clergy was not formally abolished by Parliament until 1827. For a detailed account of the history of benefit of clergy, see Beattie, *Crime and the Courts*, pp. 141–48.

33 For further details of this case, see OBP t17331205–54.

34 C. D. Linnell (ed.), *Diary of Benjamin Rogers, Rector of Carlton 1720–1771* (Bedford: Bedfordshire Historical Record Society, 1950), p. 23.

35 Turning King's (or Queen's) Evidence was a method by which accused individuals could give prosecutorial evidence against their accomplices in order to receive either a lesser sentence or a pardon. This practice dates back to at least the medieval period and is still in use today.

36 Presumably the parish constable and his assistant were either acting extra-legally or had the assistance of the local constable, as they would have had no legal jurisdiction outside their parish.

37 Thomas Turner was later tried and acquitted at the Old Bailey of aiding the escape of a prisoner – see OBP t17340116–14.

38 James Taaman is recorded as a taxpayer of 5d. at Dowgate in 1733 – see *London Land Tax Records* 1692–1932: London Metropolitan Archives, accessed through www. ancestry.co.uk.

39 OA 17331219. Taaman would appear to have been either a blacksmith or engaged in some other form of metalworking, as he was possessed of the 'red-hot iron'.

40 OA 17331219.

41 David J. V. Jones, 'The Poacher: A Study in Victorian Crime and Punishment', *Historical Journal* XXII (1974): 825–60, p. 825. For a poacher's view of the game laws, see Garth Christian (ed.), *A Victorian Poacher: James Hawker's Journal* (Oxford: OUP, 1978).

42 Charles Chenevix Trench, *The Poacher and the Squire: A History of Poaching and Game Preservation in England* (London: Longmans, 1967), p. 148.

43 A seminal article on 'social crime' remains John Rule's 'Social Crime in the Rural South in the Eighteenth and Early Nineteenth Century', *Southern History* 1 (1979): 35–53. For a succinct overview of the concept of 'social crime', see John Lea, 'Social Crime Revisited', *Theoretical Criminology* 3.3 (1999): 307–25. This article is an overview of the perceptions and definitions of social crime and aims to relate the concept to modern-day illegal activities such as street crime and the widespread protests over the poll tax. 'Social crime' has also exercised sociologists and criminologists as well as historians; for example, see Stanley Cohen and Andrew Scull (eds), *Social Control and the State: Historical and Comparative Essays* (Oxford: OUP, 1983).

44 Sharpe, *Crime in Early Modern England*, p. 122.

45 For a detailed account of the history of Customs and Excise, see W. J. Ashworth, *Customs and Excise: Trade, Production, and Consumption in England 1640–1845* (Oxford: OUP, 2003).

46 OBP t17470715–1.

47 OBP t17470715–1. The Smuggling Act's official title was 'An Act for the further punishment of persons going armed or disguised, in defiance of the laws of Customs and Excise. . .' (19 Geo. II c.34).

48 For a discussion of exactly what gibbeting involved, see Chapter 5.

49 OA 17470729.

50 OA 17470729.

51 OA 17470729.

52 OBP t17470715–1.

53 OBP t17470715–1. Two of the men who kidnapped Bolton in 1744 were eventually tried on 9 December 1747. Peter Tickner and James Hodges, described as 'ringleaders' of the Hawkhurst Gang, were both sentenced to transportation for life – see OBP t17471209–52.

54 OA 17470729.

55 OA 17470729.
56 OA 17470729.
57 Lea, 'Social Crime Revisited'.
58 A Quarantine Act was first introduced in England in 1710 (9 Anne c.2) in order to prevent the transmission of plague. The period of quarantine could last up to two months.
59 H. A. L. Cockerell and Edwin Green, *The British Insurance Business 1547–1970* (London: Heinemann Educational books, 1976), pp. 6 and 13.
60 *The Times*, 27 December 1815.
61 *The Times*, 27 December 1815.
62 *The Times*, 27 December 1815.
63 The creation and use of the force of Bow Street Principal Officers (more commonly referred to as 'Runners' is discussed in detail in Chapter 5.
64 *The Times*, 27 December 1815.
65 Rainer Behre, 'Shipwrecks and the Body: 18th and 19th Century Encounters with Death and Survival at Sea' (paper delivered at the *Controlling Bodies – the Regulation of Conduct 1650–2000 Conference*, University of Glamorgan, July 2002).
66 *The Times*, 27 December 1815.
67 Rule and Wells, *Crime, Protest and Popular Politics*, p. 159.
68 Danby Pickering, *The Statutes At Large from the 23rd to the 26th year of King George II*, Statute 26 Geo. II c.19 (London and Cambridge: Joseph Bentham, 1765).
69 Wrecking seems to have attracted far more attention in fiction than in real life. For an exploration of the myth and reality of the practice, see C. J. Pearce, *Cornish Wrecking, 1700–1860: Reality and Popular Myth* (Woodbridge: The Boydell Press, 2010).
70 *The Times*, 6 January 1817.
71 The number of provincial banks more than doubled between 1790 and 1820.
72 *Bank of England Freshfields' Papers, F2/166 AB 179/6*. It has been estimated that between 1805 and 1823 there were some 263,990 forged notes in circulation (*Report of the Constabulary Force Commissioners Police 8* [1839], p. 5).
73 *Bank of England Freshfields' Papers F2/155 AB 91/12*, various letters dated 6–21 April 1801. Thomas Glover sent back a detailed series of reports, together with his own comments on how and why the rumours had started. He visited Brixham, Totnes, Torquay, Dartmouth and Exeter in his exertions to find the culprits.
74 *First Report of the Commissioners appointed to inquire as to the best means of establishing an efficient Constabulary Force in the counties of England and Wales (169)* (London: House of Commons, 1839), p. 5.
75 Randall McGowen, 'The Bank of England and the Policing of Forgery, 1797–1821' (paper given 28 November 2003, European Centre for Policing Studies, Open University). For further details on how the Bank of England prosecuted forgery and coining, see Randall McGowen, 'Managing the Gallows: The Bank of England and the Death Penalty, 1797–1821', *Law and History Review* 25.2 (2007): 241–82.
76 Alan Cameron, *Bank of Scotland 1695–1995: A Very Singular Institution* (Edinburgh: Mainstream Publishing, 1995), pp. 102–3.
77 *Bank of England Freshfields' Papers F22/8 AB64/2: Correspondence concerning forgery in Cockermouth 15 April–8 July 1812*. This case shows that the Bank of England employed its own investigators as well as occasionally calling upon the expertise of Bow Street or the other Police Offices.
78 P. Fitzgerald, *Chronicle of Bow Street Police Office: With an Account of the Magistrates, "Runners" and Police*, 2 volumes (London: Chapman & Hall, 1888 [reprinted as a one-volume book with an introduction by Anthony Babington and index: Montclair, NJ: Patterson Smith, 1972]), vol.1, p. 111.
79 *Chester Chronicle*, 8 August 1818. Halesowen was a detached part of Shropshire until 1844, hence the trial being held in Shrewsbury. 'Toys' in the eighteenth and nineteenth century referred to any small metal objects, not necessarily children's playthings.

80 The person in question was possibly John Bradley, who was convicted of larceny at Warwick Assizes and transported for seven years on 1 April 1817.

81 Grainger must have sought the assistance of the Birmingham parish constabulary, as he would not have had the power of arrest outside his own parish.

82 Milling was (and remains) a process by which the edge of coins were given ridges in order to prevent 'clipping', whereby the edges of coins were clipped in order to obtain small off-cuts of silver or gold which could then be melted down.

83 *Chester Chronicle*, 8 August 1818.

84 *Chester Chronicle*, 8 August 1818. There was at the time no right of appeal for convicted individuals.

85 For a detailed account of the work of the Twelve Judges see James Oldham, 'Informal Lawmaking in England by the Twelve Judges in the Late Eighteenth and Early Nineteenth Centuries', *Law & History Review* 29.1 (2011): 181–220, and for their specific involvement in forgery cases, see Randall McGowen, 'Forgery and the Twelve Judges in Eighteenth-Century England', *Law & History Review* 29.1 (2011): 221–57.

86 Cohen and Scull, *Social Control and the State*, p. 62.

4   Capturing the criminal

Introduction

> It was not safe to go out at night owing to the profusion of housebreakers, highwaymen, and footpads – and especially because of the savage barbarity of the two latter, who commit the most wanton cruelties.[1]

The above words were written in 1750 by Horace Walpole, Whig politician and author of Gothic novels, during the turbulent times in England which followed the demobilization of many thousands of troops at the end of the War of the Austrian Succession (1740–48). Walpole, youngest son of former Prime Minister Robert Walpole, was speaking from experience, as he had been held up at gunpoint by highway robbers in November 1749.[2]

The reaction of men such as Walpole, who had much to fear and much to lose from both the imagined and actual threats of lawless men terrorizing the prosperous, seems to have been curiously ambivalent. On the one hand they wanted an effective executive organization that could prevent the perceived increase in offences against property and person, but on the other they did not wish to create a 'Continental'-style force in the same mould as the militaristic *gendarmerie* present in France (which had developed from the *Maréchaussée*, in existence since the Middle Ages).[3] At the same time they were aware that the cost of such a force would probably be a matter of vigorous debate.

Thanks to studies by historians such as John Beattie, David G. Barrie and Alistair Dinsmor it is now widely accepted among criminal justice and police historians that modern policing in Britain did not begin with the creation of the Metropolitan Police in London in 1829.[4] Recent research into pre-Metropolitan policing has revealed a wide range of both publicly and privately funded policing bodies. Whiggish assertions that the 'New Police' – those created by the 1835 Municipal Corporations Act, 1839 Rural Constabulary Act and the 1856 County and Borough Police Act (19 & 20 Vict. c. 69) – 'quickly ended a long period of uncontrollable crime and disorder which had lasted, in some parts of the country, for more than a century' can no longer be accepted at face value.[5] Research by historians such as Robert Reiner and Cyril D. Robinson has, as Stanley Cohen and Andrew Scull remark, 'destroyed for ever the idea of a simple, linear progression from "bad" old parish constables and watchmen to "good" new, uniformed police forces'.[6]

The eighteenth century saw a move from informal and communal responses to criminality to a more professional and officially controlled form of law enforcement; whereas 'amateur office-holding and voluntary prosecution, supported by state majesty and divine providence, were the keystones of accusatory justice in early modern England', by the end of our period several developments had begun to transform the ways in which crime and criminals were both regarded and dealt with.[7]

Historical background

From Anglo-Saxon times a communal system of policing largely based around 'hue and cry' had been in place in England. This system, David C. Cox states, 'required that all members of a neighbourhood should be responsible for pursuing and capturing suspected criminals'.[8] In 1285 this requirement was placed on a more legal footing by the Statute of Winchester (13 Edw. I, St. 2), which stated that:

> Cries shall be solemnly made in all Counties, Hundreds, Markets, Fairs and all other place where great resort of people is, so that none shall excuse himself by ignorance, that from henceforth every County be so well kept, that immediately, upon such robberies and felonies committed, fresh suit shall be made from town to town.

As John Beattie has pointed out, 'the hue and cry [. . .] depended at least in part on a broad public acceptance of the criminal law'; without such acceptance, it would have failed to function – if a community did not think that an activity was worthy of punishment, any request for 'hue and cry' would have been unsuccessful.[9]

By the time of Edward I's reign another system of law enforcement was also developing: that of the parish constabulary. This system remained the mainstay of executive law enforcement until the mid-nineteenth century. The Statute of Winchester stated that:

> A watch is to be kept in every town, parish, village and tything, every night from Ascension till Michaelmas, from sunset to sunrise, which the constables etc must constantly cause to be set, and that by two or four men, according to the greatness of the place [. . .] The watchmen must be men of body, well and sufficiently armed.[10]

In 1626 a parish constable, James Gyfronn, penned the following doggerel about his duties:

> I a constable haue tooke myne oath;
> By which shall plaine appeere

The troth and nothing but the troath,
Whoseuer my song will heere.
One greate constable of Ingland was,
Another late should haue ben;
But litle ones now is found will serue,
So they be but honnest men.
A constable must be honest and just;
Haue knowledge and good reporte;
And able to straine with bodie and braine,
Ells he is not fitting for 't.[11]

Contemporary records kept by parish constables, such as those published in Thornhill's *A Village Constable's Accounts (1791–1839)*, go some way to illuminating the wide-ranging day-to-day duties of provincial parish constables, which were often far removed from criminal investigation; they included, for example, the maintenance of public highways, the collecting of dead foxes and the paying of poor relief to soldiers, widows and others.[12]

One of the main duties of the parish constable, however, was to serve warrants on suspects and bring them before a Justice of the Peace for a summary hearing. Such a warrant, issued by magistrate W. Forester, survives from 1752:

> To the High and Petty Constables in the Hundred of Bradford South; to each and every one of them, particularly to the constables of Buildwas. This is in His Majesty's name to will and require you, or one of you, upon receipt, hereof, to bring before me or any other of His Majesty's justices of the peace for this County, the body of the desired persons in this list here annexed at the Talbot Inn in Wellington upon Wednesday next, the 22nd inst. to answer to such matters of complaint as will be objected against them by the overseers of the poor of the parish of Buildwas aforesaid and to be examined touching the several places of their last legal settlement. And further to do and receive as to justice appertaineth hereof. Fail not, as you will answer the contrary at your peril. Given under my hand and seal the 17th day of April 1752.[13]

While it would be a mistake to accept at face value portrayals of the parish constable as little more than a figure of ridicule, as memorably personified by Dogberry and Verges in *Much Ado about Nothing* (and it must be remembered that these two bumbling constables did in fact get their man), there was undoubtedly considerable and longstanding criticism of the parish constabulary system. However, it remains the case that until the end of the eighteenth century virtually no professionally organized policing system was available at any place in Great Britain; instead, the system of law enforcement was largely dependent upon the ancient parish constabulary system, and some parish constables undoubtedly did their duty honourably and to the best of their ability, often serving for several years.

Moreover, despite there remaining, as Alastair Dinsmor remarks, 'a tendency to dismiss any policing organization before 1829 as not being "real" policemen, just a collection of old nightwatchmen or bumbling parish constables', an increasing body of evidence is emerging to suggest that the system was not always ineffi-cient.[14] Work by both James Sharpe and John Styles has shown that in some loca-tions both the parish constabulary and the local magistracy occasionally proved effective in preventing and detecting crime.[15]

Similarly, R. W. England's work on the investigation of murders in Northern England in the first quarter of the nineteenth century suggests that magistrates within the Northern Circuit often relied heavily on the investigative skill and prowess of their local constables. He provides summaries of four cases showing constables' detective skills and tenacity and also indicates that this skill was not exclusive to the North of England, giving several examples from further afield. Successful prosecutions of murders in Bitton parish, Gloucestershire (1824), and in Tilhurst parish, Berkshire (1817), resulted from basic forensic examination of footprints. The former case also involved the investigation of trouser marks made by sitting ambushers, while the latter involved measuring footprints and stride lengths and comparing heel marks – boots and shoes were, at the time, all hand-made, and therefore individual.[16]

Whether or not the parish constabulary should be seen as useful law-enforce-ment officers, one of the main problems with the parish constabulary system outside London seems to have been the lack of manpower. Roger Swift's research into the policing of Wolverhampton reveals that in the first decade of the nine-teenth century the town had a population of *c*.13,000 and possessed only two parish constables, although in 1814 a night-watch of ten men was finally created to supplement this meagre force.[17] Similarly, in 1812, Stourbridge in Worcestershire had a population of *c*.4,500 and one parish constable.[18]

By contrast, at the beginning of the nineteenth century London appears to have been relatively well-served by constables and watchmen. *Jackson's Oxford Journal* of 9 October 1802 provided a detailed breakdown of the numbers involved in the parish and night-watch system:

City of London, Marshalmen, Beadles and Constables	319
City of London Watchmen and Patroles	803
City and Liberty of Westminster, Constables	71
City and Liberty of Westminster Watchmen and Patroles	302
Holborn Division, Constables	79
Holborn Division, Watchmen and Patroles	377
Finsbury Division, Constables	69
Finsbury Division, Watchmen and Patroles	185
Tower Hamlets, Constables	218
Tower Hamlets, Watchmen and Patroles	268
Liberty of Tower of London, Constables	17
Liberty of Tower of London, Watchmen and Patroles	14
Kensington & Chelsea Division, Constables	22

Kensington & Chelsea Division, Watchmen and Patroles	66
Borough of Southwark, Constables	88
Borough of Southwark, Watchmen and Patroles	79
Seven Police Offices, including Bow Street	150
Total	3127[19]

There were undoubtedly serious problems and flaws in the parish constabulary system: constables were amateurs, in that they were part-time volunteers, often serving unwillingly (they may even have paid someone else to act as a substitute); they normally served for only a short fixed period (usually a year); they were local to the area, and therefore both they and members of their family were liable to repercussions if they made an unpopular arrest; and, perhaps most importantly, they received no training for their post. As late as 1839 evidence was heard at a Parliamentary Committee from rural magistrates that:

> As far as our experience extends, we are convinced of the incompetency and inefficiency of the old parish constable. He holds his office generally for a year; he enters upon its duties unwillingly; he knows little what is required of him; is scantily paid for some things, has no remuneration in many cases; he has local connections, is actuated by personal apprehension, and dreads making himself obnoxious. His private occupation as a farmer or little tradesman engross his time, and, in most cases, render him loath to exertion as a public officer; and all these drawbacks have induced a general persuasion that, in ordinary cases, the parish constable has an interest in keeping out of the way when his services are called for.[20]

Constables were also, by their very nature, parochial; they had no powers of arrest outside their parish. This led to problems with investigating crime and capturing suspects; as David Phillips has stated, 'many property owners had great difficulty finding and arresting offenders against them in the days before organized professional police forces – particularly if the offender had travelled any distance from the scene of the crime.'[21]

'Thieftakers' and private policing

There were few alternatives to the parish constabulary until the last half of the eighteenth century. We have seen in Chapter 2 that wealthier individuals could subscribe to associations for the prosecutions of felons in order to safeguard their property and provide an affordable means of prosecution in the event of a crime. Such associations and other private associations of manufacturers or organizations did occasionally employ their own force of constables or detectives. In 1814 the Dursley Association for the Prosecution of Felons created a short-lived police force consisting of thirty-six men on night patrols, and, as noted above, Freshfields, solicitors to the Bank of England, employed their own agents for detecting and pursuing suspects.[22] Insurance companies also have a long history of employing 'in-house' surveyors, investigators and assessors, the first post of Fire Surveyor being created in 1696 by the Hand in Hand Fire Insurance Office.[23] It would seem, however, that most associations or private businesses were unwilling or unable to meet the expense necessary for the creation of such forces; Philips remarks that 'a number of associations [did] establish their own private police forces or patrols, but the majority did not go to this extent, preferring to work through their relationship with the parish constables, or later, with the new police forces.'[24]

From the late seventeenth century a system of Parliamentary rewards was established in an attempt to increase prosecution against serious crime. The Highwaymen Act 1693 (4 & 5 Wm & Mary c.8) offered a £40 statutory reward for the capture of highwaymen, rewards which could often mount up to a considerable sum. Beattie remarks that 'rewards paid in London for the conviction of street robbers, which for the twenty-five years between 1720 and 1745 were supplemented by royal proclamation [. . .] amounted to £140 for each defendant – a staggering sum that approached three or four years' income for even a skilled workman.'[25] One major change to the payment of rewards was introduced in the mid-eighteenth century when, as a result of Act 25 Geo. II c.36 (1752), it became an offence with a fine of £50 to advertise a reward with 'no questions asked'.[26] The payment of private rewards had a similarly long history.

The financial rewards available to those involved in the detection and successful conviction of a felon played a considerable part in contemporary crime detection, at least in the metropolis. The employment of private, non-attested thieftakers began in the early seventeenth century; John Beattie has found that 'the term thief-taker dates back to at least 1609'.[27] Thieftakers were individuals who operated privately, without any official status or power, attempting to capture suspected criminals in order to claim any reward money on offer from either the State or private individuals. It was widely believed that many of them operated illegally by framing innocent people or enticing weak-willed persons to commit crimes for which they were then arrested, with the thieftaker claiming any reward that was on offer.[28]

Case Study 9: Jonathan Wild, theft and compounding, 1725

By far the most famous thieftaker of the eighteenth century was the notorious Jonathan Wild (1683–1725). Although Jonathan Wild was one of the most infamous villains of the eighteenth century, little is known of his early life. He is known to have been baptized at St Peter's Church in Wolverhampton on 6 May 1683, suggesting that he was also born in that year, as infants were commonly christened within the first few months of life to ensure that they would be received within the Christian faith should they die in infancy.

He was the eldest of five children, having two brothers (John and Andrew) and two sisters. John became a bailiff and Town Crier of Wolverhampton, where he achieved a brief notoriety in 1715 by disgracing himself by taking part in a religious riot. He died in 1720. Jonathan's other brother, Andrew, emulated him to a certain extent, following a life of petty crime. Jonathan's father John was a joiner by trade, while his mother sold fruit in Wolverhampton Market. It is likely that Jonathan had at least a rudimentary education at the Free School in St John's Lane, but from his surviving letters it is clear that he occasionally struggled with the written word.[29] Little more is known of Jonathan's life in Wolverhampton apart from the facts that he possibly married a local girl and fathered a son (there was a Jonathan Wild, the son of Jonathan, baptized on 23 June 1703 at St Peter's Church, Wolverhampton), and that he became an apprentice buckle-maker.[30] At the time Wolverhampton was one of the most prominent areas for the production of steel buckles for shoes. Such buckles became popular from the mid-1600s, replacing laces or strings. Jonathan apparently completed his apprenticeship, but in his early twenties he seems to have determined that this career was not for him.

The exact date of and reason for his leaving Wolverhampton remain unclear, but within the next few years he had deserted his wife and child and was living in London. It is not known whether he continued his trade of buckle-making in London, but by 1710 he had begun a downward spiral, being imprisoned for debt in Wood Street Compter (where Charles Dickens' father John was also later to spend some time). Wild spent a total of four years in the Compter and there met Mary Milliner, a prostitute and petty thief, who was to play a significant role in his subsequent life.

Wild was extremely fortunate in that in April 1712 'An Act for the Relief of Insolvent Debtors, by obliging their Creditors to accept the utmost Satisfaction they are capable to make, and restoring them to their Liberty' (10 & 11 Anne. c.29) was passed, which granted a discharge to any debtors who could prove that they could not meet their debts while imprisoned. Wild was duly discharged in December 1712 and he took up residence with Mary in a brothel in Lewkenor's Lane, Covent Garden, a notorious haunt for prostitutes and ne'er-do-wells.

It was here that Wild learned the crafts of his new profession. Mary instructed him in the art of 'buttock and twang' (see Chapter 1), and he was also taken under the wing of Charles Hitchen, an under-marshal of Newgate Gaol and a notorious thieftaker and receiver of stolen goods. Wild soon picked up the necessary skills of the receiver and fence. However, he was not content for long to be merely a petty player in such nefarious activities; he was extremely ambitious and soon set himself up as a thieftaker, negotiating the return of stolen goods and being instrumental in sending thieves to gaol and, often, the gallows.

From 1712 Wild honed thieftaking to a new art, and in 1714 he set himself up in an office near to the Old Bailey. From here he controlled a considerable network of thieves and informers operating throughout the metropolis. He played the extremely dangerous but profitable double game of acting as a receiver for stolen goods and as the taker of thieves in order to claim the often substantial rewards available for their successful prosecution. Included in his list of numerous victims was a William Smith, who was a well-known criminal and one of the creditors who had been responsible for Wild's spell in Wood Street Compter. Wild was obviously a man who neither forgot nor forgave easily; in 1719 he managed to get Smith transported for seven years for theft. Smith escaped, but was recaptured by Wild and received a sentence of fourteen years' transportation (which he never served, dying on the journey).

Receivers were not above the law, however; an Act of 1691 (3 Wm & Mary c.9) made a receiver an accessory after the fact and liable to whipping, branding and seven years' transportation (or any combination of these punishments). The Receiving Act 1706 (6 Anne c.31) increased the sentence against convicted receivers to that of death, while an informer who successfully turned Queen's Evidence in order to convict his accomplices received both a free Royal Pardon and a reward of £40. However, Wild sidestepped these laws by cutting out the middleman (the receiver) and dealing directly with both the victim and thief. He made sure that he never personally handled stolen goods; instead, he would place carefully worded advertisements in the London newspapers stating that he knew the location of missing goods and offering to return them to their lawful owners for a price.

He became extremely wealthy, buying himself a country house, and set his thieftaking on a business footing, employing a manager and clerks: he was the self-styled Thieftaker-General. He dealt with famous and aristocratic clients, including Daniel Defoe and the 1st earl of Dartmouth, William Legge, who owned Sandwell Hall near West Bromwich. A letter dated 15 June 1724 to the earl from Wild survives in which Wild refers to the recent loss of some important correspondence and offers to retrieve the missing items (for an unstated price):

> My Lord, I am informed by Mr Woolley's man that your Lordship has lost some things on the road. I humbly beg your Lordship will please to order me a particular of them by next post and I will use all diligence I can to service your Lordship to the utmost of my power and beg leave to subscribe your Lordship's most obedient and dutiful servant.[31]

Although the earl seems to have responded favourably to this letter it appears that his steward was a more worldly and suspicious individual; a second letter from Wild to the earl, dated 11 August 1724, makes it clear that Wild was becoming frustrated with the steward's attempts to thwart him:

> To the Right Honourable The Lord Dartmouth of Sandall Hall [sic] in Staffordshire, My Lord, some time ago your Lordship suggested that you had lost some writing, which I endeavoured to discover, and after the reward of ten guineas was published, they [the thieves] demanded twenty for themselves, which your steward proposed to pay in part, if he could see all the writings, which were considerably more than your Lordship at first seemed to note, and had your steward paid all the money down your Lordship undoubtedly would have had them [the letters] before him. I was upward of six pounds out of pocket, and I would still endeavour to procure them for your Lordship would you please to order any one else to me than your

steward, he always making so many trifling and needless excuses and putting-off in paying the money and expenses I have been at [. . .]. Should your Lordship please to order your commands be supplied they shall be faithfully obeyed.[32]

By 1717 the government appeared to be in a quandary concerning Wild's activities; they were afraid of his growing operations and passed an Act to prevent the receipt of rewards for the recovery of stolen goods without a subsequent successful prosecution (4 Geo. 1 c.11), but they were also aware that his work did to a certain extent control criminality in London and provided a means for the recovery of missing property.[33] In 1720 Wild was even consulted by a Parliamentary Commission about what to do to prevent the growth of crime. Not surprisingly, Wild suggested that the reward system should be increased, with an eye to swelling his ever-growing fortune.

However, Wild finally grew over-confident in his powers and perhaps even began to believe some of his own publicity. In 1724 he petitioned the Aldermen of the City of London to make him a Freeman of the City because of his usefulness in reducing crime. However, in the same year he made the serious error of capturing the notorious and popular Cockney thief Jack Sheppard (see Chapter 7). This individual achieved lasting fame by escaping from the condemned cell of Newgate Prison not once but twice.[34] Sheppard was eventually recaptured and put to death, but Wild's popularity diminished as a result of Sheppard's death. In 1725 he was finally hoist by his own petard when he was tried on 13 May for stealing and subsequently receiving a reward of £10 for the return of forty yards of lace valued at £50. He defended himself energetically and succeeded in being acquitted of the theft.[35] However, he was found guilty of the receipt of a reward from the recovery of the lace under the provisions of the aforementioned Act of 1717 (ironically, the Act was informally known as Wild's Act).

In a desperate last-ditch attempt to escape the noose Wild wrote to several influential figures with whom he had had previous dealings, imploring them to intervene on his behalf and save him from the gallows. One of those contacted was the earl of Dartmouth, which suggests that Wild had succeeded in returning the missing documents. The letter survives and is dated 23 March 1725:

I do not doubt that your Lordship will be surprised at my presuming to write to you, but I cannot but hope your Lordship will pardon me in so doing, because I am compelled to seek protection, by the violent prosecution of some magistrates (whom I never offended) who have encouraged several notorious thieves to swear against me, and to qualify them to be legal evidence, have procured his Majesty's most gracious Pardon, for crimes for which they have been condemned. If your Lordship would be pleased to give me a letter to such person as you shall judge proper to hear and redress me, I am confident that the designs of my enemies will be frustrated and I thereby at liberty to discover, apprehend and convict numbers of notorious criminals, which will be a great service to the public.[36]

Wild also published a list of more than sixty criminals that he had convicted in an effort to swing public opinion behind his appeal for clemency, and also petitioned the king, but all his efforts proved fruitless. In the Ordinary's account of his last few days, Wild states that:

> his Business was doing good, in recovering lost Goods; that as he had regain'd Things of great Value for Dukes, Earls and Lords, he thought he deserved well. He also, before his Conviction, affirm'd that he had apprehended the greatest and most pernicious Robbers and Plunderers the Nation ever was molested by.[37]

He was sentenced to be hanged on 24 May 1725. On the night prior to the execution Wild attempted to take his own life by taking laudanum. However, he was not an experienced drug-taker and misjudged the dosage, succeeding only in making himself semi-conscious. In this state he was half-dragged from his cell and taken to Tyburn. He was unable to make a coherent final speech and the large crowd that had come to see the spectacle threatened to lynch the hangman when he attempted to allow Wild to prepare himself for his death:

> [At] about two of the Clock in the Morning [Wild] endeavoured to prevent his Execution by drinking Laudanum; but the largeness of the Draught, together with his having fasted before, instead of destroying him immediately, was the Occasion of his not dying by it. At the Place of Execution [. . .] Wild had render'd himself delirious by Poyson, but began to recover himself. They all united in the Publick Prayers, as well as the Tumult and Clamour of the Occasion would give them leave.[38]

Ruth Paley regards thieftakers as persons straddling 'the margins of the conventional and criminal worlds' who 'formed, in effect, a sort of entrepreneurial police force'.[39] However, their numbers were extremely limited and those who operated in the provinces were largely confined to major towns and cities – for example, the *Staffordshire Advertiser* reported that in January 1801 the entrepreneurial industrialist Matthew Boulton, after a series of robberies at his Soho Manufactory, 'procured some of the constables and thieftakers from Birmingham, to the number of twenty in the whole, who were well-armed, and concealed in the Manufactory' in order to arrest the offenders – but such thieftakers appear to have been localized in their operations.[40]

Bow Street and the London Police Offices

From the mid-eighteenth century onwards, however, thieftakers and parish constables were not the only men to whom victims of crime could turn. Henry Fielding is now chiefly remembered as the author of rollicking picaresque novels such as *Tom Jones* (1749), but just a few months prior to the publication of his bestseller he had been appointed as a Justice of the Peace for Westminster, moving into his predecessor Thomas De Veil's former house at No. 4 Bow Street in order to carry out the duties of his new post. Fielding had a keen interest in contemporary criminal justice and in the winter of 1748/9 he created the force that was soon to be known colloquially as the Bow Street 'Runners'. Six ex-constables of Westminster (together with a servant of Saunders Welch, High Constable of Holborn) comprised the original force based at Bow Street. These men were charged with detecting and capturing criminals throughout London and its environs, and were paid a retaining fee for their services. They were also entitled to any reward resulting from the successful prosecution of offenders that they had captured. This small group was the embryonic beginning of what would become England's first detective force.[41]

Contemporary and later commentators (notably those holding traditional views of the historical development of the modern police) have often regarded the 'Runners' as little more than glorified 'thieftakers' in the mould of Jonathan Wild:

> The Bow Street 'Runners' more nearly resembled a disreputable private detective agency than a branch of a modern police force; they accepted rewards, they often kept information about a crime to themselves in the hope of turning it to their own advantage [. . .], and their honesty was often suspect.[42]

However, Fielding regarded his force as more than mere thieftakers; despite the fact that he referred to them as such in a convenient shorthand description in his *Journey of Voyage to Lisbon* – 'a set of thieftakers, whom I had enlisted into the service, all men of known and approved fidelity and intrepidity' – both he and his immediate successor, Sir John Fielding (Henry's blind younger half-brother, who became Chief Magistrate at Bow Street following Henry's untimely death in 1754), viewed the Bow Street men as having a much wider remit than that of the 'professional' thieftakers such as Jonathan Wild and Stephen McDaniel.[43] They were acutely aware of the public's extremely low opinion of such individuals, which was often forcefully expressed by contemporary commentators such as Edward Sayer, who, in his *Observations on the Police or Civil Government of Westminster with a proposal for reform* (1784), was concerned about:

> employing mostly thieves to take thieves, thus turning their own arts against themselves. In the present situation of the Westminster government this measure may be both prudent and necessary; but at no time, and in no situation, can it be either honourable or effectual; for surely the employment of professed and generally unrepentant offenders can reflect little lustre upon the administration of justice.[44]

The Fieldings went to considerable lengths to explain the difference between such individuals and their new force. Henry Fielding, in his 1751 treatise *An Enquiry*

into the Causes of the Late Increase of Robberies, answered criticism in the form
of a series of rhetorical questions:

> I will venture to say, that if to do Good to Society be laudable, so is the
> Office of a Thief-catcher; and if to do this Good at the extreme Hazard of
> your Life be honourable, then is this Office honourable. True, it may be said;
> but he doth this with a View to a Reward. And doth not the Soldier and the
> Sailor venture his Life with the same View? For who, as a Great Man lately
> says, serves the Public for nothing? [. . .]. If to bring Thieves to Justice be a
> scandalous Office, what becomes of all those who are conven'd in this
> Business, some of whom are rightly thought to be among the most honour-
> able Officers in Government? If on the contrary they be, as it surely is, why
> should the Post of Danger in this Warfare alone be excluded from all Share
> of Honour?[45]

However, one of the most successful and famous of the late eighteenth-century
lawyers, William Garrow, held the Bow Street Principal Officers in some regard,
in contrast to his view of private thieftakers, whom 'Garrow treated [. . .] with
open contempt, presumably feeling that the jurors would have little regard for
those who were simply in the business for money and who worked without the
implicit authority that the runners derived from operating under the auspices of
magistrates'.[46] Beattie states that:

> Garrow certainly did not regard them as beyond criticism. But he seems
> rarely to have treated the Bow Street officers to the kinds of damaging cross-
> examinations to which he subjected some of the private thief-takers and
> occasionally the runners from the rotation offices, or indeed any witness
> who attempted to evade his questions. One finds few examples of his
> attempting to undermine their credibility by sarcasm or scorn or to shake
> their testimony by the powerful and insistent cross-examinations that made
> some witnesses tremble at the thought of having to face him. Indeed, one
> might characterise his attitude towards them as familiar, occasionally verg-
> ing on friendly, and at worst neutral.[47]

The Bow Street 'Runners' were not the only means of law enforcement available
to the Fieldings or their successors. Bow Street Police Office developed a complex and hierarchical structure which included regular night and day patrols in
the centre of London, horse-mounted patrols of the turnpike roads leading into
the metropolis and the aforementioned small force of experienced plain-clothes
detective Principal Officers. Occasional foot patrols around the City of
Westminster were taking place by the mid-1760s and on 17 October 1763 an
eight-man horse patrol took to the streets. This proved short-lived owing to the
perceived high cost of maintaining it and within a year the experiment had been
discontinued.[48] However, a horse patrol was re-established in 1805 by Bow Street
Chief Magistrate Sir Richard Ford and this force, which patrolled the areas

around the turnpiked roads leading into London, and which can be regarded as 'the first uniformed police force in England', continued under the aegis of Bow Street Police Office until finally being placed under the jurisdiction of the Metropolitan Police on 13 August 1836.[49]

Similarly, a more organized and permanent Foot or Night Patrol, operative during the hours of darkness in sixteen districts of central London, was established in 1790 by Sir Sampson Wright, Chief Magistrate at Bow Street, and this continued in various guises until the advent of the Metropolitan Police in 1829. In 1821 a Day Patrol, often known by its official title of the 'Dismounted Horse Patrol', was created; this force operated in the area of the metropolis between the jurisdiction of the Horse Patrol and the Foot Patrol.[50]

Bow Street continued in its unique function until 1792, when the Middlesex Justices Act (32 Geo. III c.53) created seven other Public Offices all based largely on the lines of Bow Street Public Office. The introduction of these new offices, each with three stipendiary magistrates, had far-reaching consequences with regard to policing within the metropolis, fundamentally changing the way in which law enforcement was conducted.[51] Each of the new Offices was to have its own contingent of Principal Officers and less senior personnel. The Principal Officers of the new offices were also occasionally employed outside the metropolis – usually on notorious cases such as the 1828 'Murder in the Red Barn', which involved James Lea of Lambeth Street Police Office – though to a markedly lesser extent than their colleagues based at Bow Street.[52]

With the passing of the Act the perceived advantages of the Bow Street system were to some extent officially recognized (though the status of Bow Street was still not formally encapsulated in law).[53] No specific mention of Bow Street Public Office is made in the Act, but it is clear that the other Public Offices were created in Bow Street's mould:

> Cap. XV That the justices [. . .] retain and employ a sufficient number of fit and able men, whom they are hereby authorised and impowered to swear in, to act as constables for preserving the peace and preventing robberies and other felonies, and apprehending offenders against the peace within the said counties of Middlesex and Surrey respectively [. . .]. That no greater number than six shall at one and the same time be so retained as aforesaid at any one of the said publick offices.

> Cap. XVI The Receiver to pay [. . .] to the constables so appointed as aforesaid, for their trouble and attendance as aforesaid, any sum not exceeding twelve shillings per week, and any extraordinary expenses they shall appear to have been necessarily put to in apprehending offenders, and executing the orders of the justices acting under and by virtue of this act, such extraordinary expenses being first examined and approved of by the justices attending the office in which such constables shall have been respectively appointed.[54]

The *Twenty-eighth Report from the Select Committee on Finance: Police, including Convict Establishments* of June 1798 proposed that 'the Commissions of the

Magistrates of the [. . .] eight offices of police should extend [. . .] over the whole metropolis, and the four above-mentioned counties [Middlesex, Surrey, Kent and Essex]'.[55] However, this proposal was not accepted and by 1802 the Metropolitan Police Magistrates Act (42 Geo. III c.76) still allowed jurisdiction only within Middlesex and Surrey, with constables also prohibited from voting in parish elections.[56] This situation continued until 1814, when the Police Magistrates Metropolis Act (54 Geo. III c.37) was the first to differentiate between Bow Street and the other London Police Offices, cap. XXIII stating:

> It is expected that the officers and patrol belonging to the said public office in Bow Street, should be sworn in as constables, and be empowered to act within the limits of the several counties of Middlesex, Surrey, Essex, Kent, the City and Liberty of Westminster and the liberty of the Tower of London.

This anomaly, which implicitly suggests that the Police Magistrates Metropolis Act 1814 envisaged that the majority of Bow Street's activities would occur in the immediate environs of the capital, continued until the Police Magistrates Metropolitan Act 1822 (2 Geo. IV c.118), whereby officers from all London Police Offices were given jurisdiction in all four counties surrounding the metropolis.[57]

Outside the metropolis and surrounding four counties, however, Principal Officers were regarded as ordinary citizens. If directed by the magistrates at Westminster to investigate within the provinces they had to apply to the respective local magistrates for a warrant to enable them to arrest suspects and these warrants had to be served in person by the parish constable, as 'warrants were usually directed by the justice to be executed by a constable'.[58] To further complicate matters, if the investigation crossed county boundaries the warrant had to be renewed or endorsed by magistrates in each new county.[59] In his evidence to the 1816 Select Committee Principal Officer John Vickery complained that:

> I have been obliged to wait and call in the assistance of a constable to execute a warrant. In felonies we are not constables to execute a warrant out of the county; and I have been put to great expense, where it would have been avoided, if we could have seized the party without waiting to apply for the assistance of a constable of the district.[60]

An example of the often ludicrously complex nature of warrants can be seen in the report of a trial of 1801 held at the Old Bailey. Principal Officer John Sayer conducted a search of premises for stolen goods, but, owing to the location of the house, had to be accompanied by Thomas Lawrence, a Marshalman of the City of London, who reported that 'I was with Sayer; I went in consequence of a warrant from Bow Street, backed in the City, to Haye's [the suspect's] house; the back part of the house is in the City, the other part is in Middlesex'.[61]

To a large extent the various law-enforcement agencies in London acted discretely from each other, although they could and did co-operate when it was seen as mutually beneficial, as is shown in the following case study.

Case Study 10: Solomon and Idswell Idswell,
felony and forgery, 1795

On 8 July 1795 Solomon Idswell, a Jewish watchmaker of 57 St Mary Axe in the City of London, was executed at Tyburn. This was the culmination of a complex case of forgery, deception and death that had begun several months earlier when his brother Idswell Idswell had been detained on 18 February 1795 in the New Prison at Clerkenwell on a charge of forgery of stamps to the value of six shillings each to be stamped on seamen's wills and powers of attorney.[62] Because of the dangerous nature of their employment, mariners employed by the Admiralty were encouraged to draw up wills and powers of attorney on documents often witnessed by the captain of the ship on which they were sailing. These documents were then deposited with the Navy Office, which paid out any amounts that the seaman had accrued to named beneficiaries on the document. Such wills were an obvious target for fraudsters and forgers.[63]

Idswell Idswell was a wealthy pawnbroker and silversmith, also of St Mary Axe, where he lived with his wife Sarah.[64] He was brought before Bow Street Magistrates and recommitted to New Prison on 14 March 1795. While he was held at the New Prison he used some of his considerable wealth to bribe his guardians to allow him certain privileges, including persuading them to agree to his wife Sarah spending nights with him in his private room, as she was unwell and suffered from fits.[65] He was also allowed to receive a visitor in the form of a purported 'Uncle Johnny'. Idswell's wife then informed him that her aunt was very ill in Artillery Street, and that the sick aunt

> was so ill, she could not expect she would continue long, then said that her aunt was always talking about seeing Mr. Idswell, and said that if how he could see her, it would be the cause of her giving him seven or eight hundred, or a thousand pounds; he said, the last time he saw her she made him a present of a hundred guineas.[66]

Idswell then turned to his gaoler, Under-Keeper John Day, and stated that 'if I [Day] would ask Thomas Crosswell [one of the Keepers of the prison] to conduct him to see her, he would make us both a very handsome present'.[67] Day and Crosswell originally refused this request, but did allow 'Uncle Johnny' to visit on two further occasions in return for two guineas each. The two gaolers also received other gifts, including clothes and a watch.

On 2 April they agreed to escort Idswell from the prison to see his 'sick' aunt at 13 Artillery Lane. Idswell's irons were concealed 'with four silk handkerchiefs, and Idswell had got a rough great coat on, belonging to one Myers, a prisoner at that same time'.[68] Day had concealed a small blunderbuss about his person, but Idswell was aware of this fact and communicated it by note to his accomplices waiting at Artillery Lane: 'This fellow, who goes with me, has a blunderbuss tied under his coat; so if you think it will frighten any of the family, put it off till another day. Your's, sincerely, I. I.'.[69]

Once inside the house there was a struggle between Day and Idswell's accomplices; Day was injured by the blunderbuss being discharged and Idswell received most of the discharge from the firearm. He was killed instantly. Thomas Mitchell, who lived at the next-door property, stated that:

> I see the blood boiling out of his hind parts, he lay like on his face; the next was Day, he stood about a yard space from him; I asked Day what was the matter? he said, for God's sake help, or I shall be murdered; immediately Mr. Jarvis, the headborough, came in at the door, and by knowing of me he said, Mitchell, I demand you to aid and assist; I said, it is my intention; immediately we went up stairs.

Peter Jarvis, Headborough of the Artillery Ground, called for assistance from several night watchmen and then proceeded to arrest Idswell's erstwhile accomplices at the point of his drawn cutlass.[70] He caught one of the men, John Solomons, hiding in the outside privy:

> I came to the privy door, and it was fast. I then laid hold of it by a hole that was in the door to admit the light, and it came open, whether by my shaking it or not, I cannot tell; and that man was then sitting on the seat of the privy. I asked him what he did there? – he said that he had heard a gun go off; I think those were the exact words, and that he was obliged to come in there, into the privy.[71]

In total nine men were detained by a combination of the Headborough, at least three watchmen and several neighbours. One of the latter described the scene thus:

> The neighbours hallooed, there has been murder done, don't mind what they say, they are two thieves, take them into custody; accordingly I swore that if they moved any further I would shoot them; they begged me not to shoot, they would come and tell me all about it.
>
> Q. Did you secure them? – I did.
>
> Q. Did any body assist you in conveying to the watch house? – When they were on the top of the leads I called out for assistance, and Mrs. Spencer went down stairs to get me assistance, and Day came up, and a watchman, and another person.[72]

Their trial for murder took place at the Old Bailey on 16 April 1795, but there was obviously considerable doubt as to who actually fired the blunderbuss. One of the accused, who stated that he was brother-in-law to the deceased, stated that Idswell had told him with his dying breaths that Day had shot him:

> He was then alive, and he told me Day has killed me; these are his dying words. He listed up his hand again, and pointed with his hand to Day, and said, this man has killed me. I have no more to say, I leave my cause to God and you.[73]

The jury found all nine men not guilty, but eight of them were remanded on a further charge of aiding the escape of Idswell from the New Prison. As well as these eight individuals, three other men were also indicted on a charge of aiding and assisting Idswell Idswell in escaping from prison under the Prison Escape Act 1743 (16 Geo. II c.31), which made 'aiding and assisting prisoners to attempt to escape out of lawful custody' a felony.[74] Their trial was held at the Old Bailey on 1 July 1795.[75] Simon Jacobs, one of the defendants, made the following impassioned plea:

> My lord, how can I be charged with assisting and aiding the prisoner in his escape, when the escape was made before I see him, because the moment Day took him out of the gaol the escape was made. Did I go to the gaol? No; Day is to be blamed, and none of us.

The jury found two of the defendants 'not guilty' and the other nine 'guilty' as charged after retiring for half an hour. However, judgement was respited on a technicality that the indictment had not stated the means used by the defendants in assisting any escape attempt.[76]

In the meantime, Idswell Idswell's brother Solomon had also been arrested on suspicion of his involvement with the forged stamps. He was committed to the House of Correction at Cold Bath Fields, from where he tried to escape by attempting to bribe a turnkey with fifty guineas and thirty-five watches on 7 April, but was unsuccessful. He was subsequently tried at the Old Bailey on 20 May 1795 on an indictment that:

> He, on the 1st of January, did falsely make, forge and counterfeit, and did cause and procure to be falsely made, forged and counterfeited, and did willingly act and assist in falsely making, forging and counterfeiting a certain stamp and mark, to resemble a stamp and mark directed to be used by a certain act of parliament made in the twenty-seventh year of his majesty's reign, being under the management of the commissioners for managing his majesty's stamp duties on parchment and vellum.[77]

The court heard that the Stamp Office had initiated enquiries in February 1795 and that one of the employees of the solicitors to the Stamp Office, Thomas Whittard, had travelled to Portsmouth in order to interview a jeweller and Navy agent, Gershon Wolfe, who dealt with seamen's wills and powers of attorney. The Stamp Office had received information from Thomas Bevan that he had bought some seamen's powers from the Navy agent, and that he was doubtful as to their authenticity. Mr Whittard purchased some powers from Mr Wolfe and then immediately secured him (presumably with the help of a local watchman, as Mr Whittard would not have possessed the authority to seize Wolfe). A search was made and upwards of 350 documents were discovered. Wolfe was then taken to London and delivered into the hands of St Giles' watch-house. Mr Whittard then secured the assistance of two Bow Street officers and proceeded to the house of another suspect, Joseph Moses (who had presumably been implicated by Wolfe). Moses was then arrested by the Bow Street personnel.

Christopher Kennedy, an experienced Bow Street officer, gave evidence at Solomon's trial that after he had arrested Moses he travelled to Idswell Idswell's house and took him to Bow Street after searching the house, where he found numerous watches and a silver greyhound badge.[78] The following week Kennedy went in pursuit of Solomon Idswell and found him at 'No. 8, King-street Golden-square, on the ground floor, in a closet, a small little room behind the back parlour, just room enough for a bed'.[79]

Wolfe deposed that he had come into contact with Moses in late 1794 and had ordered stamps worth £90 from him. Moses (who turned King's Evidence) was then asked when he had first met the Idswells:

> Q. When was it you first had any communication with the prisoner, on the subject of forged stamps? – About four months before I was apprehended; on calling at the late Idswell's, in St. Maryaxe, in the presence of Solomon Idswell, the late Idswell asked me, what I thought of having a six shilling stamp made? if I had anybody I could sell them to, I might make my fortune? I then told him I had a friend at Portsmouth, and mentioned one Mr. Wolfe; he then asked me whether Mr. Wolfe could be trusted, and would have no suspicion? I told him he would not, for he was a man that made use of a great many himself, and therefore he would have no suspicion.[80]

Moses went on to say that he later saw Solomon Idswell working a press in the garret of his house. An expert engraver was called upon to prove that the stamps evidenced were forgeries. Other witnesses, including two more Bow Street officers, were called against the defendant. The trial lasted eight hours, with the evidence against Solomon Idswell proving convincing to the jury, who pronounced a guilty verdict after retiring for two and a half hours.[81] He was duly sentenced to death. In a desperate attempt to avoid being hanged, Solomon Idswell confessed to recent large-scale forgery against the Bank of Denmark, but the *Telegraph* reported that 'the desired object, a pardon, was not granted in consequence of the confession'.[82] He was executed on 8 July 1785 at Tyburn.

His sister-in-law Sarah (wife of Idswell Idswell) had also been implicated in the escape attempt, and she appears to have fled from London after the death of her husband. Her whereabouts were advertised for in the papers for several weeks and as a consequence of information received at Bow Street office two experienced Bow Street officers, Thomas Carpmeal and Christopher Kennedy, were dispatched to Stubbleton near Gosport in Hampshire, where they discovered that she had been in the area for some time, pretending to be a young lady of fortune by the name of Miss Swanson.[83] It was reported that, upon the officers approaching the house where she was staying, she was 'welcomed by the officers, whom she well know, particularly Kennedy, by whom her first husband, the late Lawrence Jones, and her latter, Idswell Idswell, were both apprehended'.

Those of her husband's friends who had been found guilty of aiding and abetting his escape from New Prison were held in Newgate following the respited judgement for a considerable period; it was not until 9 July 1796 that the *Sun* reported that the nine men 'received His Majesty's most generous pardon, and were severally discharged from Newgate'. Sarah Idswell had been released on bail following her arrest, but the case against her was also subsequently dropped. Crosswell, Day's immediate superior, was also tried for aiding and abetting Idswell's escape, but was found not guilty at a trial at the Old Bailey on 22 June 1796.[85]

The role of local and central officialdom in crime detection and prosecution

As stated in Chapter Two, no system of public prosecution existed throughout the period under discussion. Douglas Hay remarks that 'the magistracy of the courts [. . .] in the absence of an organised police [. . .] bore much of the responsibility, when they were conscientious, for the detecting and capture of criminals.'[86] However, local officials (including magistrates) had no duty to instigate or control investigations into crime; it's the role of the magistracy was purely to hear the cases presented before it. R. W. England states that 'unless obliged to do so because someone initiated a private prosecution, parish officials or local magistrates were not required to investigate crimes.'[87] Until 1826, prosecutors could not even be sure of recouping any expenses arising from their efforts to prosecute suspected perpetrators of offences. Acts of Parliament had been passed in 1770 and 1818 which gave limited expenses to certain prosecutors of felonies, but it was not until 1826 that the Criminal Law Act (7 Geo. IV c. 64) made such payments the norm rather than the exception.[88]

Similarly, central government played little role in detecting crime or capturing suspects. The centralized aspects of government during the eighteenth century were very limited in comparison with the present-day civil service. Clive Emsley states that 'at the close of the eighteenth century the Home Office was a tiny organization, consisting of less than two dozen individuals', while R. R. Nelson notes that 'only four rooms made up the Home Office quarters in Whitehall'.[89] As Emsley comments, 'with no permanent police force in the country and no official centralized intelligence service, perhaps the greatest problem facing the Home Office during the 1790s, was knowing exactly what was going on in the kingdom'.[90] Nelson suggests that this problem was at least partially met by the employment of King's Messengers, who fulfilled a number of duties: 'the corps [. . .] carried important dispatches and messages both in the British Isles and abroad, but it also acted as a kind of national police.' The corps, never large in number, increased from sixteen men in 1772 to thirty in 1795. Much more research is needed to clarify the position and role of such shadowy personnel, who seem to have operated as a combination of diplomat and spy, as little of significance has been written about them.[91]

There was similarly little communication between magistrates. Patrick Colquhoun's letter to George Rose MP on 3 May 1798 regarding the formation of a Central Board of Police Revenue, in which he favoured the establishment of 'a correspondence with a select number of the most active and intelligent Magistrates in every part of Great Britain, for the purpose of communicating and receiving intelligence relative to criminal offences', suggests that such correspondence was not commonplace at the time.[92] This aspect of the local magistracy remains to be more thoroughly researched; one of the few such studies that shows the fascinating details which such research can yield is John Styles' account of the sterling efforts of Samuel Lister, Justice of the Peace for the West Riding of Yorkshire, to bring the perpetrator of several forgery offences to justice in 1756.[93] This account clearly illustrates the difficulties faced by magistrates in a time before easy communication or movement of both people and messages. In our time of virtually instantaneous communication and rapid mass transportation it is all too easy to ignore or underestimate the contemporary difficulties that must have beset even the most diligent and dedicated of law enforcers.[94]

Opposition to a national police force

Despite the fact that Bow Street Principal Officers were used throughout Britain on the investigation of serious crimes such as murder, arson and bank robberies, they were small in number (never more than eleven officers served at any one time) and were also very expensive to employ. Usually the only viable alternative remaining was the often inefficient system of the parish constabulary.

The idea of a national police force had always met with stiff resistance. The only practical attempt to create such a force took place in August 1655, when Oliver Cromwell introduced a scheme to divide England into districts under the command of Major-Generals.[95] This abortive plan, which contained an especially unpopular militaristic element, lasted less than two years and caused bitter and lasting resentment, and there was no more serious political momentum for the creation of a national police force until the early decades of the nineteenth century, by which time the reported excesses of Napoleon's militaristic gendarmerie under the control of his Minister for Police, Joseph Fouché, had immeasurably soured public opinion against the creation of such a body of men. In 1812 the earl of Dudley, referring to calls for the creation of a new police force following a series of grisly murders in the Ratcliff Highway, London, remarked:

> They have an admirable police at Paris, but they pay for it dear enough. I had rather half a dozen peoples' throats be cut in Ratcliff Highway every three or four years than be subject to domiciliary visits, spies, and all the rest of Fouché's contrivances.[96]

As late as 1829 the indefatigable commentator on policing matters, John Wade, indignantly stated that:

> The system established by Fouché and Savary, and continued under the administration of M. de Villèle, is quite sufficient to disgust us with refined

and complicated organisations of preventive justice, and cannot have the most distant resemblance to any establishment required in this country.[97]

The above views were typical of many of those in authority; there was widespread antipathy to any proposed system that would reduce the power and authority of local unpaid magistrates. Such opponents argued that a centralization of law enforcement was to be avoided at all costs, as they feared centralized control over what were considered primarily local issues of crime and punishment. They argued that such a system would lead to state coercion, with attendant spying and surveillance. These views were based on a fundamentally rural and pre-industrial outlook on crime, with little consideration being given to the burgeoning populations in rapidly industrializing towns and cities. Even a rapidly industrializing area such as the Black Country, a domain largely controlled and owned by the earl of Dudley, was still at this time fundamentally rural in nature – the population, although working in industries such as coal-mining, lived largely in small village-based communities (admittedly not always immediately distinguishable from one another to strangers) in which everyone knew nearly everyone else and outsiders were immediately noticed.[98]

Conversely, some of those directly involved in law enforcement, including Principal Officers, did perceive that benefits would accrue from the creation of a national system. John Vickery, a highly experienced and erudite Bow Street Principal Officer, tentatively suggested in his evidence to the 1816 Select Committee on the Police of the Metropolis that a force of national officers could be created: 'whether it would be considered at all a trespass upon the liberties of the subject, to make a certain number of officers constables for England, is a consideration I would submit'.[99]

Establishing the extent to which the Fieldings ever envisaged a national adoption of their plans by the creation of similar offices throughout the country is vexatious. Henry Fielding's *An Enquiry into the Causes of the Late Increase of Robbers*, together with Sir John's *A Plan for Preventing Robberies within Twenty Miles of London*, which set out the latter's views on how to provide an effective law-enforcement body, both concentrated almost exclusively on the problems resulting from perceived vastly increased criminal activity in the metropolitan area. However, Sir John made it clear in his series of notices in the *Public Advertiser* that the Bow Street personnel were available to travel throughout Britain.

There appears to be little evidence that either of the Fieldings, despite their prodigious output on the subject, or their successors ever seriously considered the creation of a nation-wide system of policing based on Bow Street lines. Stanley Palmer remarks that 'even the great police reformers, Henry and John Fielding and Patrick Colquhoun, steered clear of recommending the creation of a large, salaried, professional police force'.[100] In the event little came of any such subsequent ideas that either of the Fieldings may have held in regard to the country as a whole. Even following Peel's successful introduction of the Metropolitan Police in 1829 the appetite for a national police force remained limited.

Conclusion

This chapter has shown that the eighteenth century was a time of considerable change with regard to the development of new policing practices; the creation of the western world's first detective force in the shape of the Bow Street 'Runners' was revolutionary in its concept. It has demonstrated, however, that such developments were not without their critics and that, while there were important developments, the more traditional system of parish constables and night watchmen still continued throughout the period, especially in the provinces. The development of a professional, full-time police force was not teleological in nature: rather, it was piecemeal and hesitant, with much debate as to its role and effectiveness.[101]

The rise of private policing in the form of thieftakers and privately funded law-enforcement bodies, such as those employed by some associations for the prosecution of felons, has been shown to be the result of an increasingly concerned property-owning sector of society, which felt that it was not being well-served by the more communal or voluntary traditional system of policing. However, the exploits of Jonathan Wild and others highlighted the inherent weaknesses in reliance on such a system of rewards-based investigation.

The chapter has also highlighted the considerable amount of debate concerning the policing of England and Wales during the period and the opposition to the creation of a publicly accountable national force. The next chapter will look at how those individuals who were caught by the various law-enforcement agencies were dealt with by those in authority, and how new ideas and theories concerning the punishment of offenders were both developed and put into practice.

Notes

1 Horace Walpole, quoted in N. Rogers, *Mayhem: Post-War Crime and Violence in Britain, 1748–53* (Yale: YUP, 2013), p. 45.
2 Ibid.
3 The *Maréchaussée* was a semi-military policing body responsible to the Marshal of France. By the outbreak of the French Revolution in 1789 it numbered over 3,500 men.
4 See J. M. Beattie, *The First English Detectives: the Bow Street Runners and the Policing of London 1750–1840* (Oxford: OUP, 2012), D. G. Barrie, *Police in the Age of Improvement: Police Development and the Civic Tradition in Scotland, 1775–1865* (Cullompton: Willan, 2008), and A. Dinsmor, 'Glasgow Police Pioneers', *Journal of the Police History Society* 15 (2000): 9–11, and A. Dinsmor and R. H. J. Urquhart, 'The Origins of Modern Policing in Scotland', *Scottish Archives, the Journal of the Scottish Records Association* 7 (2001): 36–44.
5 Charles Reith, *A Short History of the British Police* (Oxford: OUP, 1948), p. 4.
6 Cohen and Scull, *Social Control and the State*, pp. 61–2. For succinct accounts of police historiography, see Robert Reiner, *The Politics of the Police*, 4th edn (Oxford: OUP, 2010), and Cyril D. Robinson, 'Ideology as History: A Look at the Way some English Police Historians look at the Police', *Police Studies* 2.2 (1979): 35–49. Although dealing primarily with the post-1829 period, David Philips and Robert Storch, *Policing Provincial England 1829–1856: The Politics of Reform* (Leicester: Leicester University Press, 1999) remains a seminal work on the state of provincial policing prior to the introduction of the County and Borough Police Act 1856.

7 Malcolm Gaskill, *Crime and Mentalities in Early Modern England* (Cambridge, CUP, 2000), p. 242.

8 Cox and Godfrey, *Cinderellas & Packhorses*, p. 13.

9 Beattie, *Crime and the Courts*, p. 37.

10 Quoted in *First Report of the Commissioners appointed to inquire as to the best means of establishing an efficient Constabulary* Force, vol. XIX, p. 105.

11 Quoted from *The Song of a Constable: made by James Gyffon, Constable of Alburye* [Surrey] *Anno 1626*. The entire text of the (much longer) song can be found online at www.quod.lib.umich.edu/e/ecco/004897833.0001.000/1:8.6?rgn=div2;view=fulltext.

12 Robert Thornhill (ed.), *A Village Constable's Accounts 1791–1839* (Derby: Derbyshire Archaeological and Natural History Society, 1957).

13 Shropshire Archives 2089/7/5/17 Order of J.P., 17 April 1752.

14 Dinsmor, 'Glasgow Police Pioneers', p. 9.

15 Sharpe, *Crime in Early Modern England*, and Styles, 'An Eighteenth-Century Magistrate as Detective'.

16 R. W. England, 'Investigating Homicides in Northern England, 1800–1824', *Criminal Justice History* 6 (1985): 105–24.

17 Roger E. Swift, 'The English Urban Magistracy and the Administration of Justice during the Early Nineteenth Century: Wolverhampton, 1815–60', *Midland History* XVII (1992): 75–93, p. 75.

18 Stourbridge population figure extrapolated from J. W. Willis-Bund (ed.), *Victoria County History of Worcestershire*, Vol. 4 (London: St Catherine Press, 1924).

19 It is interesting to note that the total number of police personnel is considerably more than the original complement of 1,011 officers that were walking the beat following the creation of the Metropolitan Police force in 1829 (although, of course, many parishes retained their own constables and watchmen). This force consisted of eight Superintendents, twenty Inspectors, eighty-eight Sergeants and 895 Constables – see Martin Fido and Keith Skinner, *The Official Encyclopedia of Scotland Yard* (London: Virgin, 1999), p. 184.

20 *First Report of the Commissioners appointed to inquire as to the best means of establishing an efficient Constabulary* Force, vol. XIX.

21 Philips, 'Good Men to Associate and Bad Men to Conspire', p. 117.

22 See Jerrard, 'Early Policing in Gloucestershire', 231 for further details of this Association employing its own police force.

23 David T. Hawkings, *Fire Insurance Records for Family and Local Historians 1696 to 1920* (London: Francis Boutle, 2003), p. 19. For a comprehensive account of the development of insurance companies, see David Jenkins and Takau Yoneyama (eds), *The History of Insurance*, 8 volumes (London: Pickering and Chatto, 2000).

24 Philips, 'Good Men to Associate and Bad Men to Conspire', p. 118.

25 J. M. Beattie, 'Early Detection: the Bow Street Runners in Late Eighteenth-century London' (unpublished essay, n.d.).

26 A. H. Manchester, *Sources of English Legal History: Law, History and Society in England and Wales, 1750–1950* (London: Butterworth, 1984), p. 237.

27 Beattie, *Policing and Punishment*, p. 229. Attested individuals were sworn in and had the power of arrest.

28 For a further discussion of Thief-takers in London, see Beattie, *The First English Detectives*, pp. 18–19 and *Policing and Punishment*, chapter 5 and pp. 401–23.

29 Although some of his advertisements detailing goods that he was prepared to return to their owners display a dextrous use of English; see an example in Ian A. Bell, *Literature and Crime in Augustan England* (London: Routledge, 1991), p. 53.

30 The surviving parish registers of St Peter's, Wolverhampton are available online at www.wolverhamptonhistory.org.uk/resources/indexes.

31 Reproduced in G. Howson, *Thief-taker General: Jonathan Wild and the Emergence of Crime and Corruption as a Way of Life in Eighteenth-Century England* (New Brunswick NJ: Transaction Publishers, 1985), p. 212.

32 Reproduced in Howson, *Thief-taker General*, p. 215.
33 Wild appears in some three-dozen larceny and burglary trials at the Old Bailey between 1716 and 1725.
34 See Chapter 7 for further details of the life and crimes of Jack Sheppard.
35 OBP t17250513–55.
36 Reproduced in Howson, *Thief-taker General*, p. 226.
37 OA 17250524.
38 OA 17250524.
39 Quoted in J. M. Beattie, *Policing and Punishment in London 1660–1750: Urban Crime and the Limits of Terror* (Oxford: OUP, 2001), p. 417.
40 *Staffordshire Advertiser*, 3 January 1801.
41 The members of the force of detective officers based at Bow Street never referred to themselves as 'Runners', considering the term derogatory and demeaning. They always referred to themselves as 'Principal' or 'Senior' Officers in an attempt to separate themselves from the lower ranks of the Bow Street policing system.
42 Francis Sheppard, *London 1808–1870: The Infernal Wen* (London: Secker & Warburg, 1971), p. 37.
43 Quoted in Gilbert Armitage, *The History of the Bow Street Runners 1729–1829* (London: Wishart & Co., 1932), p. 57. For accounts of the reputation of Thief-takers and their influence, including the notorious 'Thief-takers' Trial' of 1756, see Anthony Babington, *A House in Bow Street: Crime and the Magistracy, London 1740–1881*, 2nd edn (London: Macdonald, 1999), pp. 126–30, and Ruth Paley, 'Thief-takers in London in the Age of the McDaniel Gang c.1745–1754' in Hay, D., and Snyder, F. (eds), *Policing and Prosecution in Britain, 1750–1850* (Oxford: Clarendon, 1989), pp. 301–41.
44 Edward Sayer, *Observations on the Police or Civil Government of Westminster with a Proposal for Reform* (London: Debrett, 1784), p. 25.
45 Henry Fielding, *An Enquiry into the Causes of the Late Increase of Robbers and Related Writings*, ed. Malvin R. Zirker (Oxford: Clarendon Press, 1988), pp. 153–4.
46 Beattie, *The First English Detectives*, p. 131.
47 Ibid.
48 Patrick Pringle, *Hue & Cry: The Birth of the British Police* (London: Museum Press, 1956), p. 167.
49 Armitage, *The History of the Bow Street Runners*, p. 129. It appears that the Horse Patrol was not absorbed completely into the Metropolitan Police until September 1837; the *Morning Chronicle* of 9 September 1837 carried a report that the Horse Patrol was incorporated into the Metropolitan Police system on 2 September 1837.
50 Until as late as 1819 the less senior positions at Bow Street seem to have been part-time in nature: in a trial of that year Charles Bolton, a member of a Bow Street Patrol, states that 'I am in the East India Company's employ and am a Bow Street Patrol also' (OBP t18191201–49). In the late eighteenth century it is clear that some if not all the Principal Officers were also part-time employees of Bow Street: the list of witnesses in the Thomas Hardy treason trial of 1794 gives the other occupations of several Principal Officers (T. J. Howell, *Howell's State Trials*, Vol. XXIV [1794] [London: Longman, 1818]), pp. 1385–95, but this situation seems to have changed by the early years of the nineteenth century; certainly by 1816 the Principal Officers were all employed on a full-time basis.
51 No stipendiary magistrates were appointed outside London until 1813 (Manchester) and 1829 (Merthyr Tydfil).
52 The activities of the Principal Officers from the other London Public Offices are at present woefully under-researched, virtually nothing having been written about them.

Joan Lock's book *Marlborough Street: The Story of a London Court* (London: Robert Hale, 1980) is one of the only books to have been published that concerns itself with a London Public Office other than Bow Street, but the book concentrates heavily on events in the twentieth century and devotes little time to the early history of the Office. For a detailed account of the 'Murder in the Red Barn', see Lord Birkett, *The New Newgate Calendar* (London: The Folio Society, 1960), pp. 136–50.

53 The seven offices were: Great Marlborough Street, Hatton Garden, Lambeth, Queen's Square, Union Hall, Westminster and Worship Street. A further office, the River Thames Police Office, was created in 1798 by a separate Act of Parliament and had jurisdiction primarily over maritime policing of the capital.

54 Middlesex Justices Act (32 Geo. III c.53); full title *'An Act for the More Effectual Administration of the Office of a Justice of the Peace in Such Parts of the Counties of Middlesex and Surrey as Lie in or Near the metropolis, and for the More Effectual Prevention of Felonies'*.

55 *Reports from Committees of the House of Commons vol. XIII Finance Reports XXIII to XXXVI 1803*, Proposal 10.

56 This attempt to shield police officers from political influences continued long after the creation of the Metropolitan Police Act (10 Geo. IV c.44) and subsequent provincial Acts; constables were not allowed to vote in general or local elections until 1887.

57 Recent research has shown that the Bow Street Principal Officers operated widely throughout Great Britain and also frequently travelled to the Continent – see Cox, *A Certain Share of Low Cunning*.

58 Styles, 'An Eighteenth-Century Magistrate as Detective', p. 103.

59 Joseph Ritson, *In the Office of Constable* (London: Whieldon & Butterworth, 1791), p. 5.

60 *Report from the Committee on the state of Police of the Metropolis (510)* (London: House of Commons, 1816), vol. V, p. 175.

61 OBP t18010520–48.

62 These forged stamps purported to be from the Stamp Office, which had the monopoly for taxing legal documents by means of an official stamp; these stamps rendered the documents legal and were therefore popular with forgers. The Stamp Office's remit dated from 1694, when 'An act for granting to Their Majesties several duties on Vellum, Parchment and Paper for 4 years, towards carrying on the war against France' (5 & 6. Wm & Mar. c.21) was passed in order to assist with the cost of one of England's numerous wars with France.

63 Some 20,000 such wills are kept at TNA (ADM48).

64 Fire Insurance Registers: Fire Insurance Policy Register, 1777–1786 (accessed on Ancestry.co.uk). Sarah had been previously married to Lawrence Jones (who was executed at Tyburn in late 1793 for his part in a violent robbery – see OBP t17931030–69) and she sometimes still used her previous married name.

65 As a wealthy individual Idswell could afford to be gaoled in a private room, rather than a public cell, although he was apparently kept in irons while there (OBP t17950701–2).

66 OBP t17950416–70.

67 OBP t17950416–70.

68 OBP t17950701–2.

69 OBP t17950416–70.

70 Headborough was an ancient title, originally meaning the head of a territorial unit known as a tything or borough, but by the eighteenth century the term had become another name for a type of parish constable.

71 OBP t17950416–70.

72 OBP t17950416–70.

73 OBP t17950416–70.

74 T. Starkie, *A Treatise on Criminal Pleading: With Precedents of Indictments, Special Pleas etc.*, Vol. 2 (London: J. & W. T. Clarke, 1822), p. 136.

75 OBP t17950701–2. This trial report is relatively unusual in that it appears to be a verbatim account of the entire trial.

76 *Courier and Evening Gazette*, 2 July 1795, and Starkie, *A Treatise on Criminal Pleading*, p. 136.

77 OBP t17950520–26.

78 This badge was the official symbol of a King's Messenger, and it was an offence for it to be worn by members of the public. The use of a silver greyhound arises from a probably apocryphal story in which King Charles II broke a silver bowl decorated with four such animals and gave one of the greyhounds to each of four men that he had selected to take Royalist messages to England during his exile in France.

79 OBP t17950520–26.

80 OBP t17950520–26.

81 *Oracle and Public Advertiser*, 22 May 1795.

82 *Telegraph*, 9 July 1785.

83 *Courier and Evening Gazette*, 28 August 1795.

84 *Courier and Evening Gazette*, 28 August 1795.

85 OBP t17960622–70.

86 Douglas Hay, 'War, Dearth and Theft in the Eighteenth Century: The Record of the English Courts', *Past and Present* 95 (1982): 117–60, p. 148.

87 England, 'Investigating Homicides in Northern England', p. 113.

88 For further details of prosecutors' reimbursement in the eighteenth century, see Beattie, *Crime and the Courts*, pp. 42–8; for the early nineteenth century, see George Rudé, *Criminal and Victim: Crime and Society in Early Nineteenth-century England* (Oxford: Clarendon Press, 1985).

89 Clive Emsley, 'The Home Office and its Sources of Information and Investigation 1791–1801', *English Historical Review* XCIV (1979): 532–61, p. 532, and R. R. Nelson, *The Home Office 1782–1801* (Durham, NC: Duke University Press, 1969), p. 71.

90 Emsley, 'The Home Office', p. 536.

91 There has been only one major publication dealing with the foundation and role of the King's Messengers – see Wheeler-Holohan, V. *The History of the King's Messengers* (London: E.P. Dutton, 1935).

92 Letter reproduced in *Reports from Committees of the House of Commons vol. XIII Finance Reports XXIII to XXXVI 1803*, p. 355.

93 John Styles, 'Sir John Fielding and the Problem of Criminal Investigation in Eighteenth-century England', *Transactions of The Royal Historical Society* Fifth Series 33 (1983): 127–49.

94 For a detailed account of the functioning of magistrates' courts in the Metropolis, see Gray, *Crime, Prosecution and Social Relations*.

95 For a detailed and cogent account of the failings of the Major-Generals see Christopher Durston, *Cromwell's Major-Generals: Godly Government during the English Revolution* (Manchester: MUP, 2001).

96 Letter written by John William Ward, 1st earl of Dudley, to his sister and quoted in Clive Emsley, *The English Police: A Political and Social History*, 2nd edn (Harlow: Longman, 1996), p. 22. Fouché had been appointed by Napoleon as Minister of Police in Paris. For a further account of the Ratcliff Highway Murders, see P. D. James and T. Critchley, *The Maul and the Pear Tree: The Ratcliff Highway Murders 1811* (London: Faber & Faber, 2000).

97 John Wade, *A Treatise on the Police and Crimes of the Metropolis*, introduction by J. J. Tobias (Montclair, NJ: Patterson Smith, 1972 [original published 1829]), p. 358. General Savary succeeded Joseph Fouché as Minister of Police in 1810. The Comte de Villèle was the leader of the French Cabinet and Minister of Finance from 1821.

98 For a concise debate about changes in Georgian and Victorian attitudes to policing in the provinces, see Eastwood, *Government and Community in the English Provinces*, pp. 139–47.

99 *Report from the Committee on the state of Police of the* Metropolis, vol. V, p. 175.

100 Stanley H. Palmer, *Police and Protest in England and Ireland 1780–1850* (London: Longman, 1992), p. 72.

101 For the subsequent development of the various police forces of England, see Emsley, *The English Police*.

5 Punishment

Introduction

The punishment of offenders who were brought to justice was meted out in one of three main ways: corporal punishment and, usually reserved for less serious offences, short-term imprisonment or fines/seizure of property. The first of these varied from from detention in stocks or the pillory through public whippings to branding with a hot iron, transportation overseas or, for the most serious crimes, capital punishment in various forms (including posthumous punishment). Punishment in the eighteenth century, as we shall see, was overwhelmingly punitive, retributive and non-reformative.

Imprisonment

Although there were prisons of various descriptions in most major towns in Britain at the beginning of the eighteenth century these were used primarily as short-term holding places for those awaiting execution (e.g. Newgate, founded 1188), for debtors and bankrupts (e.g. the Clink, founded 1127, and Fleet Street prison, founded 1197) or for those who had incurred the personal wrath of the monarch (e.g. the Tower of London, founded by 1100). Edward Marston states that 'it has been estimated that in 1641 as many as 10,000 people were imprisoned for debt in England and Wales, many of them for periods of years, even though the amount they owed was relatively small at the time of arrest.'[1]

Various Poor Law acts of the late sixteenth and early seventeenth century had created bridewells or houses of correction, which were intended for 'the setting of idle and lewd people to work'.[2] Vagrants or those considered to be 'sturdy beggars' (that is, those who could work but refused to so do) were increasingly incarcerated and put to work in such institutions. However, despite the use of prisons as institutions for debtors, vagrants and 'sturdy beggars', imprisonment remained a fairly unusual punishment, especially for those who committed serious acts of crime. Imprisonment for felonies remained rare, as prisons were seen as expensive to build and maintain, and there was always the risk of cross-contamination among prisoners: that is, those imprisoned for a first offence would not be segregated from experienced and serious offenders and could therefore be taught further nefarious ways while in gaol. It was not until the early years of the nineteenth century that prison began to be seen as a suitable alternative to other punishments for certain offences.

Corporal punishment

Such punishment could be administered in a variety of forms, as will be shown below, but all the variants had several aspects in common. Corporal punishment was immediate, painful, retributive and sometimes left a permanent and visible reminder of a person's misdeeds. There was a large element of public shaming and humiliation involved in many forms of corporal punishment (much in the mould of 'rough music' or 'riding the stang', described in Chapter 2); all took place in public before often considerable crowds and were therefore intended to have a powerful psychological effect along with the more immediate element of physical pain.

Branding

Branding as a punishment in England dated back to the Anglo-Saxon period, although it had much earlier antecedents; it was recorded as a punishment for runaway slaves and robbers in the Roman period. By the early sixteenth century branding had been established as the main punishment for those convicted felons who had claimed 'benefit of clergy'. Sentencing under spiritual rather than temporal law replaced the secular death penalty for felonies with the lesser punishment of branding on the left thumb.

Branding was an obvious way of keeping 'tabs' on such offenders by visibly and permanently identifying them as transgressors. Convicted felons who had previously received benefit of clergy were indelibly marked with a permanent reminder that they had been found guilty of a criminal act and so could not claim such benefit at any subsequent court appearance.[3] Thieves were normally branded with a 'T', felons with an 'F' and murderers with an 'M'. The location of the brand was normally on the thumb of the left hand, but for a brief period in the early eighteenth century criminals were branded on the cheek. Despite the professed aim of branding being to readily identify culprits, branding on the cheek was discontinued after 1707 as it was found that it prevented ex-offenders from gaining lawful employment (and therefore increased the likelihood of both further offending and subsequent additional costs to the parish).

The use of branding or burning in any form as a punishment was not finally removed from the statute books until 1823, despite ceasing in practice from 1799 (with the exception of the armed forces, where branding of deserters with a 'D' was not abolished until 1871, as a result of the reforms of the then Secretary of State for War, Edward Cardwell).

Pillory

The pillory was another method of punishment that had persisted from well before the Middle Ages.[4] It consisted of hinged wooden boards with holes through which the offender's head and arms (and sometimes legs) would be inserted. The hinged boards would then be secured together. As the captive could neither move his head nor defend himself with his hands the pillory could be a very dangerous (and occasionally fatal) punishment, dependent upon the mood of the crowd that invariably gathered to watch the suffering of the offender. If the crowd was hostile, stones and other objects could be thrown with serious results; a newspaper report from 1810 on the reception that awaited six men who had been found guilty of 'unnatural practices' illustrates the reaction of a hostile crowd:

PILLORY. – Yesterday William Amos, alias Fox, James Cook, Philip Bell, William Thomson, Richard Francis, and James Done, six of the Vere-street gang, stood in the Pillory, in the centre of the Hay-market, opposite Norris-street. They were conveyed from Newgate [. . .in an open cart. . .] in which they were no sooner placed, than the mob began to salute them with mud, rotten eggs, and filth, with which they continued to pelt them along Ludgate-hill, Fleet-street, the Strand, and Charing-cross. When they arrived at the Hay-market, it was found that the pillory would only accommodate four at once. At one o'clock, therefore, four of them were placed on the platform, and the two others were in the meantime taken to St. Martin's Watch-house. The concourse of people assembled were immense, even the tops of the houses in the Hay-market were covered with spectators. As soon as a convenient ring was formed, a number of women were admitted within side, who vigorously expressed their abhorrence of the miscreants, by a perpetual shower of mud, eggs, offal, and every kind of filth with which they had plentifully supplied themselves in baskets and buckets. When the criminals had stood their allotted time, they were conveyed to Coldbath-fields Prison. At two o'clock the remaining two were placed in the Pillory, and were pelted till it was scarcely possible to distinguish the human shape. The caravan conveyed the two last through the Strand, then to Newgate, the mob continuing to pelt them all the way.[5]

The newspaper report concludes by demanding that such ritual humiliation and shaming accompany all pillorying:

The horrible exhibition of yesterday must prove to every considerate spectator the necessity for an immediate alteration in the law as to the punishment of this crime. It is obvious that mere exposure in the pillory is insufficient; – to beings so degraded the pillory of itself would be trifling; it is the popular indignation alone which they dread: and yet it is horrible to accustom the people to take the vengeance of justice into their own hands.[6]

However, if the crowd was sympathetic to the person being pilloried, the sentence could occasionally backfire, with cheering and collections being made for the victim(s).[7] The pillory remained in use for a wide variety of offences until 1817, following the passing of the Pillory Abolition Act 1816 (56 Geo. III c.138), when it was abolished except as a punishment for perjury or subornation (inducing a person to commit perjury). It was finally banned in 1837 following the passing of an Act to abolish the punishment of the pillory (1 Vict. c.23).

Public flogging

It was not unusual for a stint in the pillory to be accompanied by a public whipping or other forms of corporal punishment. Such punishments greatly increased both the embarrassment of and risk of serious injury to the recipient. An example of the dangers of the combination of these punishments can be seen in the case of James Lloyd, private secretary to Sir Henry Sidney, Lord President of the Council of the Marches. Lloyd was brought before the Quarter Sessions magistrates in late April 1583 charged with forging his master's signature. After being found guilty Lloyd's sentence was immediate and harsh; he was taken to the pillory that stood in Shrewsbury's Market Square, and one of his ears was nailed to the board before he was also publicly whipped – his attempts to dodge the whip presumably adding to his already considerable discomfort.

If not at a pillory, public whipping usually took place either with the victim tied to a cart which was pulled through the town or village or at specially constructed whipping posts or boards, which held the arms of the unwilling recipient fast. Public flogging was one of the last corporal punishments to be abolished; while women were not publically whipped after 1817 (and were unlikely to be privately whipped after this period), men could be publically chastized until 1862 (although in practice public whipping was rarely carried out from the 1830s onward).[8]

Stocks

The use of stocks, which were positioned in the most public of locations within a town or village in order to maximize the shame placed on the culprit, dated back to at least Elizabethan times. Stocks were generally used for petty offenders rather than felons, as the punishment, although often unpleasant, with onlookers throwing items ranging from rotten vegetables to stones at the recipient, was rarely fatal. The last recorded use of stocks in Britain was in 1872, when a notorious local drunk was placed in the stocks at the butter and poultry market at Newbury, Berkshire, for four hours.[9]

Non-corporal punishment

The above punishments were overwhelmingly retributive in nature – their main aim was to ensure that the offenders received publicly administered physical and mental chastizement in order to atone for their misdeeds. There was, however, also an element of restorative justice present in the eighteenth- and early nineteenth-century canon of punishments, and many minor transgressors were punished by the imposition of fines or the legal forfeiture of property or goods.

A fascinating *Justice's Book* kept by Thomas Netherton Parker JP, of Sweeney (near Oswestry, Shropshire), is a rare survival which illustrates the types of offences that could attract restorative fines rather than retributive corporal punishment.[10] The book was handwritten by Parker, who was sworn in as Deputy Lieutenant of Shropshire on 2 November 1803 after previously having held the same post for the county of Worcestershire since 13 November 1796 (he had considerable financial and agrarian interests in both counties).[11] The book details every one of the cases that came before him at his Petty Sessions held between 8 March 1805 and 23 July 1813, and contains an interesting cross section of the work of a fairly active and diligent magistrate. The cases, which run to well over 100 in number, are all listed with the names of the protagonists and suspects, with a full account being given of Parker's summary judgement on each. The vast majority involve either minor assaults between agricultural labourers or the fleeing from contract by servants and labourers.

An example is that of Mary Hughes, whose case was adjudged by Parker on 20 July 1805. Mary was a dairymaid who had broken her contract with her employer, Edward Minshall. She ran away from her place of employment and it took the local parish constable Edward Francis three days to locate her and bring her before the magistrate. Parker ordered that Mr Minshall pay the resultant expenses of 2s. for the drafting of an arrest warrant and the services of the clerk, along with 7s. 6d., being the amount payable to Constable Francis for his three-day search. The total sum of 9s. 6d. was then to be deducted from Mary Hughes' future wages and she was ordered to continue in Mr Minshall's service from 31 July 1805 to 11 May 1806. This must have been a severe blow to Mary, the expenses amounting to several weeks' wages.

Such a sum must have seemed large enough to the unhappy dairymaid, but on 18 March 1807 Parker imposed a far more severe financial penalty on John Owen of Whittington. Owen fell foul of the notoriously strict Game Laws that had been brought in to protect the 'sporting' interests of the landed gentry and aristocracy. He was obviously a man of some prosperity, as he was found guilty of furnishing one of his servants, John Morgan, with several guns and also of assisting him in laying them in order to take hares from a neighbouring estate. Owen was fined £5 in total, with the sum of 50s. to be surrendered to the Reverend W. W. Davies for the poor of Whittington, costs of 25s. 6d., and 10s. paid in costs to Mr Lewis Jones (presumably the owner of the land and, by extension, the poached hares).

Transportation

One of the most common punishments for felony was transportation to one of Britain's numerous colonies, where the offender would then serve a period of imprisonment and forced labour. The Transportation Act 1718 (4 Geo. I c.11) introduced penal transportation to America with a minimum sentence of seven years, but transportation had in effect existed since at least the 1610s, with various forms of indentured servitude.

As early as 1615 convicted felons who faced the death penalty were given the opportunity (by means of a Royal Pardon) for their sentence to be commuted to transportation to America or the West Indies. Governor Thomas Dale of Virginia had in 1611 written to King Charles I requesting him to 'banish hither all offenders condemned to die out of common goales, and likewise to continue that grant for three years unto the colonie (and thus doth the Spaniard people his Indes) it would be a readie way to furnish us with men, and not allways with the worst kind of men'.[12] His request was not acceded to, but on 23 January 1615 an order of the Privy Council was issued stating:

> Whereas it hath pleased his Majesty out of his singular clemency and mercy to take into his princely consideration the wretched estate of diverse of his Subjects who by the Laws of the Realm are adjudged to die for sundry offences though heinous in themselves, yet not of the highest nature, so as his Majesty both out of his gracious clemency, as also for diverse weighty considerations could wish they might be rather corrected than destroyed, and that in their punishments some of them might live, and yield a profitable service to the Commonwealth in parts abroad, where it shall be found fit to employ them [and] to reprieve and stay from execution such persons as now stand Convicted of any Robbery or felony (wilful murder, rape, witchcraft or burglary only excepted) who for strength of body or other abilities shall be thought fit to be employed in foreign discoveries or other services beyond the seas, with this special proviso: that if any of the said offenders shall refuse to go, or yielding to go shall afterwards return from those places before the time limited by us, his Majesty's Commissioners, that then the said reprieval shall no longer stand, but the said offender shall from thenceforth be subject to the execution of the law for the offence whereof he was first convicted.[13]

On 23 December 1617 a Royal Proclamation 'for the better and more peaceable government of the middle shires of Northumberland, Cumberland and Westmorland' similarly stated that:

> For the more speedy suppressing, and freeing the said countries and places of notorious and wicked offenders that will not be reformed, but by severity of punishment; We have taken order for the making out a Commission to special Commissioners, to survey, search and find out, and inform Us of the most notorious and lewd persons, and of their faults, within the said Counties of Northumberland, Cumberland, and Westmerland, Riddesdale, and Bewcastle within the same: And We hereby signify our pleasure to be upon Certificate of the said Commissioners, to send the most notorious ill-livers, and misbehaved persons of them that shall so be certified, into Virginia, or to some other remote parts to serve in the Wars, or in Colonies, that they may no more infect the places where they abide within this our Realm.[14]

These two documents were the first official sanctioning of a system that was to result in some 50,000 men, women and children being forcibly transported from Britain to America over the next 160 years, together with a further 160,000 or more transported to Australia in the period 1788–1868 following the loss of America as a colony in 1783.[15] As Bernard Bailyn has remarked, 'as a form of punishment transportation was logical enough, for the colonies were assumed to be so remote, so primitive, that merely sending people there would be punitive, and it was also economical, constructive and socially therapeutic – for Britain, that is.'[16]

Despite emerging from a common aim of ridding Britain of 'notorious and wicked offenders', the systems of transportation to America and Australia were different in several respects. As Kercher remarks, 'the punishment of transportation to America was essentially exile, to which was attached in practice a form of compulsory service modelled on [. . .] indentured labour': the convicts, while serving their sentences, were not considered to be the responsibility of the British government and were not subject to the types of official control and regulation that were imposed upon those transported to the various provinces of Australia.[17] In America, wealthy convicts could formally purchase their way out of contractual servitude upon arrival; in Australia, the system ensured that the majority of convicts served at least some of their respective terms of labour.[18]

Such a vast trafficking in human lives was not without its critics: in a starkly contrasting view to that which was expressed by Governor Thomas Dale in 1611, on 22 February 1739 the Lieutenant-Governor of Virginia, William Gooch, wrote to the Commissioners for Trade and Plantations complaining that:

> The great number of convicts yearly imported here and the impossibility of ever reclaiming them from their vicious habits have occasioned a vast charge to the country in the expense of their trial for felonies committed since their arrival, for as each of these criminals has had a jury of twelve men summoned to Williamsburg, who have been paid by the public, it became necessary to lessen the expense as there are no hopes of lessening the number, and it was of no benefit to the persons accused who are for the most part scarce known in the neighbourhood where they lived and committed the offence. So that this Act directs that when any person, being a transported convict, shall be accused of any crime the county court shall examine and certify whether he be a convict and not out of his time of servitude; and if he be, then [. . .] such convicts shall be tried by a jury of bystanders, saving to the prisoner his challenges to those jurors, and by this method the charge of jurymen will be saved which for some years has been equal almost to all the other public expenses of the government.[19]

There were also fears unrelated to the expense of maintaining convicts in the colonies; a contemporaneous commentator remarked that:

> The colonies must be peopled. Agreed: and will the transportation acts ever have that tendency? No, they work the contrary way, and counteract their

own design. We want people, 'tis true, but not villains ready, at any time, encouraged by impunity, and habituated upon the slightest occasions, to cut a man's throat, for a small part of his property.[20]

The same commentator also stated that 'there is scarce a thief in England that would not rather be transported than hanged', but the implications of being transported thousands of miles across the sea, far from one's home and family, should not be trivialized – it often had a life-shattering effect on both the transportee and his or her family and, as is demonstrated in the following case study, returning illegally from a sentence of transportation could have devastating consequences:[21]

Case Study 11: John Whalebone, larceny and returning from transportation, 1723 and 1725

John Whalebone was born *c.* 1687 in the City of London. He married Ann Lane on New Year's Day at St Dunstan, Stepney, and they had four children: John, christened 1715, Duke, christened 1717, Thomas, christened 1719, and David, christened 1721. He seems to have served in the Royal Navy for a short spell, but, deciding that a mariner's life was not for him, he returned to London, where he lived in Rosemary Lane, St Botolph-without-Aldgate and eked out a living as a hawker of old clothes.

In 1715 he had his first brush with the law, being tried at the Old Bailey for stealing a brass pestle and mortar, five brass candlesticks and sixteen shillings. He was found guilty to the value of 10d. and sentenced to a whipping.[22] This was a clear example of jury mitigation, or what Beattie has called 'pious perjury', in which a jury could prevent the offender facing the death penalty.[23] During both William and Mary's and Anne's reigns a series of Acts of Parliament steadily decreased the number of offences to which benefit of clergy could be applied; in 1691 an Act (3 and 4 Wm and Mary c.9) removed the offence of breaking into houses and shops and stealing to the value of 5s. or above, while in 1713 another Act (12 Anne c.7) removed theft from a house (even when no one was present within the house) to the value of 40s. or above, theoretically sentencing the offender to either the death penalty or, from 1718, following the passing of the Transportation Act, the prospect of transportation to America.

As Whalebone had been accused of stealing money and goods to a total value of more than 40s. he was therefore liable to the death penalty. By valuing the goods at 10d. the jury exercised their opportunity of discretion and thereby prevented the judge from passing such a sentence. Beattie has demonstrated that such actions were 'a central element of criminal administration throughout the [18th] century' and that 'the scale of undervaluation was frequently staggering', and quotes an example of gold and jewellery worth £300 stolen from a shop being valued by the jury at 39s.[24] Clearly, in the majority of such cases there must have been a certain amount of judicial direction to the jury by the judge during his closing remarks, as it is unlikely that jurors would have otherwise been aware of such fine legal distinctions.

Unfortunately Whalebone appears not to have learned any lessons from this fortuitous brush with the judicial system. Two years later he was again in trouble, being confined in Bridewell Hospital and Prison awaiting trial for pickpocketing a handkerchief from a goldsmith. He was punished (probably by another whipping) and then discharged from Bridewell.[25]

In April 1720 he was in court once more, this time accused of burglary with co-defendant John White. He was indicted at the Old Bailey

> for breaking the Dwelling-House of John Crofts, on the 29th of December last in the Night-time, and taking thence a Warming Pan, 24 Ounces of Silk, 2 Shirts, 2 pair of Leather Breeches, &c. the Goods of the said John Crofts.[26]

He seems to have ridden his luck again at this appearance; insufficient evidence of his involvement was proved and he was therefore acquitted. In the same year he decided to try his hand at soldiering, albeit with a private company rather than in a regular regiment. He signed up as a soldier with the Royal African Company in late 1720, but was subsequently involved in a riot that occurred in the Savoy prison and was seriously injured.

The Royal African Company had been created in 1672 by the duke of York (brother of Charles II) with a Royal Charter to impose martial law on areas of the west coast of Africa (primarily Gambia and Guinea). It was empowered to build forts and employ its own soldiers in order to enforce such law. Its main trading items were gold and slaves and it was responsible for the forcible export of over 100,000 West African slaves from the Gulf of Guinea to the New World.[27] By 1720, despite the tumultuous financial events of the South Sea Bubble, the Royal African Company was flourishing and needed to enlist more soldiers to maintain its enterprises in West Africa.[28]

Whalebone, together with some seventy-odd other men, had been induced by the offer of a bounty of £4 to enlist in the company's troop. He and his new comrades were accommodated at the former Savoy Palace (then a run-down military prison) to await their ship to Gambia. However, their bounty was not forthcoming and on 2 November the men argued with their officers and a riot ensued in which Whalebone was stabbed in the stomach by a bayonet fixed to a musket.[29] He was in grave danger of his life for several days, but subsequently recovered. Despite a public outcry and considerable publicity in the newspapers of the day, no charges were subsequently brought against Whalebone's assailant and many of the men did eventually sign up for the Royal African Company and went to the Guinea coast. It is not clear from the surviving records whether Whalebone was among these men, but in August 1723 he appeared once again in the court records, this time on two charges of theft, one of a periwig valued at 40s. and other goods, and the other of stealing sheets and other goods worth 45s. from a dwelling house.[30] Although the jury valued the goods in the second charge at 39s., Whalebone's luck appears to have temporarily deserted him and in consequence of the first charge he was sentenced to seven years' transportation to America. On 5 October 1723 he was taken aboard the *Forward* galley to begin his enforced emigration to the New World. The *Forward* galley was owned and operated by Jonathan Forward, a London merchant who traded extensively in slaves and tobacco to the West Indies and who, from 1718, was granted an exclusive government contract to oversee convict transportation at a cost of £3 per head for English convicts and £5 per head for convicts from Ireland.[31] As a transportee to North America, Whalebone was one of some 40,000–50,000 individuals who suffered this fate between 1718 and 1776.[32]

Whalebone proved to be a difficult individual to control; in later evidence Jonathan Forward stated that 'I remember him well, for he was so unruly, that we were forced to put him in double Irons.'[33] After making the Atlantic crossing Whalebone was sent to a South Carolina plantation owner, but quickly found that such a life was not to his liking. Although a contemporary biographer optimistically stated that transported convicts 'are [. . .] exposed to no more hardships than they would have been obliged to have undergone at home, in order to have got an honest livelihood', Whalebone determined to return to England, despite:

> the kind usage of his master, the easiness of the life which he lived, and the certainty of death if he attempted to return home, could not all of them prevail upon him to lay aside the thoughts of coming back again to London, and there giving himself up to those sensual delights which he had formerly enjoyed.[34]

As a former mariner, Whalebone appears to have had little difficulty in coming to an arrangement with a sea-captain, and he returned to the shores of England in 1725. Unfortunately for him, he could not stay away from his old haunts and it was reported in the *Evening Post* of 25–28 September 1725 that 'one John Whalebone, who sometime since was a ringleader in a Riot at the Savoy, is committed to Newgate for returning from Transportation before due Time.'

On 13 October Whalebone appeared before a judge and jury at the Old Bailey, where a parish constable gave the following evidence:

> Mr. Jones: About two Years ago I apprehended him for robbing Mr. Moor: He was Try'd, Convicted, and Transported. I afterwards heard that he was committed to Bridewell. I went thither, and ask'd how he dared appear again? He said, he knew he should be hang'd, but he would do as much Mischief as he could first.[35]

Whalebone's luck had finally run out and as a returned transportee he was sentenced to death, despite pleading ignorance of the offence of returning before his time. His contemporary anonymous biographer had no time for this excuse, stating that:

> Transportation is a punishment whereby the British law commutes for offences which would otherways be capital, and therefore a contract is plainly

presumed between every felon transported and the Court by whose authority he is ordered for transportation, that the said felon shall remain for such term of years as the Law directs, without returning into any of the King's European dominions; and the Court plainly acquaints the felon that if, in breach of his agreement, he shall so return, that in such case the contract shall be deemed void, and the capital punishment shall again take place. To say, then, that a person who enters into an agreement like this, and is perfectly acquainted with its conditions, knowing that no less than his life must be forfeited by the breach of them, and yet wilfully breaks them, to say that such a person as this is guilty of no offence, must in the opinion of every person of common understanding be the greatest absurdity that can be asserted; and to call that severity which only is the Law's taking its forfeit, is a very great impropriety, and proceeds from a foolish and unreasonable compassion. This I think so plain that nothing but prepossession or stupidity can hinder people from comprehending it.

On Wednesday 3 November 1725 John Whalebone was taken from Newgate Gaol and executed by hanging at Tyburn at the age of 38.[37]

Transportation as a punishment did not cease with the loss of America following Britain's disastrous war with its former colonists between 1776 and 1783. Instead, the British government looked elsewhere and decided that the newly discovered territory of Australia would be a perfect place in which the system could continue.

Often those sentenced to transportation served a considerable portion of their sentence on board 'prison hulks', rotting former man-of-war ships that had been stripped to their basics and moored in areas near where public works were being undertaken in order to provide the government with a ready supply of convict labour. Conditions, as illustrated by the following testimony, could be appalling. On 17 January 1794 Edward Moseley, a prisoner aboard the hulk *Stanislaus* (moored at Woolwich) wrote the following letter to Permanent Under-Secretary of State for the Home Department, Sir Evan Nepean:

Honoured Sir,

I am a young man of twenty-two years of age, by trade a bricklayer, and was convicted by Judge Gould at Chelmsford, in the year one thousand seven hundred and ninety-two, to seven years' Transportation beyond the seas, for stealing a game-cock. 1 am no lawyer, but suppose my crime to be of that heinous nature as to be incapable of pardon, I do not ask it: all I petition for is to he taken from this floating hell, and sent in the next ship to Botany Bay. I am lame from a fall, but stout and robust, and every day go through laborious work. I have three times had the gaol fever, which is another reason for my importunity, In granting this my reasonable request I shall ever consider myself,

Yours

Edward Moseley.[38]

However, if one survived the prison hulks there were, as illustrated in the following case study, opportunities to make good of one's enforced new life in Australia.

Case Study 12: Charles Beasley, highway robbery and shoplifting, 1793

Charles William Beasley, the son of Henry and Susannah, was born in the Leicestershire village of Kibworth Beauchamp and christened on 6 December 1776.[39] He seems to have been trained as a stocking weaver (possibly in Derbyshire), but by the age of fifteen he had, like so many of his contemporaries, gravitated to London.[40]

On 19 July 1793 he was brought to Bow Street Magistrates Court by the Beadle of Brentford after being apprehended the previous day by a watchman in New Brentford, who stated in his evidence that 'on the 18th of July there was an alarm come down, that a gentleman had been robbed in a postchaise; between eleven and twelve o'clock this Beazley [*sic*] came down with a hat and I stopped him, and put him in the cage.'[41] No one was prepared to swear against him at that time, however, and he was released without charge. On 15 September he was again taken into custody on both the same charge and another one of shoplifting, this time by Christopher Kennedy, a Bow Street Principal Officer. On this occasion he was remanded into custody and in late October 1793 he was once more brought before Bow Street Magistrates Court, this time being suspected of involvement in another highway robbery in June 1792, in which Elbro Woodcock, a lawyer, was knocked down on the way from his chambers and robbed of almost £100 and a gold watch.[42]

Beasley was suspected of being one of a criminal gang of footpads referred to as 'the Floorers'. This sobriquet derived from the cant term 'floorer', described in a contemporary newspaper as one 'who always knock the person down before they relieve him of his money'.[43] He was brought before Sir William Addington, Chief Magistrate of Bow Street, and again remanded in custody.

Investigations into the activities of 'the Floorers' continued, with one of the gang, Daniel Driscoll, turning King's Evidence and providing damning testimony against his erstwhile accomplices at their subsequent trial at the Old Bailey on 4 December 1793. The gang of which he was a member was suspected of involvement in a number of violent robberies, including one in which the victim was subsequently reported to have died:

> Joseph Howe, Law stationer of Chancery Lane died on Wed 30 April 1793 – his death was occasioned by having been robbed of his watch and purse, and much hurt by some villains in Symond's Inn Passage on the 17th instant.[44]

The gang also had a sideline in theft from shops; Beasley was charged along with two other suspected gang members, John Rabbitts and William Brown aka Bartlett, with shoplifting on 14 September 1793 and taking watches worth over

£60 from the premises of John Coward in Cornhill. The three individuals were all positively identified by the victim and Driscoll stated that he had gone to Mr Coward's shop where Beasley had 'observed to him that a glass case [containing the watches], which was in the shop, would be very easily stolen'.[45]

Driscoll's evidence against Beasley proved equally damning with regard to another case heard on the same day in which Beasley was accused, along with Rabbitts, of highway robbery committed on 18 July 1793 near the Brentwood Turnpike; this was the case for which he had originally been taken to Bow Street from Brentford. The two men were charged with

> feloniously making an assault, on the King's highway, on James Sayer, on the 18th of July, and putting him in fear and feloniously taking from his person, and against his will, two guineas, half a guinea, and nine shillings in monies numbered; the monies of the said James Sayer.[46]

Driscoll stated that he, Rabbitts, Beasley and another man, Randall (who by the time of this trial had already been executed as the result of being found guilty in another trial), had 'agreed to purchase a pair of pistols each, to go on the road with', and they had subsequently purchased one pair for 15s. and another for £1 from a pawnbroker.

In his cross-examination at the first trial held that day Driscoll stated that he had 'followed the medical line for a number of years' but had drifted into a life of crime through economic necessity.[47] He was clearly perfectly aware of the consequences of his turning King's Evidence; when asked by the barrister 'don't you know that you have saved yourself from hanging by these confessions?' he replied that 'I harbour this opinion in my own breast. I was informed that if I gave up the right parties that I was concerned with, I should save my life and be useful to the public.'[48] He appeared unrepentant at his actions, stating that 'I am an unfortunate young man, I have been seduced by the greatest villains in this kingdom.'

Toward the end of the trial William Brown aka Bartlett launched a verbal attack on Driscoll, stating 'in the first place, consider my life is at stake, will you positively swear, and take upon yourself to say, that I was the person that was in the shop?' Driscoll calmly replied 'I will. He was the very identical person that asked for the chain, I am very positive of it, I saw him. I would not say any thing that was wrong.' Brown then stated 'in the second place, you would wish to save your own life, and to hang us; though you wish to save your own life, do not swear false; God forgive you.' Brown then protested that 'I was dragged away, and had not money to employ counsel, or any thing; and that man that stands there, he knows, that I am innocent of the very charge that he lays against me.'[49]

Both Rabbitts and Brown aka Bartlett were sentenced to death for their part in the highway robbery, as was Beasley. Beasley and Rabbitts were further both sentenced to death on the charge of shoplifting.[50] However, owing to Beasley's age, the jury in the shoplifting case recommended mercy. This resulted in a respite for him and a conditional pardon on 10 February 1794 which commuted his death sentence to that of one for transportation for life. Rabbitts and Brown were not so fortunate and both were hanged at Tyburn within forty-eight hours of the sentence being passed upon them.[51]

Beasley was committed to Newgate Gaol, where he remained for eight months, then being transferred to the prison hulk *Stanislaus*. He spent three years on the *Stanislaus*, before being put aboard the 796-ton former East India merchant ship *Barwell* in November 1798. On 7 November the *Barwell* embarked from Portsmouth with 296 convicts, 33 soldiers and 18 free settlers aboard. A letter from an anonymous officer aboard the *Barwell*, dated 21 November 1797, paints a somewhat rosy picture of the voyage:

> Off Madeira
>
> All manner of good order (through the activity and unremitted attention of our Captain) prevails; and you would hardly know that there was a Convict on the ship, but that now and then he is obliged to order some of them a gentle chastisement for petty thefts. The ship's Company are very well, and my brother Officers are a set of good, steady, blunt, honest fellows.[52]

However, this picture of harmony proved false and in February 1798 an attempted mutiny involving some twenty-five of the soldiers on board was thwarted.[53] Ensign George Bond of the New South Wales Corps was identified as the ringleader and clapped in irons. After an arduous journey the *Barwell* arrived at Sydney on 18 May 1798, with nine convicts dying *en route*.[54] Ensign Bond was due to be court-martialled for his part in the attempted mutiny, but he resigned his commission before his trial.

Beasley survived this trying journey of 192 days and seems to have completely desisted from criminal activities. On 7 April 1804 he is recorded as joining the recently formed Sydney Loyal Association, a local part-time militia force created to help keep order in the new colony.[55] In 1806 he gained a Ticket of Leave and three years later he was granted the lease of land at Bell Row Street, Sydney. On 12 February 1810 he sent a petition for mitigation of his sentence together with a memorial requesting a grant of land to support himself and his family to the Governor of New South Wales, stating that he had been imprisoned for upwards of sixteen years and in Australia for the last twelve, having a wife and four young children to support.[56] He requested a few acres of land and confirmation of the free pardon recently granted to him by the Lieutenant Governor. He received this along with 80 acres of land. Beasley also benefited from an edict issued on 12 July 1810 by the Governor that:

> The principal brewers at Sydney having represented that it would be a great accommodation to the labouring people and to the lower classes of inhabitants in general to have plenty of good wholesome beer brewed for their drinking and permitted to be retailed to them at a moderate price, His Excellency the Governor, in view to their convenience, as well as to encourage the settlers throughout the colony to grow barley for this and other

purposes, has been pleased to direct licences to be granted to fifty persons at Sydney to vend and retail beer on the terms stipulated in their respective securities, namely each person paying an annual tax of five pounds for his licence and finding security, himself in twenty-five pounds and one surety in the like sum.[57]

Beasley was one of the fifty retailers who received a licence to sell beer, and this concession undoubtedly helped him prosper as a businessman. On 9 September 1811 he was licensed to carry a cargo of cedar on the government's behalf in his new sloop *Windsor*, and on 28 July 1812 he took out a £500 bond with the Naval Officer of the territory of New South Wales:

> Not to take out or bring in any person without written consent of Governor, not to depart port without clearance, not to navigate outside territorial limits, not to receive deserters from gangs, not to fail to provide suitable provisions for the gangs they transport, etc.[58]

He appears to have cohabited with Mary Thomas (herself a former convict sentenced to seven years in April 1801 for larceny at Carlisle) for a number of years before marrying her on 4 September 1815 (they had six children born before their marriage and one after), and appears to have flourished as a businessman; by 1817 he was holding the licence of the Lord Nelson public house at Windsor and in August 1821 he gained an auctioneer's licence.[59]

In December 1821 his wife died and in November 1823 he requested permission to marry in church at Windsor. On 8 December 1823 he remarried and had a further four children with his new wife. On 4 October 1824 he was recorded as 'free by servitude and has raised 9 children, has 72 head of horned cattle, employs 7 Government servants', and was petitioningf for additional land to be granted to him. On 21 November 1825 a further 320 acres of land was granted to him.[60]

His business interests may have faltered over the next few years, as there are several advertisements in 1828 concerning the insolvency of a Charles Beasley at Windsor, but by the early 1830s he had recovered financially; in 1831 he is recorded as being the licensee of the Rising Sun public house in George Street, Windsor, and by the time of his death on 30 November 1837 he is described in his obituary as 'an old inhabitant of the colony in his 61st year'.[61]

Capital punishment

This remained the ultimate punishment for those found guilty of committing the most serious offences. From the mid-seventeenth century to the middle of the eighteenth the number of offences attracting the death penalty rose from around fifty to well over 150.[62] Hanging was by far the most common form of capital punishment, but death could also be meted out by various other methods, including burning at the stake (usually reserved for those found guilty either of Petty Treason – the murder of one's husband – or of heresy), hanging, drawing and quartering (an excruciatingly painful and slow death), beheading with an axe or sword (usually reserved for members of the nobility) or being pressed to death with heavy weights placed on the victim's chest until their internal organs were crushed (this punishment, known as *Peine Forte et Dure*, was usually reserved for those accused who refused to plead and instead 'stood mute').[63]

The litany of multiple offences carrying the death penalty later became known as the 'Bloody Code'. Sir William Blackstone, lawyer and commentator on criminal justice matters, remarked in 1765 that:

> It is a melancholy truth, that among the variety of actions which men are daily liable to commit, no less than a hundred and sixty have been declared by Act of Parliament to be felonious without benefit of clergy; or, in other words, to be worthy of instant death.[64]

Despite the presence of the 'Bloody Code' and the large number of death penalties recorded at the various Assizes throughout the eighteenth and early nineteenth century, it became increasingly apparent to the authorities that it would be counter-productive for all of the death penalties to be carried out. Following the removal of the benefit of clergy from many offences (thereby greatly increasing the number of capital offences) trial juries often mitigated their verdicts in order to ensure that the offender escaped the noose. Beattie gives numerous examples of such jury mitigation, including an instance at the 1699 Surrey Summer Assizes where two men, who had been charged with shoplifting goods to the value of £3 15s. were tried and found guilty by the jury of stealing goods to the value of 10d. This verdict ensured that they would be publicly whipped rather than executed, as the recently passed Shoplifting Act 1699 (10 and 11 Wm III c.25) designated any theft from a shop to the value of less than 5s. to be a non-capital offence.[65]

With regard to the latter part of the period under discussion, Gatrell has calculated that during the period 1811–15, of the 2,760 capital convictions, 374 people were executed, with 86 per cent of those sentenced being pardoned (this did not mean a complete pardon, rather that their sentences were commuted).[66] How much this 'benevolence' was due to genuine sympathy for the plight of the individual rather than a realization that too many executions would diminish their overall effect in terms of fear or 'shock value' is open to interpretation, but it is clear that the death penalty was increasingly being replaced by other sentences for many lesser crimes throughout the period.[67]

Executions by hanging were carried out in public until 1868. Following the passage of the Murder Act in 1752 all such sentences had to be carried out within forty-eight hours (except if the sentence was passed on a Friday or Saturday – no hangings were permitted on Sundays). The general perception that the condemned man or woman was allowed a hearty breakfast is a misguided and apocryphal one: Article VII of the Murder Act 1752 states that 'until the execution

[...] such offender shall be fed bread and water only, and with no other food or liquor whatsoever'.[68]

The 'Bloody Code' and capital punishment in particular were coming under some question by the late eighteenth century, but many contemporary defendants of this system agreed with Archbishop William Paley (1743–1805), who in his *Principles of Moral and Political Philosophy* had argued that 'the end of punishment was not justice [. . .]. It was deterrence – and deterrence through terror'.[69] He also argued that if the wrong man was occasionally hanged by mistake, then the unfortunate victim could be considered to have died for the greatest good. By this Paley meant that the main reason for the continuation of what could be seen as a draconian system was for the benefit of society as a whole, rather than simply punishment as retributive justice against an individual. This system of deterrence was what the sociologist and philosopher Emile Durkheim (1858–1917) would later argue was a 'collective consciousness' and that this collective set of beliefs demands that offences against it are punished:

> Crimes are offences against society's sacred moral order which in turn corresponds to deeply held sentiments within society's individual members [. . .] The result is a passionate, hostile reaction on the part of the public which demands the offender be punished [. . .] vengeance is the primary motivation which underpins punitive actions.[70]

The spectre of the disintegration of the existing social order can be seen as one of the main reasons for the continuation and promulgation of the 'Bloody Code'. Douglas Hay, among others, argues that the hegemony of the rulers of England in the eighteenth century was perceived as being threatened by such disintegration, and that consequently 'the increasing arsenal of death laws provided the Whig rulers of England with a functional combination of threat, terror and mercy that established their hegemony over the "loose and disorderly" mass of the population'.[71]

Hay has remarked that 'the rulers of eighteenth-century England cherished the death sentence'.[72] His influential chapter in *Albion's Fatal Tree* is perhaps the most purely Marxist interpretation of the existence of the death penalty published at the time, and was undoubtedly one of the most successful in terms of stimulating further debate. Hay argues cogently that the rulers of England managed to successfully promulgate the majesty and terror of the law throughout the eighteenth and into the nineteenth century in order to defend their own interests.

The working classes, he argues, were ruthlessly subdued by the socio-political elite by means of a carefully controlled judicial and legal system that served explicitly to protect all equally by parading a communal sanction against communally perceived criminal acts, but in fact implicitly protected the rights of propertied men. He remarks, satirically, that 'the trick was to extend that communal sanction to a criminal law that was nine-tenths concerned with upholding a radical division of property'.[73]

Hay is supported in this view by contemporary historians such as Frank McLynn, who concedes that 'the occasional aristocratic victim like Lord Ferrers had to be offered up', but argues that the system was implicitly designed to maintain deference and inequality – the fact that there was neither publicly funded prosecution nor a national police force reinforces the view that the 'ruling class was happy with the fundamentally feudal system of law enforcement and did not want any form of centralisation or reform to occur'.[74] V. A. C. Gatrell argued passionately from a similar viewpoint in his meticulously researched book *The Hanging Tree*, which covers most aspects of England's system of capital punishment from 1770 to 1868 in often grim and disturbing detail.[75]

There was always the fear on the part of the authorities that friends or accomplices of the condemned might try to snatch them either before or after the sentence had taken place. To dissuade such individuals, the Murder Act 1752 made explicit the ferocity of the law should anyone be found guilty of such an action: attempts to rescue the condemned person before the sentence was carried out would result in the automatic death penalty, while cutting down the body of the condemned after hanging carried a sentence of seven years' transportation, as did a failed attempt at rescuing the body from the anatomists prior to dissection.

Posthumous punishment

Anatomical dissection was the normal means of disposing of the body of a hanged person; a Christian burial was not permitted in the hope that the fear of not being allowed to rest in consecrated ground (and thereby assure one's path into Heaven) would also act as an added deterrent to those considering a serious criminal act. Ruth Richardson has put forward an intriguing argument that anatomical dissection in itself was a most feared and reviled posthumous punishment, and gives an account of several serious attacks carried out on anatomists by relatives and friends of the subject being dissected. She also remarks, somewhat controversially, that 'although this was of course an extreme reaction, it was certainly the case that hanging the corpse in chains on a gibbet was popularly regarded as preferable to dissection'.[76]

This latter view seems not to have been shared by the authorities, however, as in some cases the death penalty and subsequent dissection was not considered to be an end of the individual's punishment. The Murder Act 1752 contains a reference to the discretion awarded to judges in order to protect society from a perceived threat to its continued existence:

> Whereas the horrid crime of murder has of late been more frequently perpetrated than formerly [. . .] and whereas it is thereby become necessary, that some further terror and peculiar mark of infamy be added to the punishment of death.[77]

The choice of gibbeting as a 'further terror' was not new to the eighteenth or nineteenth centuries; according to the Rev. J. Charles Cox, the gibbeting or hanging in chains of bodies of executed offenders 'was a coarse custom very generally prevalent in medieval England'.[78] The reasons why this medieval 'custom' was still present in nineteenth-century England are still the subject of discussion, but many historians hold the view expressed by Radzinowicz that:

> Its purpose – like that of public executions – was to increase the deterrent effect of capital punishment; to achieve it, the process of executing the capital sentence was, as it were, prolonged beyond the death of the delinquent.[79]

To this end, several measures were often taken to prevent the removal of the body from the gibbet, which was a substantial structure, often of a considerable height and studded with hundreds of nails in order to prevent anyone from either cutting it down or climbing it to remove the body from the iron cage. The body was fixed to the gibbet by means of iron hooks drilled into the bones of the cadaver.

Cesar de Saussure, a contemporary commentator, remarked (in contrast to Richardson) that 'the lower classes [. . .] have a great horror of the hanging in chains, and the shame of it is terrible for the relatives of the condemned'.[80] Conversely, other views held that for the family of the victim(s) the gibbet could present a 'comforting sight to the relations and friends of the deceased'.[81] In general, however, the public spectacle of a gibbeted body seems to have engendered a range of emotions and reactions in the mind of the public, as the following case study illustrates.

Case Study 13: William Howe (aka John Wood), murder, 1812

Stourbridge in 1812 was a burgeoning small town with a population of around 4,000 on the south-western edge of the Black Country. It was already experiencing rapid growth and urbanization, mainly as a result of to the presence of glass-making, coal mining and fireclay mining in the surrounding area. However, it was still predominantly agriculture that supported the local economy and society. The weekly Friday market, which had existed in Stourbridge since at least the sixteenth century and was known by 1812 as the 'Old Market', drew a large number of prosperous farmers into the town, and both contemporary and later evidence suggests that a considerable number of financial transactions took place on these occasions.

It was on such a Friday market day – 18 December 1812 – that Benjamin Robins, a well-respected gentleman farmer who lived at Dunsley Hall near Kinver, carried out his particular business in the bustling town. Mr Robins was a popular and active member of the local gentry, with several respected friends, and from 1798 had been a member of the Stourbridge Local Volunteer Association of Cavalry, providing his own horse, uniform and weapons.[82] Perhaps mindful of the cost of the forthcoming seasonal festivities, which he was no doubt looking forward to sharing with his family, he was carrying on his person two £10 notes from Messrs Hill, the Old Bank, Stourbridge, a £1 note from a Dudley bank and 8s. in silver. He left the town at around 4.30 p.m., so that he should get home before the snow that had been falling throughout the day made travelling too difficult.

He set off on the relatively short journey along the unpaved but direct route to Dunsley via the Stourbridge–Bridgnorth road. At around 5 p.m. he heard a man's voice behind him requesting him to stop. Being somewhat short-sighted, in the failing light Mr Robins at first mistook the well-dressed man for one of his brothers, Jeremiah. He consequently waited for the figure to catch up with him, to discover that the man was in fact a stranger who asked directions for the Kidderminster road. Mr Robins told him that they were not far from the required road, and asked the stranger to accompany him as they were both going in the same direction.

This proved to be a fateful act of kindness: a contemporary account of what happened next is given in the *Staffordshire Advertiser* of Saturday 26 December 1812:

> On Friday evening, about five o'clock, as Mr B. Robins of Dunsley, was returning from Stourbridge Market; he was overtaken by a man who walked and conversed with him for some distance; but when within less than half-a-mile of Mr Robins' house, the villain drew behind Mr Robins and discharged a pistol at him, the ball, it is supposed, struck Mr Robins on the backbone, which caused it to take a direction round his ribs to near the belly; the place it entered, to where it was found, was from fourteen to sixteen inches. The villain, as soon as he had fired, demanded Mr Robins' money, who said, 'Why did you shoot me first? If you had asked me for it before, you should have had it.' Mr Robins then gave him two £10 notes, a £1 note, and 8s. in silver.[83]

The robber also demanded Mr Robins' silver watch, threatening to shoot him again with a companion pistol, before he ran off. Mr Robins managed to stagger back to his home, where the alarm was immediately raised and two surgeons sent for to attend his injuries. He managed to give a fairly detailed description of his attacker and a handbill offering a reward of £100 above and beyond any statutory government-funded reward was hastily printed and also published in the local newspaper. Despite clinging to life for ten days, Mr Robins unfortunately succumbed to his wounds on the morning of 28 December.

The period during which the attack had taken place was a particularly unsettled one; mainland Europe had recently witnessed a cataclysmic revolution and Britain was at that time in the middle of the Peninsular Wars, with the concomitant problems resulting from a long-term international conflict. The pages of many of the national newspapers were taken up with lists of deserters who had either broken ranks abroad or (perhaps of more immediate concern to the propertied and relatively well-heeled section of the populace who could afford to read of such events) absconded from their barracks in England. The Luddite uprisings were in full swing and staple food prices were rapidly rising beyond the pockets of those most in need, leading to increased tensions in many areas.

As the incident took place almost thirty years before Staffordshire gained a County Police force, responsibility for the investigation of the crime fell on the local Justices of the Peace – in this case the magistrates who sat at nearby Stourbridge, and who would almost undoubtedly have known Mr Robins personally – and the attack undoubtedly unnerved many members of the upper echelons of local society. As magistrates and farmers, the worthy Justices of the Peace at Stourbridge had a vest interest in ensuring that the perpetrator of the attack upon one of their fellow 'gentlemen farmers' was brought swiftly to justice. The worried Stourbridge magistrates, also conscious of the striking similarities of the attack on Mr Robins to the murder of another gentleman farmer, Mr Edward Wiggan, at Eardington, near Bridgnorth, Shropshire (only a dozen or so miles away), on 25 November 1812, consequently decided that their local constable, no matter how eager, was not up to the job, and therefore decided to bring in the 'professionals', writing a letter to London requesting the services of one or more Bow Street 'Runners'.

The two Principal Officers despatched to Stourbridge were among the most well known and respected of the eight Officers employed by Bow Street Office at the time of the murder. Harry Adkins had been a witness to the assassination of Spencer Perceval earlier in 1812, and eventually became Governor of Warwick Gaol, while Samuel Taunton continued as an Officer until 1835. Adkins, in his evidence to a Parliamentary Select Committee in 1816, stated that he had been employed at Bow Street since 1801.

Adkins and Taunton arrived in Stourbridge immediately after Christmas. Suspicion had by then fallen on William Howe (aka John Wood), a 32-year-old journeyman carpenter working at the marchioness of Downshire's country estate at Ombersley Court, Worcestershire, who had been seen by several witnesses in the vicinity at the time of the attack. Howe by all accounts was a bit of a 'dandy', with 'airs and graces' and a preference for fancy clothes – his colleagues apparently nicknamed him 'Lord Howe', after his famous namesake Sir William Howe, who had been Commander-in-Chief of British forces during the American War of Independence.

An exhaustive investigation by the two diligent Officers followed, during which they travelled over 400 miles in pursuit of the suspect. Howe was found to have left his employ at Ombersley on 15 December 1812 and not returned until 22 December, when he had then arranged for boxes containing his clothes and tools to be sent 'in the name of John Wood, to be left at the Castle and Falcon, Aldersgate Street, London, till called for'. The Bow Street Officers, through a combination of diligence and good fortune, traced these boxes (which contained a pistol and bullets) and lay in wait for Howe, who was subsequently arrested on 13 January 1813. He denied having been in Stourbridge and refuted the charge that he had been involved in the attack upon Mr Robins. He was brought back to Stourbridge by Adkins and Taunton and was interviewed by Stourbridge magistrates on 19 January. He was transferred to Stafford Gaol on 26 January, where he awaited trial at the Lent Assizes in March 1813.

The inhabitants of Stourbridge seemed to have made up their minds of Howe'sculpability before he went to trial: the *Staffordshire Advertiser* of 6 February 1813 reported that 'A numerous meeting of persons resident in Stourbridge and the neighbourhood was held in Stourbridge last week, when £50 was collected for Adkins and Taunton, the Bow Street Officers, as a reward for their vigilance in apprehending Howe'.

While in gaol Howe made a desperate attempt to hide further evidence of his misdeeds by asking another prisoner to pass a letter to his wife via Elizabeth Barlow, an intermediary. This illustrates that Howe was by no means a criminal genius, as unfortunately for him his newly wed wife (whom he had probably married bigamously, as circumstantial evidence suggests that another wife was living in Norwich) was illiterate and had to have the letter read out to her by one of the other residents at the lodging house where Elizabeth Barlow was residing. The letter gave details regarding a a pistol, bullets and a bullet mould that had been hidden in a hayrick at Oldswinford, near Stourbridge, this being either the murder weapon or its companion piece. Mr Vickers, the landlady's husband, read the letter after it had been given to him and immediately left for Stourbridge, where he informed Mr William Robins, a nephew of the victim. It is not recorded whether or not Vickers subsequently received a share of any reward. The letter had been given back to Mrs Howe, who apparently had sense enough to burn it to prevent its use as further evidence.

The pistol and bullets were duly found and later produced as evidence at Howe's trial, which took place at 8 a.m. on 16 March 1813 under the jurisdiction of Justice John Bayley and lasted until 4.30 p.m. More than thirty witnesses were called for the prosecution, and a compelling case was built up by Mr Jervis, the prosecuting counsel. The prisoner objected to one juror who was from the Stourbridge area (and who was subsequently replaced), but otherwise said nothing in his defence (at this time, the accused was not allowed to give evidence on oath). The jury took just seven minutes to find Howe guilty and Justice Bayley sentenced him to death by hanging and subsequent dissection of his body for anatomical research. Howe apparently received the verdict impassively and 'appeared indifferent about his fate.'

Following the dictate of the Murder Act 1752, the sentence had to be carried out within forty-eight hours of the verdict – there was no appeal procedure and, in this case, little chance of a Royal Pardon. Incidentally, Howe was hanged by one Thomas Johnson, who was in 1816 himself found guilty of receiving stolen goods and sentenced to fourteen years' transportation. Howe apparently confessed to the murder at the gallows, declaring the 'badness of his heart', and went to his end 'with firmness and composure'.[84]

However, the Stourbridge magistrates (possibly with the backing of Robins' family) were dissatisfied with the fate of Howe's body and successfully campaigned for the by then very unusual step of his body being gibbeted at the scene of the murder. This request was sanctioned by the Home Secretary, doubtless in an attempt to dissuade other would-be evil-doers. Howe's body was therefore transported back in an open cart to the scene of the crime at Fir Tree Hill, Dunsley, where a large iron and wood gibbet had been hastily constructed. The body was fixed to the gibbet (which cost £22, with the irons costing another £7 19s. 6d.), as described above, by means of iron hooks drilled into its bones.[85]

Gibbets were invariably public and exposed in their siting, presumably in a deliberate attempt to imbue the viewing public with a sense of fear and respect for the terrible power of the law. The *Wolverhampton Chronicle* expresses the view that this attempt to instil terror into those contemplating a criminal act was terrible but necessary:

> Dreadful as most certainly is the enforcement of this part of the law of our country, it is most ardently to be wished, that it may operate as a memento to such as are pursuing a career of vice, and lead them to those timely reflections which can also rescue them from the retributive hand of public justice.[86]

This view was also shared by others such as John Townsend, who, in his answers to a Parliamentary Select Finance Committee, was in no doubt as to the fear and power exerted by the sight of a gibbeted corpse. When asked the direct question 'Do you think any advantages arise from a man being put on a gibbet after his execution?' Townsend replied that he was in favour of gibbeting, as 'the thing [awareness of the murder] is kept alive. If it was not for this, people would die, and nobody would know anything of it.'[87]

Contemporary attitudes among the general public to gibbeting seem to indicate that such events were indeed remembered, but not necessarily for the reasons given by Townsend and other supporters of the practice; rather, there seems to have been almost no end to the members of the public who were willing to travel considerable distances to see such a sight. There are several accounts of the large numbers of people who flocked to see the macabre sight of William Howe's body, among which A. J. Standley remarks that:

> The body of Wood [Howe] thus suspended, excited considerable interest and crowds of people were reported to have visited the part of the heath where the body could be viewed. Not wishing to overlook the opportunity of spreading the Gospel, a Minister, believed to have been of the Methodist persuasion, was said to have attended at three consecutive Sundays and to have preached an appropriate sermon to the crowds who had gathered.[88]

The level of the crowd's ghoulish interest can perhaps be gauged by their willingness to give up part of their only day of rest, Sunday, to visit the site. Robert Southey, the soon-to-be Poet Laureate, who refers several times to the gibbeting in his writings, indicates this desire to see the body of the hanged man:

> For the information of Roseanne [Southey's housemaid], who is sadly disconcerted at remaining in ignorance of what all the country knows but herself, I have made a drawing of the scene, but I am sorry to say she would rather see the original. Roseanne is an old servant, too old to go six miles to see the sight.[89]

He also recorded that the sight drew 'more than 100,000 people [. . .] and a kind of wake continued for some weeks for ale and gingerbread'.[90]

The name of the lane where the murder and subsequent gibbeting occurred was later changed to Gibbet Lane and was marked as such on the 1882 Ordnance Survey County Series map. As a gruesome postscript, accounts state that Mr Downing, one of the surgeons who had attended Mr Robins' wounds, returned to the gibbet over a year after the event and removed the bones, reconstructing the skeleton in his hall as a rather peculiar practical joke on his visitors. Howe was one of the last men in England to be gibbeted, the very last being James Cook in Leicestershire on 10 August 1832.

Bodies of condemned individuals were also occasionally subjected to other acts of public and ritual posthumous humiliation. After his suicide while awaiting trial in late December 1811 it was decreed that the corpse of John Williams, suspected perpetrator of the infamous and brutal Ratcliff Highway murders, was to be 'publicly exhibited in procession through the neighbourhood which had been the scene of his crimes, provided there was no risk of a disturbance'.[91] His body was then buried at a crossroads in order that his soul would not know in which direction Heaven was, and a stake was driven through his heart.

Some particularly brutal punishments bridged the gap between life and death; the process of hanging, drawing and quartering an individual involved both living torture and posthumous humiliation. The identity, status and respectability of the offender were ritually and dramatically removed in a horrifying public spectacle that dated back to the late thirteenth century and continued until the last quarter of the eighteenth.

Case study 14: David Tyrie, High Treason, 1782

David Tyrie has the dubious distinction of being the last man in England to suffer the full punishment of hanging, drawing and quartering. The story of how he met this end is a complex one. He was born *c.* 1746 at Leith, Scotland, and served an apprenticeship (for an unknown trade) in Edinburgh. By the late 1770s he seems to have plied numerous trades, including that of merchant, lottery office keeper in Edinburgh (under an assumed name) and stationer's clerk. The *London Chronicle* remarked that 'he was ever remarkable for an avidity to get, and a carelessness in the disposition of money.'[92]

By 1778 he had settled in London, where he became embroiled in a complex and long-winded bankruptcy claim. The *London Gazette* of 8–12 September 1778 carried the following advertisement:

> Whereas a Commission of Bankrupt is awarded and issued forth against John Parker, sometime since of the Parish of St James Westminster in the County of Middlesex, Robert Crowe, and David Tyrie, both sometime since of Chad's-row in the Parish of St James in the said County, and all later of London, Merchants, and they being declared Bankrupts, are hereby required to surrender themselves to the Commissioners in the said Commission named [. . .] to make a full Discovery and Disclosure of their Estate and Effects; when and where the Creditors are to come prepared to prove their Debts. . .

Tyrie and the other bankrupts had, it was claimed, been partners in an unsuccessful distillery venture in Clerkenwell. It appears, however, that Tyrie, despite being heavily in debt, continued to trade as a merchant; he is listed as trading as such from Batson's Coffee House in Cornhill in a directory of 1780.[93]

However, in a long-running legal argument that continued until late 1781 Crowe and Parker claimed that they had never been partners with Tyrie and that Tyrie had persuaded their solicitor to examine a witness whose evidence was later found to be perjured. The Commission of bankruptcy against them was later superseded. Crowe and Parker subsequently sued their assignees and their solicitor, but were unsuccessful, their business activities appearing to the court to be highly suspect. However, as a result of this action Tyrie was declared liable to the sum of £5,000.[94]

In late 1780 Tyrie moved to Gosport in Hampshire, where he set himself up as a naval agent while also keeping up lodgings in London. There he appears to have hatched a plan by which he attempted to free himself of his heavy debts and impending financial ruin. He had entered into correspondence with a Monsieur Bonnier of Cherbourg, who was acting on behalf of the French Minister of Marine, and offered to supply him with up-to-date lists of the movements of the Royal Navy to and from their main port in Portsmouth.[95]

Tyrie also became reacquainted with James Mailstone, a fellow former apprentice from Edinburgh. Mailstone was subsequently employed by Tyrie with 'commissions to buy poultry and livestock for the East India ships'.[96] Mailstone later stated that Tyrie also 'desired me likewise to send me an account of all the ships of war that were come into port, or sailed from Spithead. I was to let him know what ships sailed with convoys, and what arrived.'[97]

Tyrie appears to have gathered a considerable amount of information about the movements of the Royal Navy from Mailstone's and others' reports to him, but in February 1782 his plans began to fall rapidly apart. On 13 February Maria Hervey, who ran a school at Scotland Yard in London, was given a bundle of letters by a woman that she knew as Mrs Askew, the sister of a woman who sent two children to Mrs Hervey's school, for delivery to a Mr Page at Westminster. Mrs Hervey stated that Mrs Askew 'appeared very much flurried [and that] the gentleman who had delivered them to her was in trouble and wished to get them off'.[98] Mrs Hervey delivered the letters to Mr J. Page at Westminster, who examined them and found them to be a list of naval movements in Tyrie's handwriting totalling some fifty papers. Mr Page then took the letters to the Secretary of State, who instigated further investigations.

Mrs Askew was in fact living with David Tyrie as his wife.[99] It is not clear from whom she had received the papers, but it is unlikely to have been Tyrie himself, as he would not have wished the matter to be made public. It seems more probable that someone else involved in Tyrie's scheme had got cold feet and wished to be finished with the matter, and had persuaded Mrs Askew of the benefit of distancing herself from Tyrie.

Tyrie's troubles deepened when another packet of incriminating documents was delivered on 20 February to the office of the Secretary of State by a Captain

Harrison, owner of a ship which had been commissioned by Tyrie ostensibly to collect wine from Ostend, but which was in fact a cover to deliver documents to the French authorities. Harrison had been brought the packet by one of his friends, Captain James, who had been approached by Tyrie to deliver it following the sinking of Harrison's ship on a previous voyage on the way back from Boulogne. Harrison opened the packet and immediately realized the significance of its contents. Bow Street Office was immediately contacted and Tyrie's lodgings in London were searched by Moses Morant, a Principal Officer. Tyrie was subsequently arrested and placed in Newgate gaol. He was then indicted on a charge of High Treason and transported to Winchester gaol to await his trial.

The trial took place at Winchester Assizes on 10 August 1782.[100] Tyrie was indicted for:

> Falsely, wickedly, and traitorously (being a subject of Great Britain) compassing, imagining, and intending, the King of and from the royal state, crown, title, power, and government of Great Britain, to depose and wholly deprive; and the King to kill, and bring and put to death; and to fulfil, perfect, and bring to effect, his treason, compassing, and imaginations, as such false traitor, falsely, wickedly, and traiterously, composing, and writing, and causing to be composed and wrote, divers letters and instructions in writing, to shew and inform Lewis the French King (who for a long time, and still carries on and prosecutes, by land and by sea, an open an public war against our present King) and his subjects, enemies of our King, of the stations of divers squadrons of ships of war of our King, employed in prosecuting and carrying on said war. . .[101]

He was found to have compiled detailed lists of the movements of the English navy in and out of Portsmouth and also to have given instructions as how to employ other spies in order to compile further lists:

> I should imagine that proper persons could be found at Portsmouth and Plymouth, for five guineas per month, including all extra expenses, to furnish every information wanted; and one person, on the same terms, to supply for both Chatham and Sheerness, as the communication between them is frequent, and the distance but small. Harwich being a more inconsiderable dock, two or three guineas per month would be sufficient. Woolwich and Deptford, being at a short distance from town, may be furnished by the agent there.[102]

Several dozen similar letters and communications were read out at the trial and, despite Tyrie's lawyer putting up a spirited defence in which he stated that the majority of the details of the movements of the Navy's ships were public knowledge, at the conclusion of the trial the jury almost immediately returned a 'guilty' verdict.

Mr Justice Heath, the Assize judge, then pronounced the following sentence:

> You, David Tyrie, are to be led from hence to the gaol from whence you
> came; and from thence you are to be drawn, upon a hurdle, to the place of
> execution; and there you are to be hanged by the neck; and being alive, to be
> cut down, and your privy members to be cut off, and your bowels to be taken
> out of your belly, and there burnt, you being alive; and your head to be cut
> off, and your body to be divided into four quarters; and that your head and
> quarters be disposed of where his Majesty shall think fit.[103]

The reasons behind the very particular nature of this form of punishment are
revealed in a contemporary account of the similar fate of several of the Gunpowder
Plotters in 1606:

> First, after a Traitor hath had his just Trial, and is convicted and attainted, he
> shall have his Judgement to be drawn to the place of Execution from his
> Prison, as being not worthy any more to tread upon the Face of the Earth
> whereof he was made: Also for that he hath been retrograde to Nature, there-
> fore is he drawn backward at a Horse-Tail. And whereas God hath made the
> Head of Man the highest and most supreme Part, as being his chief Grace
> and Ornament [. . .] he must be drawn with his Head declining downward,
> and lying so near the Ground as may be, being thought unfit to take benefit
> of the common Air. For which Cause also he shall be strangled, being hanged
> up by the Neck between Heaven and Earth, as deemed unworthy of both, or
> either; as likewise, that the Eyes of Men may behold, and their Hearts con-
> temn him. Then he is to be cut down alive, and to have his Privy Parts cut off
> and burnt before his Face, as being unworthily begotten, and unfit to leave
> any Generation after him. His Bowels and inlay'd Parts taken out and burnt,
> who inwardly had conceived and harboured in his heart such horrible
> Treason. After, to have his Head cut off, which had imagined the Mischief.
> And lastly, his Body to be quartered, and the Quarters set up in some high
> and eminent Place, to the View and Detestation of Men, and to become a
> Prey for the Fowls of the Air. And this is a Reward due to Traitors, whose
> Hearts be hardened.[104]

After he was taken down from the court it was reported that the gaoler found a
razor concealed upon Tyrie's person.[105] It was also reported that during his confinement at Newgate Tyrie had hatched a daring escape plan with one of his colleagues to be rescued from the coach which was to transfer him between Newgate
and Winchester, but the plan was never put into operation.[106]

After being returned to Winchester Gaol to await his fate Tyrie made another
escape attempt. He had bribed a man named John Deadman to smuggle tools to
him in order for him and fellow prisoners to tunnel through the walls of the
gaol,[107] a plan that might have succeeded had Tyrie not aroused the suspicions of
the keeper of the prison by enquiring about the thickness of the wall.

During his confinement Tyrie admitted the offence, claiming that he was no traitor and that 'my poverty lost me my life', and supplied further details of the scheme by which he had endeavoured to act as a spy for the French government.[108] On 24 August he was taken from Winchester Gaol to meet his death. A contemporary account gives an impression of the sombre pomp of the occasion:

> David Tyrie was brought from Winchester Gaol in a coach and six, accompanied by the Sheriff of Hants and his attendants; he was met by the officers and constables of Portsmouth at the Green Post, and in solemn procession to the White House, where he was taken out and immediately put on a hurdle with a sledge, drawn by four horses and proceeded to South Sea beach, where after some little time, he suffered the whole punishment according to the dreadful sentence pronounced upon him.[109]

Tyrie appears to have undergone the complete punishment of hanging, drawing and quartering, the only modifications being that his body was placed in a coffin after quartering and that he appears to have been dead as a result of the hanging; the *Hampshire Chronicle* of 2 September 1782 recorded that he was left hanging for exactly twenty-two minutes.

The terrible process, designed to instil fear and loathing in its spectacle, seems to have quickly turned into a desperate and callous struggle to obtain parts of Tyrie's body:

> He was then put into a coffin, and buried among the pebbles by the sea-side; but no sooner had the officers retired, but the sailors dug up the coffin, took out the body, and cut it in a thousand pieces, every one carrying away a piece of his body to shew their messmates on board.[110]

A letter from Plymouth corroborating this account was also published soon after the event:

> The populace had the liberty of cutting and hacking any part they thought proper, such as fingers, toes and ribs. This abominable shock to human nature, must certainly have been the neglect of the sheriff: and what was most palpable, to suffer the gaoler of Gosport to take away Tyrie's head, and which he is now making a show of at his own dungeon. Many of the bodysnatchers, as they are called, bid high for the head; however, Buck – either having more interest, or being quicker than the rest, whipped it away into a bag, and some of his worthy emissaries conveyed it away.[111]

Conclusion

The above discussion has shown that there was a gradual shift in terms of the type of punishment meted out to offenders during the eighteenth century. From an overwhelming emphasis on immediate physical retribution, both corporal and capital, the bodily removal of offenders under the system of transportation grew to become the most popular means of punishment for those judged guilty of felonies. There was also a move from extreme methods of capital punishment to a standardization in the form of the relatively more humane death by hanging.

We have also seen that, despite the presence of the 'Bloody Code' and the large number of offences theoretically punishable by the death penalty, both juries and judges could and did (at least to a certain extent) mitigate the punishment of offenders by massively undervaluing stolen goods, issuing recommendations to mercy or exercising other forms of judicial discretion. However, it is clear that punishment of serious offences during the period remained punitive and did not usually include incarceration as an option. It was not until the beginning of the nineteenth century that reformers and commentators began to make serious inroads into the prevailing views that punishment should be immediate and retributive rather than reformatory and carceral.

The next chapter continues the discussion on punishment by detailing how men and women were regarded differently by the law and how this affected their respective positions within the criminal justice system.

Notes

1 Edward Marston, *Prison: five hundred years of life behind bars* (Kew: National Archives, 2009), p. 44. Debt was of course a civil rather than a criminal offence.
2 Statute quoted in S, Webb and B. Webb, *English Poor Law Part 1 – The Old Poor Law* (London: Cass, 1963), p. 50. For a detailed study of the poor and the ways in which they could fall foul of the law, see Tim Hitchcock, *Down and Out in Eighteenth-Century London* (London: Hambledon, 2004), and for a detailed account of the development of buildings designed to control and house the poor, see Kathryn Morrison, *The Workhouse: A Study of Poor-Law Buildings in England* (London: Royal Commission on the Historical Monuments of England, 1999).
3 Branding was normally reserved for those who had been found guilty of serious offences (felonies) rather than less serious offences (misdemeanours).
4 The earliest reference to the use of a pillory appears in the *Utrecht Psalter* of the ninth century (www.pilloryhistory.com/history.html).
5 *London Chronicle*, 28 September 1810. For further details of this case, see Chapter 6.
6 *London Chronicle*, 28 September 1810.
7 See, for example, various reports of sympathetic onlookers (and indeed officials) cheering and aiding the offender in the pillory, cited by the earl of Lauderdale in the Parliamentary debate over the Pillory Bill reported in the *Caledonian Mercury*, 10 July 1815.
8 For example, there are no sentences of private whipping of females recorded at the Old Bailey after 1817 and only forty-six cases of men being publically flogged after that date – see OBP for further details. One of the best-preserved whipping posts can be found at Much Wenlock, Shropshire, where an information board states that its last use was in 1852, when a Thomas Lloyd was its final unfortunate occupant.
9 See *Lloyd's Weekly Newspaper*, 16 June 1872, for a full account of this event.
10 Shropshire Archives 1060/168–170 Justice's Book 1805–1813.
11 Justices of the Peace had to meet certain financial criteria before they could be appointed. For further details on how magistrates were chosen and appointed during the eighteenth century, see David J. Cox, 'The Shropshire Magistracy in the Eighteenth

Century', in Cox, D. J., and Godfrey, B. (eds), *Cinderellas & Packhorses: A History of the Shropshire Magistracy* (Almeley: Logaston Press, 2005), pp. 23–42.

12 Quoted in James Davie Butler, 'British Convicts Shipped to American Colonies', *American Historical Review* 2 (1896): 12–33, p. 16.

13 E. G. Atkinson (ed.), *Acts of the Privy Council of England volume 34 – 1615–1616* (London: HMSO, 1925).

14 Quoted in Clarence S. Brigham (ed.), 'British Royal Proclamations Relating to America, 1603–1783', *Transactions of the American Antiquarian Society* 12 (1911): 52–5.

15 For histories of the transport of convicts to America, see A. Roger Ekirch, *Bound for America: The Transportation of British Convicts to the Colonies, 1718–1775* (Oxford: Clarendon Paperbacks, 1987); Anthony Vaver, *Convict Transportation from Great Britain to the American Colonies* (Westborough, MA: Early American Crime.com, 2009); Peter Wilson Coldham, *The King's Passengers to Maryland and Virginia* (Westminster, MD: Heritage Books, 1997); Peter Wilson Coldham, *Emigrants in Chains: A Social History of Forced Emigration to the Americas of Felons, Destitute Children, Political and Religious Non-Conformists, Vagabonds, Beggars and Other Undesirables, 1607–1776* (Baltimore, MD: Geneaological Publishing, 1992); and Gwenda Morgan and Peter Rushton, 'Running Away and Returning Home: The Fate of English Convicts in the American Colonies', *Crime, Histoire & Sociétiés/Crime, History & Societies* 7.2 (2003): 61–80.

16 Bernard Bailyn, *The Peopling of British North America: An Introduction* (London: I B Tauris, 1987), p. 121. It has been estimated that the cost of transporting the 50,000 convicts worked out at roughly £4 per head – see Bruce Kercher, 'Perish or Prosper: The Law and Convict Transportation in the British Empire, 1700–1850', *Law and History Review* 21.3 (2003): 527–84, p. 532. If this figure is correct then it is clear to see why the British government remained in favour of the system despite other disadvantages.

17 Kercher, 'Perish or Prosper', p. 540. Kercher also states that 'During the course of the eighteenth century, the link between the convict's sentence of transportation and the period of the contract of service was broken. No matter what the original sentence, all convicts came to be sold for seven-year terms of service' (ibid., p. 534). For a detailed examination of the legal rights of convicts transported to America, see Ekirch, *Bound for America*, and Alan Atkinson, 'The Free-Born Englishman Transported: Convict Rights as a Measure of Eighteenth-Century Empire', *Past and Present* 144 (1994): 88–115.

18 Recent research has shown, however, that few of the Australian convicts (even those serving life sentences) actually served their full terms – see Barry Godfrey and David J. Cox, 'The "Last Fleet": Crime, Reformation, and Punishment in Western Australia after 1868', *Australia and New Zealand Journal of Criminology* 1.2 (2008): 236–58. Convicts transported to Australia for other than a life sentence were allowed to return to Britain following the expiry of their sentence at their own expense. Those sentenced to transportation to Australia for life were not allowed to return, even if they were later pardoned.

19 Quoted from 'America and West Indies: February 1739, 16–28', *Calendar of State Papers Colonial, America and West Indies, Volume 45: 1739* (1994), pp. 37–50 – see www.british-history.ac.uk/report.aspx?compid=115263.

20 William Smith and Anon., *A History of New-York, from the First Discovery to the Year 1732: With a Continuation, from the Year 1732, to the Commencement of the Year 1814* (Albany, NY: Ryer Schermerhorn, 1814), p. 320.

21 Recent research has shown that a number of convicts offered a commuted sentence of transportation refused to accept such a pardon, ostensibly preferring the original sentence of death – see Simon Deveraux, 'Imposing the Royal Pardon: Execution, Transportation, and Convict Resistance in London, 1789', *Law and History Review*

25.1 (2007): 101–38, and Lynn MacKay, 'Refusing the Royal Pardon: London Capital Convicts and the Reactions of the Courts and Press, 1789', *London Journal* 28.2 (2003): 21–40.

22 LL, ref. t17150713–32.

23 Beattie, *Crime and the Courts*, p. 424.

24 Ibid., p. 424; quoting L. Radzinowicz, *A History of English Criminal Law and its administration from 1750*, Vol. 1 (London: Stevens & Sons, 1948), p. 95 n. 52.

25 LL, ref. BBBRMG202040338.

26 OBP t17200427–13.

27 For a comprehensive history of the Royal African Company, see K.G. Davies, *The Royal African Company* [Vol. 5 of the 7-volume series *Emergence of International Business 1200–1800*] (London: Taylor & Francis, 1999).

28 The South Sea Bubble of 1718 was a Stock Market crash that resulted from the activities of the South Sea Company. This company had entered into an agreement with the British government in 1711 and had been offered exclusive rights with Spain's colonies in southern America – then known as the South Seas – in return for financing government debt at 6 per cent. The company was hugely successful at first and people flocked to invest in it. However, through a combination of bad management, fraud and the fact that in 1718 Britain and Spain declared war on each other, thereby ending the lucrative trade agreement, the company's finances and investments collapsed, resulting in a huge financial crisis from which Britain took nearly a century to recover.

29 *London Journal*, 29 Oct–5 Nov 1720.

30 OBP t17230828–34.

31 See www.earlyamericancrime.com/category/convict-transportation for further details of Forward's career. He became notorious as a confidante of Jonathan Wild: he was in a unique position to inform Wild of returned convicts whom Wild would either blackmail or capture, thereby claiming the £40 reward for handing in a returned convict. Not all those who were commissioned to transport convicts were of such dubious status as Forward; between 1771 and 1775 the Scottish commission to transport convicts to Maryland and Virginia was held by the highly respected judicial reformer and commentator Patrick Colquhoun (see Chapter 7).

32 Absolute numbers are impossible to verify owing to the paucity of records and the difficulties in compiling surviving figures, but this estimate is generally accepted by historians. For more detailed accounts of the history of transportation to North America, see A. Vaver, *Bound with an Iron Chain: The Untold Story of How the British Transported 50,000 Convicts to Colonial America* (Westborough, MA: Pickpocket Publishing, 2011); Coldham, *Emigrants in Chains*; Ekirch, *Bound for America*; and A. E. Smith, *Colonists in Bondage: White Servitude and Convict Labor in America, 1607–1776* (New York: Norton, 1971).

33 OBP t17251013–53.

34 A. L. Hayward (ed.), *Lives Of The Most Remarkable Criminals Who have been Condemned and Executed for Murder, the Highway, Housebreaking, Street Robberies, Coining or other offences, Collected from Original Papers and Authentic Memoirs, and Published in 1735* (New York: n.p., 1927). For a more critical account of the life of transported convicts and a comparison with slave life and conditions in North America, see S. Christianson, *With Liberty For Some: 500 Years of Imprisonment in America* (Boston: Northeastern University Press, 2000).

35 OBP t17251013–53.

36 Hayward, *Lives Of The Most Remarkable Criminals*.

37 In a postscript to John Whalebone's criminal career and eventual death by hanging, it appears that at least one of his children did not heed these warnings; his second son Duke was himself transported to Virginia for seven years in 1737 after being found guilty of robbery. However, Duke settled in Virginia, married and eventually became a respectable landowner of 150 acres. He died in 1804 in Caswell County, North

Carolina, and the Whalebone name is to this day commemorated in the form of Whalebone Branch, a subsidiary stream of Pumpkin Creek on the North Carolina/ Virginia border.

38 Edward Moseley to Under-Secretary Nepean in F. M. Bladen (ed.), *Historical Records of New South Wales*, Vol. 2 (Sydney: Charles Potter, 1895), 102. 41. It is not known whether or not Moseley's plea was successful.

39 This village is one of the three that featured heavily in the recent BBC television series *A History of England*, presented by Michael Wood, and Australian descendants of Charles Beasley were interviewed in one of the programmes.

40 In his trial he claimed to have a brother living at Windsor and so may well have followed him down to the south-east of England.

41 OBP t17931204–17.

42 *The Times*, 29 October 1793. Beasley was never charged with this offence and the other members of 'the Floorers' also denied any involvement.

43 *Northampton Mercury*, 8 Feb 1794.

44 *True Briton*, 17 May 1793.

45 *The Times*, 6 December 1793.

46 OBP t17931204–17.

47 OBP t17931204–21.

48 OBP t17931204–21.

49 OBP t17931204–21.

50 This was a very unusual verdict in a shoplifting case, despite the offence being a capital one. Deidre Palk states that during the period 1780–1823 these two men were in fact the only individuals on whom the death penalty was carried out from a total of 680 cases heard at the Old Bailey. She also points out that the last previous recorded execution for shoplifting was in 1763 – see Palk, *Gender, Crime and Judicial Discretion*, pp. 48–50.

51 OBP t17931204–21.

52 *Bell's Weekly Messenger*, 7 January 1798.

53 See *Autograph letter signed from Richard Dore, Judge Advocate of New South Wales, to Sir Michael Le Fleming, from on board the Barwell, Table Bay, Cape of Good Hope, regarding a convict, William Lindsay, the voyage, the ship Lady Shore, and life at the Cape, 5 February 1798*, partially reproduced at www.jenwilletts.com/dore_1798.htm.

54 For a full list of the 296 convicts on board, see www.historyaustralia.org.au/twconvic/ Barwell+1798. For the most up-to-date research into mortality rates on convict ships to Australia, see H. Maxwell-Stewart and R. Kippen, 'Morbidity and Mortality on Convict Voyages to Australia', available at www.hsmt.history.ox.ac.uk/ecohist/seminars/ Papers2011–12/Morbidy_Mortality_atsea.pdf.

55 *New South Wales, Australia, Colonial Secretary's Papers, 1788–1825*, online database available at www.Ancestry.com. He served as a private in the Association for at least six years.

56 Ibid.

57 Ibid.

58 Ibid.

59 Ibid.

60 Ibid.

61 *New South Wales, Australia, Certificates for Publicans' Licences, 1830–1849*, online database available at ancestry.com; obituary in *Sydney Monitor*, 8 December 1837.

62 Known as the 'Bloody Code', this system of laws and punishments reached its zenith in the early nineteenth century, when over 200 crimes were (at least theoretically) punishable by death.

63 Burning at the stake was outlawed by the Treason Act 1790 (30 George III. c.48). The last person to be beheaded in Britain was Lord Lovat in April 1747 (for taking part on the losing Jacobite side at the Battle of Culloden in 1746). The last person pressed to

death in Britain was John Weekes, who had been found guilty of murdering a woman in Petworth, Sussex. He was executed after being found guilty at the Lewes Assizes (see *Gentleman's Magazine*, vol. 5, August 1735, p. 497) This method of capital punishment was withdrawn in 1772 (12 Geo. II c.20) and in 1827 'standing mute' was decreed to be taken as a plea of 'Not Guilty' – for a brief history of this type of punishment see Andrea Mckenzie, 'This Death Some Strong and Stout Hearted Man Doth Choose': The Practice of *Peine Forte et Dure* in Seventeenth- and Eighteenth-Century England', *Law and History Review* 23.2 (2005): 279–313.

64 Sir W. Blackstone, *Commentaries on the laws of England*, Vol. 4 (Oxford: Clarendon Press, 1765), p. 18.

65 See Beattie, *Crime and the Courts*, p. 420, n. 34.

66 Gatrell, *The Hanging Tree*, p. 616.

67 By 1837 the death penalty had been removed from most offences, and in practice only murder remained a capital offence – see Gatrell, *The Hanging Tree*, p. 618, for further details of the dates of non-capitalization of offences.

68 A. Barrett and C. Harrison, *Crime and Punishment in England* (London: UCL Press, 1999), p. 153.

69 Quoted in Gatrell, *The Hanging Tree*, p. 202.

70 Quoted in David Garland, *Punishment and Modern Society: A Study in Social Theory* (Oxford: OUP, 1997), p. 31.

71 Quoted in Robert P. Weiss (ed.), *Social History of Crime, Policing and Punishment* (Aldershot: Ashgate, 1999), p. 59.

72 Hay, 'Property, Authority and the Criminal Law', p. 17.

73 Ibid., p. 35.

74 McLynn, *Crime and Punishment*, p. xviii. Lord Ferrers was tried and executed in 1760 for the murder of his steward. His execution was a scene of ostentatious pomp (he was dressed in his wedding suit and asked to be hanged with a silk rope), drawing huge crowds.

75 Gatrell, *The Hanging Tree*.

76 Ruth Richardson, *Death, Dissection and the Destitute* (London: Routledge & Kegan Paul, 1987), p. 76.

77 Barrett and Harrison, *Crime and Punishment in England*, p. 152.

78 Quoted in W. Andrews, *Bygone Punishments* (London: W. Andrews, 1899), p. 41.

79 L. Radzinowicz, *A History of English Criminal Law and its Administration from 1750*, Vol. 3 (London: Stevens & Sons, 1956), p. 323.

80 Quoted in L. Moore, *Con Men and Cutpurses: Scenes from the Hogarthian Underworld* (Harmondsworth: Penguin, 2001), p. 18.

81 Quoted in ibid.

82 Such Local Volunteer Associations were created as a response to the perceived threat of imminent invasion by Napoleon's forces and were popular among the gentry; as well as being an obvious statement of loyalty to the Crown, they also provided an opportunity to be seen in military uniform on horseback, thereby increasing their social status.

83 Robins had previously been the victim of petty theft several years earlier – see Stafford Archives Q/SB 1797 T/ *Information of William Raybould of Stourbridge, Worcestershire, about the theft by Edward Sidaway of iron cletts from a plough in Kinver belonging to Benjamin Robins*, 30 Jun 1797.

84 Anon., *The Trial of William Howe, alias John Wood, for the Wilful Murder of Mr. Benjamin Robins of Dunsley, near Stourbridge on the 18th of December 1813* [sic] (Stourbridge: J. Heming, 1813), pp. 29–30.

85 Stafford Archives, Q/SB 1813 T/195 Money order listing expenses to be paid out, including salaries, goods for the maintenance of prisoners, conveyance of female convicts, hanging William Howe in chains upon Dunsley Hill, Jul 1813.

86 *Wolverhampton Chronicle*, 24 March 1813.

87 *Report from the Committee on the state of Police of the Metropolis*, vol. V, p. 139.

88 A. J. Standley, *Stafford Gaol: The Chronological Story* (Stafford: Standley, 1990), p. 51.

89 Robert Southey, *Southey's Common Place Book (Fourth Series): Original Memoranda etc.* (London: Longman, Brown, Green and Longman, 1851), p. 355. Southey became Poet Laureate in 1813, succeeding William Wordsworth.

90 Gatrell, *The Hanging Tree*, p. 268, quoting R. Southey, *Letters from England*.

91 Radzinowicz, *A History of English Criminal Law*, Vol. 3, p. 323.

92 *London Chronicle*, 24–27 August 1782.

93 T. Lowndes, *The London Directory for the Year 1780. Containing an Alphabetical List of Names and Places of Abode of the Merchants and Principal Traders of the City of London*, 15th edn (London: T. Lowndes, 1780).

94 *St. James's Chronicle or the British Evening Post*, 2–4 August 1781.

95 Britain was at war with France because the French sided with the Americans during the American Revolutionary War.

96 J. Gurney, *The Trial of David Tyrie for High Treason at the Assize at Winchester on Saturday August 10 1782* (London: M. Gurney, 1782), p. 15.

97 Ibid., p. 15.

98 Ibid., p. 4.

99 There is some doubt as to whether or not they were legally married; in her evidence Miss Hervey stated that Mrs Askew was upset at being addressed as such, stating that 'if Mr Tyrie was here, he would be very angry with you for calling me Askew, for he took me to church for a name' (ibid., p. 4).

100 A 24-page account of the trial compiled from shorthand notes was published by an enterprising publisher, J. Gurney, and was available for sale for one shilling within a week of the events – see ibid.

101 Ibid., p. 1.

102 Ibid., p. 9.

103 Ibid., p. 23.

104 T. Salmon, *The Complete Collection of State-trials, and Proceedings for High-treason, and other Crimes and Misdemeanours: From the Reign of King Richard II to the end of the Reign of King George I*, Vol. I (London: J. Walthoe, 1730).

105 *Whitehall Evening Post*, 10–13 August 1782.

106 *Morning Herald and Daily Advertiser*, 13 September 1782. The letter was found on the person of a John Graham, who had been arrested on forgery charges. Graham was later found guilty of forgery and himself executed.

107 Deadman was later tried and convicted for supplying the tools to aid Tyrie, while a fellow prisoner Captain Maynard was later acquitted of procuring them – see *London Chronicle*, 12–15 October 1782.

108 *Public Advertiser*, 6 September 1782.

109 *Caledonian Mercury*, 31 August 1782.

110 *Hampshire Chronicle*, 2 September 1782.

111 *Morning Herald and Daily Advertiser*, 28 August 1782.

6   Gender and the criminal justice system

Among other eccentricities of the day is a female constable in the Borough of Southwark, who keeps a Lock-up House for persons arrested for debt.[1]

Introduction

Men and women were not considered to be equal in the eyes of the law in England and Wales during the period under discussion and the law was extremely detrimental to women's rights and property. Married women and any property or goods that they brought to the marriage were deemed to belong to their husbands and divorce was unobtainable except in exceptional circumstances; it was not until the Matrimonial Causes Act 1857 (20 & 21 Vict. c.85) that the law enabled men and women to apply for legal divorce without having to resort to the introduction of private Acts of Parliament.[2] Such laws made it very difficult for women to bring legal challenges to their husbands' authority in cases of domestic violence or sexual abuse (including rape). Equally, any act of sexual misconduct by a woman (especially if married) was dealt with more severely than had the protagonist been male.

This chapter discusses the roles of gender within the criminal justice system. It begins by investigating women's position both as offenders and as victims/prosecutors. It also discusses crimes involving gender identity and the problems that such activities caused the authorities.[3]

Women as law-enforcement officials

That the use of a female as a minor agent of law enforcement was deemed worthy of comment in *The Times*, from which the quotation at the head of this chapter is taken, illustrates that women played almost no official part in the criminal justice system of the eighteenth century. It was not until the latter decades of the nineteenth century that women became more visible in this sphere. Apart from the aforementioned use of a female 'constable' to operate the lock-up in Southwark in 1792, it is not until 1828 that reports of another female acting as an official agent of law enforcement appear in the press. The *Standard* of 21 April 1828 brought the following account to its readers' attention:

PETTICOAT GOVERNMENT

The good people of the township of Urmston, being persuaded of the superiority of the 'petticoat form of government' to all others, have, for two successive years, made choice of a female constable as a 'terror to evil-doers' within the bounds of the township. Last year, the lot fell upon Miss Clementina Trafford, who, in person or by deputy, discharged the office to the high satisfaction of the inhabitants; and the appointment of Miss Catherine Newton, as constable for the ensuing year, was last week, duly confirmed by the court and jury at the Salford leet.[4]

Six years later, Robert Jones, the well-respected and long-serving Constable of Stafford, took the highly unusual and inspired decision to use a female deputy to spy on the activities of a female pickpocket.[5] And, according to Emsley, in 1883:

The Metropolitan Police began to employ a female visitor to visit women convicts on licence and under police supervision [. . .] in March 1889 fourteen more women were employed to act formally as Police Matrons. Their duties, hitherto undertaken largely by the wives of policemen, were to supervise and search female and child offenders while in police stations and the courts'.[6]

These examples are noteworthy and of intrinsic interest, but remain very much the exception to the rule; in general females had no say and played no part in the eighteenth- or early nineteenth-century criminal justice system (except as victims or offenders). They had no vote, did not have the right to sit on a jury or to act as magistrates or judges, and, if they were married, could not testify against their husband.

Female prosecutors

Female prosecution of offences during the seventeenth and eighteenth centuries has attracted surprisingly little attention from historians of crime and the criminal justice system. D'Cruze and Jackson comment in their recent study of women and criminal justice from 1660 that 'whilst a large number of studies have concentrated on women's presence in criminal justice statistics across time, less attention has been paid to long-term trends in their numerical involvement as prosecutors and complainants.'[7] Their work is hopefully among the earliest evidence of a long-overdue emergence of interest in the role that women played as both victims and prosecutors in the criminal justice system in the early modern and modern period.[8]

Cruze and Jackson's research includes a search of the Old Bailey Session Papers, which 'shows that, numerically, female prosecutors/complainants were active across the eighteenth and nineteenth centuries although they formed a minority compared to men'.[9] Between 1725 and 1824 prosecutions by female complainants accounted for 12.83 per cent of total prosecutions, with a declining trend through-out the period.[10] These findings are very similar with Gowing's with regard to the Sussex Quarter Sessions records for 1633, in which she found 13 per cent of pros-ecutors to be women.[11] D'Cruze and Jackson note that, by contrast, Gowing found that 'Women formed over half of all litigants in the London Church Courts in 1633', and quote her conclusion that this 'testifies to women's maximization of a rare opportunity of speech, complaint and legal agency'.[12] They also point out that:

> It is possible of course that their lower level of activity reflected a lower like-lihood of being a victim of crime. Furthermore, given that the property of married women was frequently held in their husbands' name, the theft of goods that were used by a woman but not necessarily owned by her might also be concealed within a simple search (by gender) of 'victims'.[13]

Cox's work into the activities of the Bow Street Office between 1792 and 1839 has also revealed that women rarely played a part in the prosecutorial system in provincial cases involving the Principal Officers:

> There are [. . .] few documented cases where Bow Street Principal Officers were employed directly by or on behalf of women; for example, in January 1817, Daniel Bishop was employed by the Countess of Orkney to recover jewellery stolen from her residence in Taplow, whilst in August 1835, [Henry] Goddard investigated a burglary at Lady Harvey's house in Chigwell.[14] In July 1823 Mr Minshull, magistrate at Bow Street, gave a distraught mother from Chichester free use of [George] Ruthven in an attempt to trace her runaway daughter.[15] However, such examples are very much the exception to the rule, and in an age where women were rarely in control of their own finances and had little say in the legal process, the dominance of men as employers of Bow Street's services is perhaps unsurprising.[16]

Apart from D'Cruze and Jackson's research and Gowing's work on the sixteenth and seventeenth centuries there remains little written about female prosecutors; as Deirdre Palk remarks:

> Only relatively recently has writing on the history of crime and the criminal justice system in England broached the difficult question of the relationship between gender and law-breaking, and gender and judicial decisions in the early modern and modern periods.[17]

Female offenders

The research situation with regard to women as offenders in the eighteenth cen-tury is, by contrast, comparatively healthier. Recent work by Palk, D'Cruze and

Jackson, and King has built upon previous research by Beattie, McLynn and others into both the proportion of prosecuted offences carried out by women and the specific types of these offences, and such research has moved the study of female offending on over the past few decades.[18]

In the eighteenth-century criminal justice system the male-dominated order continued unabated; as Elizabeth Ewan has stated with regard to the sixteenth century, 'the authorities were concerned with maintaining a world of good order and regulation, of social and gendered hierarchy', and this concern was still paramount in the eighteenth century.[19] Women were therefore extremely disadvantaged by their gender in the eyes of the legal system of the eighteenth century. Olwen Hufton, in her comprehensive study of the roles of women in the early modern period, succinctly sums up this situation:

> Judges, prosecutors and, where they exist, jurors, are all men. They have never been beaten or abused not themselves experienced an unwanted pregnancy. [. . .] They approach accuser and accused with an assumption of a particular God-ordained order (which it is their job to interpret and maintain) in which women are under the control of husband or father who is their initial judge.[20]

D'Cruze and Jackson state that 'women in England were most likely to appear before the courts in urban areas for theft, drunkenness (or public order offences) and prostitution-related offences (soliciting charges tended to be applied exclusively to women).'[21] Sharpe suggests that larcenies committed by women in the early modern period tended to involve goods of less value than those committed by men and that 'larceny, burglary, murder and assault in early modern England were overwhelmingly male activities.'[22]

Feeley and Little, in an article published in 1991, suggested that the prosecution of females declined sharply during the eighteenth century, but this view has been cogently challenged and refuted by other historians, including Peter King.[23] He argues that there was little if any change to the rate of female prosecution during the eighteenth century, stating that 'the data for many counties suggests long-term stability in female involvement in recorded crime between 1750 and 1850 and the data for London itself during this period suggests a very small decline and possibly no decline at all.'[24] King also found that the proportion of female offenders brought before the courts in Essex between 1740 and 1807 remained relatively consistent, averaging out at 13.65 percent,[25] and remarks that Samaha's work on Essex during the period 1668–1713 produced an average of female offending of 13.5 per cent.[26] Palk echoes these findings, stating that 'the ratio of men to women indicted for felony/serious offences appears to remain relatively constant from the Middle Ages onwards.'[27] Studies of the more recent past also tend to reinforce the stability of the offending ratio of men and women. Godfrey, Cox and Farrall found in their study of prolific offenders prosecuted in Crewe for minor offences between 1880 and 1940 that the female ratio remained fairly constant, at around 18 per cent.[28]

Both offending patterns and the types of punishment meted out varied by gender in the eighteenth century. For example, women were treated very differently in regard to infanticide cases; until the passing of Lord Ellenborough's Act 1803 (42 Geo. II c.53) any unmarried women who concealed the birth of their child were considered to be guilty until proven innocent. Infanticide was by its very nature much more likely to be carried out by women than by men, although the offence was not gender-exclusive.[29]

Similarly, until an Act of 1691 (3 & 4 Wm and Mary c.9) benefit of clergy was not available to women (with the exception of nuns), and it did not apply to either Petty or High Treason, the penalty for both being death by burning at the stake, as illustrated in the following case study.

Case study 15: Joyce Hodgkis (née Mancefield), Petty Treason, 1714

Joyce Mancefield was born in Staffordshire *c.* 1672 but moved to Shadwell, London, when she was still a young girl. On 14 July 1700 she married John Hodgkis at St Dunstan's Church, Stepney.[30] John was a cordwainer, London-born and bred, and the newly married couple lived in Limehouse. It is not known whether or not the couple had any children, but according to Joyce the marriage was not a happy one; she stated that John 'prov'd a very cruel Husband to her all the time she was his Wife, which was Fourteen Years'.[31]

On 18 August 1714 John and Joyce had been arguing about the fact that John's mother was living with them. According to Joyce, John picked up a carving knife and threatened her with it. She stated that she ran away from him and on turning to see whether he was following her, found that he had tripped and accidentally stuck the knife in his own left thigh, near to his groin, and soon afterwards expired.[32] However, unfortunately for Joyce, the argument between the couple had been overheard by a lodger who came down the stairs because of the commotion and saw 'the Prisoner run at him [John] with a Knife, and immediately saw Blood run out at his Breeches'.[33]

Joyce was consequently arrested and was tried at the Old Bailey on 8 September 1714. Another witness, a near neighbour, stated that:

> she liv'd over the Way, and hearing an Out-Cry, ran over to the House, where she heard the Man groaning, and saw the Blood run violently out of his Breeches, and asking the Prisoner how it came, she told her that cursed Knife had done it (shewing her an old Butcher's carving Knife) and that he would have stab'd her with it; and that the cursed Wretch had been the Ruin of her and himself too.[34]

Joyce's defence that the wound was self-inflicted was not believed by the jury, and she was found guilty on a charge of Petit Treason. Such a charge carried the penalty of death by burning at the stake. The offence of Petit (also known as Petty) Treason dated back to 1351 and applied to the murder of a superior by a subordinate. Although the charge was occasionally brought against a cleric who killed his prelate, most charges related to the murder of masters by servants or, as in Joyce's case, of a husband by his wife.

As a married woman Joyce was regarded in law as her husband's subordinate. As such, she had very few independent legal rights and was subject to her husband. This was known as coverture and a married woman had the legal status of a *'feme covert'*, as opposed to a single woman's status of *'feme seule'*. Both terms originate from Anglo-Norman and respectively mean 'covered woman' (as in covered by her husband) and 'single woman'. In practice this meant that a married couple was one person in the eyes of the law, and that person was exclusively male. Coverture, which has been referred to as 'the lack of a legal identity', meant that if a married woman murdered her husband she was guilty of treason against a superior and therefore faced both the death penalty and the additional penalty of being burnt at the stake.[35]

Joyce protested vehemently at her trial that she had been abused by her husband for many years, but this was no legal defence. The Ordinary of Newgate echoed the popular view that 'she ought not to have taken his Life away for that, but have endeavour'd by some proper Means (as having the Minister of their Parish, or some other serious Person, to discourse him) to bring him to a better Temper'.[36] As Marisha Caswell states, 'while people saw the abuse of authority as problematic, they were even more troubled by a wife's usurpation of authority, especially if that usurpation ended in a husband's murder.'[37] Caswell's research shows that 'of the twenty-two cases of married women accused of Petty Treason at the Old Bailey between 1674 and 1760, juries acquitted eight (36.36 per cent), convicted seven (31.82 per cent), and delivered partial verdicts in the remainder.'[38] Petty Treason ceased to be a separate offence from murder following the passing of the Offences against the Person Act 1828 (9 Geo. IV c.31), which still allowed for the further penalty of hanging and drawing in such cases.

Joyce was one of two women and eight men who received the death penalty at the Old Bailey on that day, and she was sent to Newgate to await her fate. Two of the men were reprieved and both Joyce and the other woman, Katherine Priest, 'pleaded their bellies'.[39] This was a common-law facility that allowed pregnant women (but only those in the later stages of pregnancy) to claim a respite from the death penalty until after any babies that they were carrying were born; this prevented an unborn but developed foetus being killed by proxy. This form of respite had existed since at least 1387 and often resulted in the new mother's sentence being commuted.[40] Those women who pleaded their belly were then subject to inspection by a 'jury of matrons', who were normally chosen from women who had observed the trial. These women, normally six in number, examined and questioned the supposedly pregnant woman in order to verify her claim and to see if she was indeed 'quick with child' – that is, whether the foetus could be felt moving within the woman's belly.[41] Katherine Priest (who had been sentenced to death for stealing 40s. 6d.) was indeed found to be in the advanced stages of pregnancy, but Joyce was found not to be pregnant. Consequently she was part of the grim procession of condemned individuals that made its way to Tyburn on 22 September 1714.

The Ordinary, Paul Lorrain, recorded that Joyce was penitent before her imminent death:

> And in that her Denial she persisted for a great while after she had received Sentence of Death; but at last she confess'd it, saying, That in her Passion she gave him the Wound he dy'd of, but did not design to have killed him.[42]

He also recorded that he had conscientiously attempted to ease each of the condemned individuals' path to final judgement:

> While they were under this twofold melancholy State of Guilt and Condemnation, I constantly visited them, and had them, twice every day (save one Afternoon) brought up to the Chapel of Newgate, where I pray'd with them, read and expounded the Word of GOD to them giving them out of it such Instructions and Animadversions as were proper for them, in order to their making a due Preparation for their approaching Death and Judgment, that by a lively Faith and sincere Repentance, wrought in them by the Divine Spirit, and their devout Attention to that Sacred Word, they might obtain Mercy, Pardon, and Salvation, thro' Jesus Christ, the Redeemer of all them that truly Believe and Repent.

However, he found Joyce to be:

> very ignorant in Matters of Religion, tho' she said she went frequently to Church; but not being able to read, she had not that Advantage of understanding Good Things, which they have who were brought up to Reading, and to know the Principles of the Christian Religion from their Youth.[43]

The Ordinary impassively recorded the final minutes of Joyce's life:

> After the Men were thus turn'd off, the Woman [i.e. Joyce Hodgkis] was ty'd to a Stake, set up for her at a little distance from the Gallows, where I pray'd by her; And when I had done, then the Fuel and combustible Matters, that were there prepared, being placed round her, and set on fire, she was burnt.[44]

It is not recorded in Joyce's particular death, but in many cases of death by burning at the stake the executioner showed some compassion by strangling the woman with the cord used to tie her to the stake. Burning at the stake (which remained a punishment until 1790) was itself seen as a more humane method of execution for treason for women as it did not involve unseemly interference with their bodies.

Joyce Hodgkis seems to have been unfortunate in both her choice of husband and the extreme bias of the law against women with regard to both domestic violence and her punishment. Other women, despite their initial bad luck in being caught and sentenced, at least seem to have been ultimately more successful in their choice of partner, as is illustrated in the following case study.

Case study 16: Sarah Bellamy, larceny, 1785

Sarah Bellamy was baptized on 3 February 1770 at Holy Trinity church, Belbroughton, Worcestershire, the sixth child of Richard and Elizabeth. Her family had fallen on hard times and are recorded as living in a cottage 'occupied by paupers of the said parish' and receiving irregular subsistence payments of a few shillings a week from the Overseers of the Poor.[45] At the age of nine Sarah was apprenticed to James Spurrier, an overseer and farmer in nearby Bell End, but by 1785 she had left the Spurrier household and was working as a domestic servant for Benjamin Haden, a weaver living in Dudley.

On 9 July 1785 Sarah appeared at Worcester Summer Assizes on a charge of grand larceny. She was accused of having stolen a linen purse, fifteen and a half guineas and two promissory notes valued at £15 5s. from Benjamin's house on 29 May 1785. Until 1718 theft of property or money to the value of more than 40s. was classed as a capital offence and therefore (at least theoretically) punishable by death.[46] However, from the passing of the Transportation Act 1718 the courts were authorized to exile grand larcenists to the colonies for a fixed period as an acceptable alternative to the death penalty. At the conclusion of her trial Sarah was found guilty. She begged the judge, Baron Beaumont Hotham, to be lenient and sentence her to be publicly whipped in Worcester Market place on two consecutive days, but he refused and instead sentenced her to seven years' transportation.[47]

Sarah's sentence of transportation came at a time of great flux and consternation for the British government. Between 1718 and 1776 an estimated 50,000 people had been transported to various outposts of the British Empire, including the West Indies and the west coast of Africa, but most notably North America. Following the American War of Independence (1776–83) the newly independent country made it clear to the British government that no more transportees were to be accepted. Consequently, one of the most recent additions to the British Empire, namely Australia (and New South Wales in particular) became the chosen destination for transported convicts.

It is likely that Sarah was imprisoned at Worcester County Gaol immediately after her sentence but in January 1787 she was transferred (probably via Southwark Gaol in London) to the convict ship *Lady Penrhyn* at Gravesend, which then sailed for Portsmouth, arriving on 31 January.[48] The *Lady Penrhyn* was a new ship of some 338 tons, constructed the previous year and contracted by the East Indies Company to return from Australia by way of China with a cargo of tea. Sarah was one of just over 100 female convicts to board the ship, together with the crew and a handful of marines. On 13 May 1787 the *Lady Penrhyn* and her cargo of female convicts embarked from Portsmouth as part of the First Fleet to sail to Australia.

The journey took just over seven months and, while the ship was newly constructed, it was found to be fairly unstable at sea, with conditions being rudimentary on board. The newly appointed Governor of New South Wales, Arthur Phillip, who was also in charge of the arrangements for the sailing and

provisioning of the First Fleet, was a capable and compassionate man who complained bitterly of the state of the convict women who were brought aboard the
Lady Penrhyn. He stated in a letter to the Under-Secretary of State that:

> The situation in which the Magistrates sent the women on board the Lady
> Penryhn stamps them with infamy – tho' almost naked and so very filthy
> that nothing but clothing them could have prevented them from perishing
> [. . .] which could not be done in time to prevent a fever.[49]

Despite this inauspicious start, Sarah (along with the vast majority of her fellow
convicts, both male and female) survived the undoubtedly arduous journey and
a report in the log of the *Lady Penrhyn* dated 19 January 1788 stated 'in sight
of land'.[50] The ship docked at Port Jackson (to be renamed Sydney a few months
later), but the female convicts were not disembarked there until stores were
unloaded and preparations for habitation completed. The complement of ninety-
eight female convicts and ten children (including one Joseph Bellamy, who is
listed as a 'convict's child', the probable offspring of an illicit liaison between
Sarah and Joseph Downey, the ship's quartermaster) were consequently not
allowed on shore until 6 February 1788.[51]

Sarah was subsequently assigned to work as a housemaid to Second Lieutenant
William Faddy, who had also travelled as part of the First Fleet on the smallest of
the vessels, *Friendship*.[52] In August 1789 she was charged with breach of the
peace after a curious incident in which Captain James Meredith of the Royal
Marines had tried to enter her bedchamber after a social event at the nearby
Governor's house. Meredith was clearly drunk and made improper advances
towards Sarah, who resisted him by screaming 'Murder!' until a night watchman, John Harris, fortuitously appeared. Meredith was escorted away, but coun-
tered by bringing a charge of breach of the peace against Sarah, who insisted that
she was the wronged party and was merely defending her honour. Despite
Meredith's and Sarah's respective positions in society, Sarah's version of events
was believed by the court (she was assisted by the testimony of another witness,
convict Matthew James Everingham) and the charge against her was dismissed.[53]

Shortly after this incident Sarah appears to have met and set up home with
another First Fleeter, James Bloodworth. He had been sentenced to seven years'
transportation on 3 October 1785 at Kingston-upon-Thames, Surrey, after being
found guilty of stealing poultry. Bloodworth, a brickmaker, was almost eleven
years older than Sarah, being baptized on 7 March 1759, and had left a wife and
three surviving children behind at Kingston.[54] James arrived at Port Jackson
on the *Charlotte* on 26 January 1788 and was immediately put to work as a
brickmaker and builder.

Sarah subsequently bore James eight children, four of whom (two sons and
two daughters) survived infancy. The couple never married (probably owing to
his previous marriage to Jane Marks), and this caused Sarah considerable difficulty in later life; in 1806 she had to appear in court and swear that her children
were all James' offspring. This was due to the compilation of a *Female Register*

(also known as the 'Concubine Index') by the Reverend Samuel Marsden in 1806 in order to demonstrate the level of immorality present in the new colony of New South Wales. Marsden included only women married by him or according to Church of England rites, thereby damning women who were nonconformists, Catholics, Jews and so on, as well as those in 'common-law' relationships, as concubines. Sarah was therefore listed as such, despite having being in a stable relationship with James Bloodworth for almost two decades. Marsden recorded 395 married women and 1035 concubines.[55]

James received an absolute pardon on 16 December 1791 and in the same year was appointed Superintendent of Buildings. He was responsible for most of the first brick-built edifices to be constructed in Sydney, including the original Governor's House, and rose to a position of considerable influence and respect. He and Sarah received grants of land in Sydney and lived for many years in a house built by James in South Row (now O'Connell Street).

James died on 21 March 1804 at the age of 45 after contracting pneumonia and was given the honour of a State funeral; the *Sydney Gazette and Morning Advertiser* carried the following details:

On Wednesday last died, generally lamented, Mr. James Bloodworth, for many years Superintendent of Builders in the Employ of Government. He came to the Colony among its first inhabitants in the year 1788, and obtained the Appointment, from his exemplary conduct, shortly after his arrival; the first house in this part of the Southern hemisphere was by him erected, as most of the Public Buildings since have been under his direction. To lament his loss he has left a Widow and five Children, the youngest an infant now only one week old; and the complaint which terminated in his dissolution was supposed to proceed from a severe cold contracted about two months since. The attention and concern which prevailed at the interment of the deceased were sufficient testimonies of the respect with which he filled, and the integrity with which he uninterruptedly discharged the duties of a Public Trust during so long a period. His EXCELLENCY was pleased to order that the Funeral should be provided for at the Public Expense, and to show other marks of attention to so old a Servant of the Crown. Four in the afternoon of Friday being as the wish of the widow appointed for the Funeral, the Relics of the deceased were at that hour removed from his house in South-street, and conveyed to the place of interment, at tended by a great number of friends, among whom were most of the Sydney Loyal Association, in which he had been appointed Serjeant. Opposite to his old residence a Procession was formed, which moved in the following order:

12 of the Loyal Association, arms reversed
Serjeant of the Association

Drum muffled & Fife

THE BIER

Two Sons, chief Mourners followed by an
Infant Daughter,
Fourteen Female Mourners,
Twenty-four Male ditto,
A number of respectable inhabitants in Rank.
The Non-commissioned Officers of the New South Wales Corps,
And a crowd of spectators.

When near the Burial Ground the Association were obliged to file off, for the accommodation of the friends of the deceased, and the populace, who were become very numerous; and when the remains were deposited approached the grave and performed Military Honours.

James' sudden death caused considerable financial problems for Sarah; despite his elevated position in New South Wales society his financial affairs seem to have been somewhat chaotic and he died almost insolvent. A notice in the *Sydney Gazette and NSW Herald* of 24 June 1804 stated:

SARAH BELLAMY having obtained Letters of Administration of the Goods, Chattels Credits and effects of the deceased Mr. JAMES BLOODWORTH, requests that all those who have any Claims or Demands against the estate do forthwith send their Accounts to her, that Means may be adopted for discharging such as appear just: Any those indebted to the Estate are likewise requested to discharge their respective Debts immediately, to avoid any coercive measures being taken for that purpose.

This notice seems to have had little effect, however, as Sarah appears to have been forced to sell some of James' effects in order to make ends meet. This appears to have caused problems for those who had provided sureties for her in respect of her claims on James' estate, and on 28 October 1804 the following warning was printed in the *Sydney Gazette*:

NOTICE,

We whose Names are hereunto subscribed
Sureties for Sarah Bellamy for her due

Administration of the Effects of Mr. James Bloodworth, deceased, do hereby caution the Public not to purchase any part of such Effects from the said Sarah Bellamy, as such Effects so purchased must be returned, and the Purchasers abide by the loss: and such as have already made Purchases are hereby directed to return the article; —Those withholding any article already made Purchase of will be prosecuted as the law directs.

James John Grant

David Bevan.

The legal arguments over James' estate dragged on throughout the next few months, with the following two notices appearing on 9 December 1804 in the *Sydney Gazette*:

1) NOTICE.

Mrs. Sarah Bellamy, Administratrix of the Goods, Chatels and Effects of the deceased Mr. James Bloodworth do hereby request, that all those who may have any claim or demand against her, as Administratrix, do attend at the House of Mr. David Bevan, on Tuesday the 18th Instant, at 11 in the fore-noon, in order to ascertain what Dividend can be made from his Estate; and such as will not then attend will be precluded from the benefit of a dividend provided they are within the Territory; and those who are not, that may have claims, the proportion of such Creditors (as it may be ascertained at such Meeting), will be lodged in hands of a Public Officer, to answer their Demands, provided that such Demands be made within 12 Months from the date of her Administrationship.

2) By Order of the Trustees for the Management of the Estate of Mr, WILLIAM COX.

In consequence of an application from the Sureties for the due Administration of Mrs Sarah Bellamy to the Estate of the deceased Mr. J. BLOODWORTH, the Trustees have agreed to SELL by AUCTION certain CATTLE, for the Liquidation of a Debt due from the Estate of the late James Bloodworth to that of Mr Cox: the Stock consisting of 3 Cows in Calf; 1 Heifer ditto; 1 female Calf about six months old; and 1 male ditto two months. And, if required to make up any balance that may of such Debt be due to Mr. Cox's Estate, there will also be sold 1 Mare in foal, and 1 Filley Foal. The sale to commence on Saturday the 15th Instant, at ten o'clock. Approved Bills only will be required in payment; and 3 months credit on good security.

It appears that this resolved the legal claims and counter-claims (at least tempo-rarily), but left Sarah only with the house in which she resided. In December 1824 she petitioned Sir Thomas Brisbane, Governor of New South Wales, stating that she had lived in the colony at No. 4 O'Connell Street for upwards of 34 years, that she had lived with the late James Bloodworth, who had been appointed Superintendent over the Bricklayers, that by his last will and testament she was left sole executrix of his estate and that she had paid off his debts of £350 and was left with nothing but the house.[56] Her two sons were now grown men and both qualified shipwrights, and both daughters were married. The house was leased to her eldest son James shortly after her husband's death and the lease had recently expired (on 2 May 1824), and James Bloodworth the younger now claimed it as his sole property despite his father's wishes for the residue of his estate to be split four ways, and he requested that his mother and sister quit the property. Sarah requested a new lease divided equally between her four children with the proviso that she lived in the house until her death. Sarah appears to have remained illiterate until her death – she signed the petition with an 'X'. However, her petition was successful and resulted in the house being re-leased in Sarah's name until the time of her death, when it would revert to her eldest son. In the 1825 general muster Sarah is described as a single householder and a washerwoman. She died at Lane Cove, Sydney, on 24 February 1843, and is recorded on her death certificate as Sarah Bloodworth.[57]

Some crimes, such as shoplifting or, most notably, prostitution, were seen as being almost exclusively the preserve of women. The latter offence was also often closely linked with female pickpockets, who frequently combined the two activities; as D'Cruze and Jackson remark, 'the enclosed, private and dark places in which women successfully operated are in almost total contrast to the busy, public, day haunts of the male pickpockets.'[58] However, not all female pickpockets operated in such a fashion; some were much more subtle and ingenious in their methods, as illustrated below.

Case study 17: Mary Young (aka Mary Webb, Jane Webb, Jenny Diver), larceny, 1741

Mary Young became one of the most infamous female pickpockets of the eighteenth century thanks to her daring escapades and flouting of the law. She is best known by one of her many aliases, Jenny Diver.[59] Although several historians, among them Lucy Moore, claim that '[John] Gay used her name for one of Macheath's loose women in *The Beggar's Opera*', it is far more likely that she acquired the alias from Gay's character; Gay published his most famous play in 1728, at a time when Mary Young was barely known either to the authorities or the public.[60]

She appears to have been born in Ireland *c.* 1705, though she denied being Irish to the Ordinary of Newgate, 'calling herself an English Woman, being unwilling to declare either her Country or Family, desiring to be excused in that Point'.[61] She claimed that from the age of ten she received rudimentary education, being taught to read and write and becoming a more than competent seamstress.[62] However, at the age of fifteen she quarrelled with the woman who was looking after her (having been deserted by her mother and never knowing her father) and sought a new life in London. The Ordinary's *Account* recounts that she made an agreement with a manservant (who had stolen over £80 of his master's goods to finance their new life) that they would abscond together to London.[63] Unfortunately, upon landing at Liverpool, they tarried there owing to seasickness and her putative beau was recognized and captured by a man whom his former master had sent to look for the runaway servant. Mary managed to escape detection and made her way to London, where she fell in with Anne Murphy, the leader of a gang of female pickpockets.

Mary proved to be a quick and willing pupil; she appears to have used ingenious methods to distract onlookers while their pockets were being picked or their purses cut, and she utilized her seamstress skills to construct a costume which made her appear to be a genteel pregnant lady with her arms resting upon her swelling belly. In fact, her 'pregnancy' was an overstuffed pillow, while her folded arms were false, leaving her real arms free under her petticoat in order that she could relieve unknowing victims of their goods while sitting between them at church services or other gatherings.[64] When the thefts were discovered she appeared to be innocently sitting between the injured parties. She also perfected the art of creating a distraction by apparently fainting in the middle of a crowd while wearing her 'pregnancy' disguise. In the ensuing confusion her partners would move about the concerned onlookers, relieving them of their valuables.

However, Mary did eventually fall foul of the law, being tried at the Old Bailey on 5 June 1728 and sentenced for larceny under an assumed name (her real name was not revealed to the court) of Mary Webb:

> *Mary Webb*, of St. Martin's in the Fields, was indicted for stealing a Holland Shift, value five Shillings, the Goods of Elizabeth Gibbs; four Shifts, the Property of Barbary Pinfold, and five Aprons, with other Things, the Property of other Persons; which Goods being found in her Custody by the Constable who apprehended her, and she giving but a very indifferent Account of herself, the Jury found her Guilty to the Value of 10d.[65]

She was accordingly sentenced to transportation to Virginia, but was subsequently confined in Newgate for a period of some months, awaiting a ship to carry her overseas. The Ordinary's *Account* states that:

> During the Time of her Confinement she turned Fence, and bought such Things as came in her Way, she having a quantity of Money by her, and knowing this Business could no ways affect her, she being Cast already; and when she went away she had as many Goods of one Sort or other, as would almost have loaded a Waggon. When she came on Board she was treated in a quite different Manner from the rest of the Transports, and was put ashore at the first Port they came to in Virginia. Jenny staid no longer there than to see the Country, for Business in her Way could not be transacted there; so after she had diverted herself as long as she thought proper, she agreed with a Gentleman for her Passage who was bound for England, who brought her over.[66]

She had therefore returned from transportation before her sentence had expired and soon returned to her old ways, but seems to have successfully avoided detection for almost a decade. The *London Evening Post* of 11–13 April 1738 records that:

> Jane Webb, alias Jenny Diver, was committed to Newgate [. . .] for picking a pocket at the North Door of St. Paul's of 8s. 6d. As she was carrying to Newgate in a coach, she attempted to stab the person who apprehended her. She is one of the expertest [sic] Hands in Town at Picking Pockets; she used

to attend well-dressed, at the Opera House, Play-Houses etc and it's reckon'd made as much annually by her Practice, as if she had had the fingering of the Publick Money.

She was accordingly sentenced to transportation in the name of Jane Webb. By this time it appears that her previous sentence of transportation and her subsequent avoidance of it had become public knowledge; the *London Evening Post* of 18–20 May 1738 stated that:

Great Interest is making to get the famous Jenny Diver, alias Murphy, alias Webb, off from her second sentence of Transportation; the Gang [the pick-pocketing gang to which Mary belonged] spares no Pains or Cost, well knowing that in six Months Time she'll pick Pockets enough to pay all Charges; Such an excellent Hand as she, is a sure Thousand at the ensuing Installation at Windsor.

However, such attempts proved futile and it was reported on 9 June 1738 that:

This Morning about One o'Clock 126 Convicts were carried from Newgate and put on board a close Lighter at Black-Fryars, and from thence conveyed and shipped in the Forward Galley bound to Virginia and Maryland. Among this infamous Crew is the noted Jenny Diver.[67]

Despite this, the second attempt by the authorities to ensure that Mary served a sentence of transportation was once more thwarted; by December 1738 it was reported that:

The celebrated Jane Webb, alias Jenny Diver, who was transported last April for picking of Pockets at St Paul's is returned from her travels; as is Wreathcock and others of that Gang, of whom only Bird is yet taken, who is now in Newgate. It's said the Inducement to these People to return from Transportation, is, that Vaughan, nick-named Lord Vaughan, and several others who have returned, are taken no Notice of, but appear publicly, as if they had never been transported. Besides, as there's no Reward for appre-hending those who do return, People don't care to run any Hazard to take them, and be at the Expense and Trouble of prosecuting them too. – Justice has been here, but is fled the Kingdom again.[68]

Mary managed to evade the authorities for a further two years, but on 17 January 1741 she was caught with another woman, Elizabeth Davis, in the act of robbing a woman and sent to Newgate to await trial. She was tried at the Old Bailey on 20 January and under her real name was sentenced to death.[69] Both Mary and Elizabeth pleaded pregnancy in a desperate attempt to avoid the gallows, but the press reported that 'a Jury of Matrons being immannelled thereon, they were found Not Quick with Child'.[70]

On 18 March 1741 Mary was taken to Tyburn to be hanged; the Ordinary of Newgate reported that:

> The Morning she went to Execution she seem'd very composed; but when the Officer came to halter her in the Press Yard, she was very much shocked. [. . .] She declared that Elizabeth Davis had no Hand in the Robbery which she suffered for, and that she would persuade the World (if possible) that she was not the Woman, that she was represented to be; but had always lived a sober Life (if you believe her) but she could not deny the robbing of Judith Gardener, on the 17th of Jan last, and that she was Transported by the Name of Jane Webb, in April Sessions 1738. She believed in Christ her only Saviour, repented of all her Sins, and was in Peace with all the World. [. . .] After she had hung the usual Time, she was cut down, and convey'd to Pancras, in order to be interr'd in the Church-yard.[71]

Gender-identity crimes[72]

One area that caused the authorities of the eighteenth century considerable difficulties was that of gender-identity crimes, especially those involving cross-dressing or impersonation of the opposite gender (usually, but not exclusively, women impersonating men).[73]

Reports of such cases are very rare; Olwen Hufton suggests that only a handful of English women who lived and worked as men (and who lived as 'man and wife' with a partner) came before the courts in the period 1500–1800. She states that 'these women usually came before the magistrates charged with fraud, a serious offence and were in almost all cases brought before the courts by their "wives" who wished to annul the union.'[74] However, Rictor Norton's extensive research into this aspect of criminal behaviour suggests that cases of cross-dressing were somewhat more prevalent than Hufton states.[75]

There were many reasons why a woman would want to impersonate a man; many simply wanted to improve their working prospects by entering male professions such as the army or navy, some undoubtedly wished to pursue a homosexual relationship, while others appear to have used cross-dressing simply as yet another means to a fraudulent end.

In 1760 a 20-year-old woman named Betty Blandford was committed to Bridewell after being discovered working as a soldier in a light-horse regiment. She had apparently enlisted in London and had been sworn in, but her sex was soon discovered and she was subsequently discharged.[76] Other women, however, were more successful in their attempt to live a male life. The *Lancaster Gazette* of 29 May 1813 reported the following case:

> An American seaman taken in the American schooner *Revenge*, by the *Belle Poole*, 36, on finding he was got to Mill Prison, discovered himself to be a woman, and that she had worn men's clothes these three years. She was examined and sent to the hospital to be clothed. The account she gives of

herself is as follows: Going coastways with her master, mistress and family about three years since, the vessel was wrecked, and all on board perished except herself. [. . .] She conceived the idea of dressing herself in men's apparel, and then begged her way home as a shipwrecked seaman to the nearest seaport. She got relieved, and also got employment as a landsman on board a vessel, and from thence into the *Revenge* schooner, on breaking out of the war. She says her share of prize-money and wages is about 200 dollars.[77]

Some women were completely open about wishing to improve their employment prospects. In a somewhat unusual case Margaret Eyres was indicted at the Old Bailey on 20 February 1805 on a charge of grand larceny (the theft of a wheelbarrow from a Richard Howell) and was apprehended 'drest in men's apparel [. . .] in men's clothes; coat, waistcoat, and breeches' at 2 a.m.[78] Margaret was known to the complainant as a woman who had been a servant who married 'a respectable man of fortune' from whom she had parted about ten years previously. She denied attempting to steal the barrow, saying that she had sat down in it for a rest. She further stated that she had fallen on hard times and that:

the reason why I appeared in men's apparel (as has been stated by my husband's friends) is, that I being able to execute the work of a gardener, and being dressed as a man, I had the same wages as a man had; I had no intention of stealing it; the prosecutor knew me in better circumstances; it is all spite and malice.[79]

Her story was believed and she was acquitted.

Other women clearly used cross-dressing as an opportunity to commit offences; the *Daily Advertiser* of 8 July 1777 reported that:

On Saturday last a Woman was convicted at the Guildhall, Westminster, for going in Men's Cloaths, and being married to three different Women by a fictitious Name, and for defrauding them of the Money and Cloaths: She was sentenced to stand in the Pillory at Charing-Cross, and to be imprisoned six Months.

The anonymous woman was convicted of fraud rather than bigamy, as none of her 'marriages' would have been deemed legal in law.[80]

Transsexual relationships between men also occasionally made the headlines, perhaps the most famous being the 'Vere Street' scandal of 1810. This centred around a public house called the White Swan, which became well known as a haunt of cross-dressing and homosexual men. In this respect it was not unique, as Ian McCalman states:

Low-life guides to urban life produced by hacks like Ned Ward reported the existence of transvestite homosexual brothels around the Strand or in garrison towns and ports (an especially notorious one in Vere Street, London, was said in 1812 to hold transvestite marriage services conducted by an ex-Methodist parson called John Church).[81]

The *Morning Post* of 10 July 1810 reported that this venue had been raided the previous day by several members of the Bow Street Office:

POLICE. Bow-Street, July 9. – In consequence of its having been represented to the Magistrates of the above office, that a number of persons of a most detestable description, met at the house of James Cooke, the White Swan, in Vere-street, Clare-market, particularly on a Sunday night, a privy search-warrant was issued, and was put in execution on Sunday night last, when 23 persons, including the landlord of the house, were taken into custody, and lodged in St. Clement's watch-house, till yesterday, at eleven o-clock, when they were brought before Mr. Read for examination; but the circumstance having transpired, a great concourse of people had collected in Bow-street, and which was much increased by the mob that followed the prisoners when they were brought from the watch-house. It was with the greatest difficulty the officers could bring them to and from the Brown Bear to the Office; the mob, particularly the women, expressing their detestation of the offence of which the prisoners were charged. [. . .] Two of the Patrole gave an account of their being in the house last night previous to the execution of the warrant, and stated the particulars of the conversation and actions that passed while they were in the parlour, but it is of too horrible a nature to meet the public eye.[82]

The same report indicates that the general populace expressed revulsion at the reported offences:

The crowd had, by this time, become so great in Bow-street, particularly facing the Office, that it was almost impossible to pass, and most of those who were discharged, were very roughly handled; several of them were hunted about the neighbourhood, and with great difficulty escaped with their lives, although every exertion was used by the constables and patrole to prevent such dangerous proceedings; and, in doing which, many of them were very roughly treated.

Several of the apprehended men were eventually tried and found guilty, and were sentenced to imprisonment and/or being stood in the pillory. A contemporary newspaper report illustrates the public opprobrium and 'rough music' to which they were subjected on their journey between court and prison:

On sentence being pronounced they were all handcuffed, and tied to one chain in Court, and ordered to Cold Bath-fields prison. On leaving the Court, a numerous crowd of people, which had collected at the door, assailed them with fists, sticks, and stones, which the constables could not completely prevent, although they were about 40 in number. The prisoners perceiving their perilous situation, immediately ran in a body to the prison, which they reached in a few minutes, and the constables, by blockading the streets, prevented the most fleet of their assailants from molesting them during their inglorious retreat.[83]

Conclusion

This chapter has demonstrated that much more research is needed before the often complex relationships between gender and prosecution, gender and offending, and sex and gender in the eighteenth century are more thoroughly understood. It is already clear, however, that women in particular were often at a considerable disadvantage both as complainants/victims and as offenders; the legal system remained extremely biased against them throughout the period under discussion. As Bridget Hill has memorably stated, 'their legal existence, in so far as they had one at all, was that of under-age children'.[84]

It has also been shown here that some offenders and their offending caught the eyes and ears of the public. Mary Young, for example, was unusual in becoming well known during her own relatively brief lifetime; most offenders (male and female) either served their sentence or died in obscurity. Some, however (such as the members of the Vere Street case), were destined for notoriety either while still alive or posthumously. Crime was often a best-selling component of popular literature in the eighteenth century, and it is this aspect of crime history that is discussed in the next chapter.

Notes

1 *The Times*, 29 March 1792.
2 Prior to this date the only way in which men or women could be divorced was by getting a private Act passed through Parliament. This was a time-consuming and extremely expensive procedure and as a result only a very small number of wealthy individuals were granted a divorce. There was also considerable social stigma attached to the whole process of divorce and this was especially directed towards a divorced female. It was not until the Matrimonial Causes Act 1923 (13 and 14 Geo. V, c.19) that equal rights in divorce were established for men and women, making it possible for wives to divorce husbands for simple adultery; up to this date wives also had to prove an aggravating factor. Married women were not allowed to retain possession of their property until the Married Women's Property Act 1870 (33 & 34 Vict. c.93), which allowed women to legally be the rightful owners of the money they earned and to inherit property up to £200.
3 Rictor Norton (ed.), *Homosexuality in Eighteenth-Century England: A Sourcebook*, available online at www.rictornorton.co.uk/eighteen/.
4 The 'leet' was an ancient manorial court that appointed local officials such as ale-taster, constable and so on in a similar manner to that of a parish vestry. Clementina Trafford was a member of the influential Trafford family of Lancashire and died in 1834 at the age of 51. The post may have been little more than an honorary one, as it refers to her deputies, but her appointment remains highly unusual.

5   *Staffordshire Advertiser*, 8 February 1834.

6   Emsley, *The English Police*, p. 127.

7   S. D'Cruze and L. Jackson, *Women, Crime and Justice in England since 1660* (Basingstoke: Palgrave Macmillan, 2009), pp. 25–6.

8   For an examination of the role of women as prosecutors and victims in the late sixteenth and early seventeenth century, see L. Gowing, *The London Church Courts, 1572–1640* (London: University of London, 1993). For female victims of violent offences, see Beattie, *Crime and The Courts*, pp. 124–32. For research into female offenders, see Palk, *Gender, Crime and Judicial Discretion*; Beattie, *Crime and the Courts*; King, *Crime, Justice, and Discretion*; and Garthine Walker, *Crime, Gender and Social Order in Early Modern England* (Cambridge: CUP, 2003).

9   D'Cruze and Jackson, *Women, Crime and Justice in England since 1660*, pp. 26–7.

10 Abstracted from Table 1.2 'Complainants/victims' by sex, Old Bailey Proceedings, 1725–1899 in ibid., p. 27.

11 Figures quoted in ibid., p. 26.

12 Quoted in ibid., p. 26.

13 Ibid., p. 27.

14 *The Times*, 6 January 1817 and 12 August 1835.

15 *The Times*, 28 July 1823.

16 Cox, *A Certain Share of Low Cunning*, pp. 172–3.

17 Palk, *Gender, Crime and Judicial Discretion*, p. 3. Palk's work is important with regard to the study of females within the criminal justice process, but itself contains little mention of the role of women as prosecutors.

18 See Palk, *Gender, Crime and Judicial Discretion*; D'Cruze and Jackson, *Women, Crime and Justice in England since 1660*; King, *Crime, Justice, and Discretion*; and Beattie, *Crime and the Courts*. For research into Scottish female offenders see Galloway Brown and Ferguson, *Twisted Sisters*.

19 E. Ewan, 'Crime or Culture? Women and Daily Life in Late-Medieval Scotland', in Galloway Brown, Y., and Ferguson, R. (eds), *Twisted Sisters: Women, Crime and Deviance in Scotland Since 1400* (East Linton: Tuckwell Press, 2002), pp. 117–136: p. 117.

20 Hufton, *The Prospect Before Her*, p. 262.

21 D'Cruze and Jackson, *Women, Crime and Justice in England since 1660*, p. 17.

22 Sharpe, *Crime in Early Modern England*, p. 109.

23 M. Feeley and D. Little, 'The Vanishing Female: The Decline of Women in the Criminal Process 1687–1912', *Law and Society Review* 25 (1991): 719–57.

24 King, *Crime, Justice, and Discretion*, p. 220 – for further details of his argument, see pp. 196–226.

25 Figures abstracted from King, *Crime and the Law in England*, p. 201.

26 Peter King, *Crime and Law in England, 1750–1840: Remaking justice from the margins* (Cambridge: CUP, 2006), p. 201, quoting J. Samaha, *Law and Order in Historical Perspective. The case of Elizabethan Essex* (New York: Academic Press, 1974), p. 140. These figures are for only one county and King points out the pitfalls of confusing the specific with the general.

27 Palk, *Gender, Crime and Judicial Discretion*, p. 6. Palk's work concentrates on London and Middlesex; prosecution levels in the provinces remain under-researched.

28 Godfrey *et al.*, *Criminal Lives*, p. 35.

29 For an example of an 1823 infanticide perpetrated by a man, see Cox, *Foul Deeds & Suspicious Deaths*, pp. 35–44.

30 St Dunstan's parish register, London, England, Baptisms, Marriages and Burials, 1538–1812, available online at Ancestry.co.uk).

31 OA 17140922.

32 OBP t17140908–35.

33 OBP t17140908–35.

34 OBP t17140908–35.
35 Marisha C. Caswell, 'Married Women, Crime, and Questions of Liability in England 1640–1760' (unpublished PhD thesis, Queens University, Kingston, Ontario, 2012): abstract.
36 OA 17140922.
37 Caswell, 'Married Women, Crime', p. 214. For further details of coverture, see Frances Dolan, 'Battered Women, Petty Traitors, and the Legacy of Coverture', *Feminist Studies* 29.2 (2003): 249–77.
38 Caswell, 'Married Women, Crime', p. 214.
39 OA 17140922.
40 For further details of 'pleading the belly', see C. Means, 'Pleading the Belly 1387– 1931. The Phoenix of Abortional Freedom: Is a Penumbral or Ninth-Amendment Right about to Arise from the Nineteenth-century Legislative Ashes of a Fourteenth-century Common-law Liberty?', *New York Law Forum* 17 (1971): 335–410.
41 The practice of pleading one's belly continued sporadically until the twentieth century, when the Sentence of Death (Expectant Mothers) Act 1931 c.24 replaced the practice in common law. This Act was itself not repealed until 1998.
42 OA 17140922. Paul Lorrain was Ordinary of Newgate from 1698 until his death in 1719. He had previously been diarist Samuel Pepys' secretary and copyist.
43 OA 17140922.
44 OA 17140922.
45 1783 Indenture, loaned to Belbroughton History Society by Mr W. A. Allen. I am indebted to Belbroughton History Society for their help with research into Sarah's antecedents. For a more detailed account of Sarah's family and her life, see M. Vaughan and David J. Cox, *From Belbroughton to Botany Bay: The story of a Worcestershire girl's transportation to Australia on the First Fleet and her life in the new colony* (Kingswinford: Dulston Press/Belbroughton History Society, 2013).
46 We have already seen in Chapter 5 how this gave rise to frequent massive undervaluations of goods by juries in cases of grand larceny.
47 Beaumont Hotham, 2nd baron of Hotham (1737–1814), was called to the Bar in 1758 and sat as an Assize judge from *c.* 1775 to 1805.
48 A. Frost, *The First Fleet – The Real Story* (Collingwood, Victoria: Blacks Inc., 2012), p. 131.
49 This was almost undoubtedly 'gaol fever' – either typhus or typhoid – contracted as a result of the appalling conditions in which convicts awaiting transportation were kept. Thanks to the prompt attention of Phillip and the surgeons on board the First Fleet ships the outbreaks of fever were dealt with and the fleet sailed free of fever.
50 TNA ADM 51/4376, Captain's Log, *Lady Penrhyn*, 27 October 1786–28 March 1788.
51 Joseph Bellamy was baptized on 10 February 1788, but the infant unfortunately survived only for a few days afterwards (Madge Gibson, *From Belbroughton to Botany Bay* (Belbroughton: Belbroughton History Society, 1987), p. 14). From the child's appearance in the ship's muster it is likely that Sarah and Joseph consummated their liaison either while the *Lady Penryhn* was still in Gravesend or shortly after it had arrived at Portsmouth.
52 William Faddy RN had a fascinating but short life, being killed in action during the Battle of the Nile in 1798 – see www.firstfleetfellowship.org.au/stories/lieutenant-william-faddy/ for further details of his life.
53 Everingham had been sentenced to seven years' transportation for false pretences at the Old Bailey on 7 July 1784. He later rose to become a constable and accidentally drowned during an investigation on Christmas Day 1817. Captain Meredith was held in custody from 14 October 1789 to the time of his court martial at Plymouth on 2 October 1792, when he was charged with 'behaviour highly improper in an Officer'. The charge was found to be 'groundless and malicious' and he was honourably acquitted (*The World*, 5 October 1792).

54 He had married Jane Marks on 9 December 1782 at Shoreditch, London – see Ancestry.co.uk.

55 The *Register* has been described as 'an inspired piece of creative bigotry' – see Hughes, R., *The Fatal Shore*, p. 247. For the views of transported convicts to previous marriages and to marriage within the colony, see Tony Rayner, *Female Factory Female Convicts* (Dover, Tasmania: Esperance Press, 2005), pp. 79–81.

56 Colonial Secretary's Papers December 1824, available online at www.Ancestry.co.uk.

57 For further details of Sarah's life, see Vaughan and Cox, *From Belbroughton to Botany Bay*.

58 D'Cruze and Jackson, *Women, Crime and Justice*, p. 167.

59 'Diver' was a common eighteenth-century slang or cant word for a pickpocket – see N. Bailey, *The Universal Etymological English Dictionary*, Vol. II (London: Bailey, 1737).

60 Moore, *Con Men and Cutpurses*, p. 101.

61 OA 17410318.

62 OA 17410318.

63 OA 17410318.

64 OA 17410318.

65 OBP t17280605–9.

66 OA 17410318.

67 *Daily Post*, 9 June 1738. A 'lighter' was a manually powered boat that was rowed by a 'lighterman' and his assistant on the River Thames.

68 *London Evening Post*, 21–23 December 1738.

69 OBP t17410116–15.

70 *London Evening Post*, 20–22 January 1741.

71 OA 17410318.

72 Some of the most comprehensive accounts of homosexuality and cross-dressing in the eighteenth century can be found in 'Some Cross-Dressing Women' in Norton, *Homosexuality in Eighteenth-Century England*, and Rictor Norton, *Mother Clap's Molly House: The Gay Subculture in England, 1700–1830* (Stroud: History Press, 2006).

73 For details of a famous cross-dressing case where a man impersonated a woman, see Ruth Paley and Simon Fowler, *Family Skeletons: Exploring the Lives of our Disreputable Ancestors* (Kew: National Archives, 2005), pp. 130–31 for the story of Charles d'Eon (1728–1810).

74 Hufton, *The Prospect Before Her*, pp. 255–6.

75 Norton, *Homosexuality in Eighteenth-Century England*.

76 *London Chronicle*, 5–7 September 1760.

77 Britain was at war with America from 1812 to 1815. The *Belle Poole* was a twenty-eight-gun frigate that had been recently captured from the French (and which was later used to transfer Napoleon's body to France).

78 OBP t18050220–62.

79 OBP t18050220–62.

80 For a historical study of the offence of bigamy, see David J. Cox, '"Trying to get a good one": Bigamy Offences in England and Wales 1850–1950', *Plymouth Law & Criminal Justice Review* 4 (2011): 1–32 [www.research.plymouth.ac.uk/plr/].

81 I. McCalman (ed.), *Oxford Companion to the Romantic Age: British Culture 1776–1832* (Oxford: OUP, 2001), p. 547. Ned Ward was the most famous of a number of eighteenth- and early nineteenth-century pedlars of scandal, his best-known publication being *The London Spy*, published in 1703.

82 The Brown Bear was a public house near to the Bow Street office, which had cellars which were used as a lock-up by the Bow Street Officers.

83 *Jackson's Oxford Journal*, 29 September 1810.

84 B. Hill, *Eighteenth-Century Women: An Anthology* (London: Allen & Unwin, 1984), p. 108.

7   Crime in contemporary literature and culture

Introduction

> We do not know that any circumstance could have occurred, which was better calculated to exhibit the utility of newspaper reports of the proceedings in courts of justice, than the discovery which we detailed last week, of the innocence of three persons, two of whom had been left for execution, on a charge of highway robbery. Had not the attention of persons residing at Wolverhampton and Oswestry been attracted by seeing the trial of the people reported in the newspapers, the probability is, that two innocent men might have lost their lives on the gallows.[1]

The above report referred to a case in 1830 at Lancaster Assizes in which newspaper reports of the proceedings and the verdict of capital sentences issued to two men led directly to their reprieve and subsequent acquittal. A Wolverhampton constable read of the case and visited Lancaster for the purposes of making inquiries that proved that the two men under sentence of death were innocent, as the prosecutor of the case was found to be a fraudster. Although the report refers to a case outside our period, it aptly illustrates the growing role that literature (including newspapers) played in the reporting of, and responses to, crime and criminals throughout the eighteenth and early nineteenth century.

This chapter investigates the various roles played by the many forms of popular literature, including newspapers, trial reports, Ordinarys' Accounts and plays, as well as more insightful and serious treatises on the subject of crime and criminals.

Newspapers

Jeremy Black states that 'the first successful daily paper, the *Daily Courant*, began publication in March 1702, and the first provincial paper, probably the *Norwich Post*, in 1701'.[2] By the end of the eighteenth century newspapers had become increasingly popular among the emergent middle class.[3] The *Staffordshire Advertiser* reported in 1795 that:

> There are at this time one hundred and fifty-eight newspapers published in Great Britain and Ireland viz. 38 in London, 72 in the county towns of

England. 14 published daily in London, 10 three times a week, 2 twice a week and 12 weekly.[4]

Owing to their relatively high cost newspapers were not readily available to the majority of the public; provincial newspapers such as the *Staffordshire Advertiser* and the *Wolverhampton Chronicle* cost 6½d., as did *The Times* and *Hue & Cry and Police Gazette*, and were consequently too expensive for general consumption; studies suggest that in the last half of the eighteenth century 'well-established papers may normally have sold between one thousand and two thousand copies.'[5] These small circulation figures, of course, ignore the possibility that such publications would have been read by more than just the purchaser, and also that articles or reports may well have been read aloud either in public venues or the increasingly popular coffee houses.

The main reasons for newspapers' comparatively high cost were Stamp Duty (imposed by the government and set at a rate of 3½d. per copy), causing the majority of newspapers, both provincial and metropolitan, to be priced at either 6d. or 6½d., and the high production costs involved in printing. It has been calculated that it took a compositor 'twenty hours work for a four-page newspaper, and it took about one hour for about two hundred copies of a four-page newspaper to be printed'.[6]

Raymond Williams suggests that Stamp Duty was kept deliberately high 'to restrict readership of newspapers to the middle class, by inflating newspaper prices', and the resultant effect certainly played a part, by design or not, in keeping newspaper circulation low.[7] The extent to which provincial newspapers were circulated among the local populace is still not known precisely, but research suggests that between 1.6 per cent and 1.8 per cent bought or read a weekly newspaper; daily newspapers were at this time almost unknown owing to the limitations of transport and printing methods.[8]

Both provincial and metropolitan newspapers of the late eighteenth and early nineteenth centuries devoted a considerable amount of their typeface to criminal matters. In London newspapers regularly reported on the proceedings of the Old Bailey and the other courts within the metropolis, while provincial papers often devoted several columns in each issue to important national or local trials. Provincial papers were not above brazenly 'lifting' accounts of interesting criminal cases directly from the London weeklies, often not even crediting the source. Similarly, *The Times* was quite happy to reprint verbatim accounts of criminal activity from numerous provincial papers, usually, but not always, acknowledging the source. Then, as now, as Jeremy Black remarks, 'crime was a major draw in the press'.[9] Provincial papers in particular also carried numerous adverts of rewards offered by victims or relatives of victims after a crime had been perpetrated, and these contained often quite detailed descriptions of the suspected offender(s). As Ian Bell states, 'the cultural and ideological importance of law in eighteenth-century England ensured that it remained at the centre of public discussion throughout the period.'[10]

Those cases that were reported reflected the perceived interests of the various publications' readerships; as Jeremy Black states: 'the press was largely read by upper and middle-class consumers' and consequently 'reflected the interests and views of the middling orders'.[11] Cases that were considered of limited interest to the readership of the various publications may well therefore have been unreported in either national or local newspapers or journals. Conversely, cases involving high-profile and prominent people such as members of the aristocracy or well-known political figures often merited a considerable degree of attention. Sir Nathaniel Conant (Chief Magistrate at Bow Street), in his evidence to an 1816 Parliamentary Select Committee, was of the opinion that serious offences, 'where they are of any importance, are universally known through the newspapers'.[12]

Then as now, sensational or particularly horrific cases often made headlines. Esther Snell's recent research into the crime reporting of the *Kentish Post* in the eighteenth century has revealed a high degree of editorial selectivity in the crimes reported, with particular emphasis placed on violent crime, which accounted for 67 per cent of such reports, and murder being the third most frequently reported crime.[13] Such research suggests that even in local cases newspapers reported only those crimes that it was thought would interest their readerships. Cases occurring in other parts of the country would have had even less appeal to provincial readers (or newspaper editors), thus making it unlikely that local publications would report such instances.[14] However, misdemeanours of extremely limited local interest were often published in local newspapers in the form of formal apologies or letters disputing another correspondent's viewpoint. This was certainly the case in eighteenth- and early nineteenth-century Yorkshire, where there are several examples of advertisements placed by individuals seeking redress or absolution for offences, such as the very public apology issued by a prospective defendant in an assault upon a Worsted Inspector in 1821 in exchange for the dropping of a prosecution for assault:

> PARDON ASKED – WHEREAS I, LEVI WARD, of Clayton, in the County of York, Weaver, did, on the 31st Day of July last, assault and ill-treat Mr Benjamin Wood, of Bowling, Inspector of Worsted Yarn, for which Offence he has commenced a Prosecution; but on my agreeing to ask his Pardon and pay Expenses, he has consented to stop the Prosecution. I do, therefore, most humbly ASK his PARDON, and thank him for his Lenity, and promise never to be guilty of the like Offence again.[15]

The reporting of criminal cases did not always meet with the approval of all those involved in the criminal justice system, as is illustrated in the following case study.

Case study 18: Reverend Robert Bingham, fraudulent arson, 1811

On Sunday 16 December 1810 the Reverend Robert Bingham, the 43-year-old curate of Maresfield, Ashdown Forest, Sussex,[16] alleged that he was riding down the main street towards his home when he saw a piece of paper on the ground in front of his horse. He picked it up and found that it contained the following threatening letter:

MURDER! FIRE! and REVENGE!

Fifty of us are determined to keep our lands or have revenge. Therefore Parson, Churchwards and Farmer your Barns and Houses shall burn if you take over Lands, your lives two shall pay Your Sheep we will eat – Your Oxen we can mame your Stacks shall blaze and DICK you shall be shuted as you return home from the market or fare. We are united and sworn to stand by one another. Fifty good fellows.[17]

Bingham took the note to his friend and neighbour, Richard Jenner, who was a farmer and thought to be the 'Dick' referred to in the letter. Both Bingham and Jenner were therefore disturbed by the letter, as there was also continuing trouble between the residents of Maresfield and the Ashdown Foresters, described in one contemporary account as 'a set of people who established themselves in the Forest, and lived chiefly on plundering the farmers'.[18] The Foresters had enclosed several parts of Ashdown Forest in order to create small-holdings, thus angering the local farmers, who relied on the Forest for pannage and other benefits.[19]

After the contents of the threatening letter were made public 200 guineas were offered in reward, but no one came forward with information. On the night of 17 January 1811 Reverend Bingham's house and outbuildings were set alight and many of the contents of the house were apparently consumed by fire. Lord Sheffield immediately contacted Bow Street and on 21 January 1811 Harry Adkins, an experienced Principal Officer, arrived at Bingham's badly damaged house to investigate the arson attack.

Adkins examined the available evidence and rapidly came to the conclusion that Bingham had in fact both written the threatening letter and set fire to the house himself in order to claim the £1,050 for which he had insured the property in 1810 with the Union Fire Office. Bingham was accused of burying considerable amounts of his property (including a quantity of silver plate) before and during the fire. He was also reported as saying that he was unable to get water with which to attempt to extinguish the fire except from a 75-foot-deep well. However, the jury at his subsequent trial was told by prosecuting counsel that 'there was a pond of water close by, and also a bucket in the wash-house, and he might have helped himself to water'.[20]

In his evidence to the court Harry Adkins stated that when he arrived at the burnt-out house he was asked by Bingham if he had a warrant. He had, and Bingham then demanded a sight of it. Adkins then stated:

He says, now then I must submit. Immediately upon that, he said, if you will burn that warrant, I will give you all the information you want. I told him it would answer no purpose to burn the warrant, as I could take him without it'.[21]

Bingham's trial took place on 26 March 1811 before Chief Baron Archibald McDonald at Horsham General Assizes. He was tried on two separate offences – writing a threatening letter to his neighbour, Richard Jenner, and for arson committed on his own property. After a trial lasting twelve and a half hours, in which Bingham conducted his own defence, he was acquitted of the first charge after the jury had retired for half an hour. He was then immediately tried with the second offence of arson and again found not guilty, the jury this time taking just one minute to consider their verdict.

The Reverend Bingham clearly had influential friends and contacts; several Reverends were called by him as character witnesses, as were his brother, Richard, who was himself a magistrate and clergyman, and his other brother, Joseph, who held senior rank as a Post-Captain in the Royal Navy.[22] He also utilized his relationship with Lord Sheffield to its maximum potential, with Sheffield providing Bingham with a good character reference, although there is circumstantial evidence that Sheffield thought Bingham may have been guilty, as Sheffield's solicitor, Edward Verrel of Lewes, expressed grave doubts about Sheffield defending Bingham.[23]

The trial judge, Archibald MacDonald, clearly took these character references seriously, stating in his summing up of the case to the jury that 'if you entertain serious doubts, you will throw the excellent character he has received from the honourable and respectable witnesses into the gale.'[24] The judge continued, suggesting that Reverend Bingham was a gentleman and a man of the cloth and, as such, had impeccable moral credentials:

> The character and morals [. . .] of the Reverend were of such a nature that he did not know, nor could conceive what motive he could have for committing such a dreadful crime [. . .] he could not surely commit such an act of ingratitude and injustice.[25]

After the 'not guilty' verdicts had been given Bingham must have hoped that he would be allowed to stay as curate at Maresfield, but this was clearly thought to be inadvisable by his superiors. Lord Sheffield corresponded with the bishop of Chichester, John Buckner, on Bingham's fate and the two men jointly refused to accede to Bingham's two brothers' entreaties that Bingham be allowed to continue at Maresfield. Bishop Buckner suggested a curacy in 'some distant county', or a mission, either in the West Indies or North America. Bingham's eventual fate is unknown.[26]

The trial was extremely well publicized, generating considerable interest in the London press as well as the local newspapers. At least two accounts of the trial were printed for circulation, with one enterprising printer advertising his pamphlet of thirty-two pages for sale at 2s. 6d.[27]

Accounts of the case also appeared in the London papers well before the trial had begun, some within a few days of Adkins' investigation. This was much to the chagrin of the presiding judge, who was extremely concerned about the prejudicial nature of much of the reporting, as illustrated in the following report:

> Upon the officer's arrival, after making inquiries, he strongly suspected that Mr Bingham had set his own house on fire, and in consequence placed several men to watch. One of them he stationed in the steeple of the church, when they discovered him [Bingham] to bring a great quantity of books from the stable, and bury them in the garden. From a variety of other suspicious circumstances, a warrant was granted against Mr Bingham, and one to search his premises, when Adkins found in the roof of the privy, a variety of valuable papers concealed, together with other suspicious circumstances of his having set his premises on fire for the purpose of defrauding the Union Fire Office. . .[28]

Bow Street was heavily implicated in this respect, the judge questioning Officer Adkins as to how the London press could have got hold of some of the more private facts about his investigation. Adkins was asked if his examination – that is, his questioning of Reverend Bingham – was conducted in private. Adkins confirmed that the interview had taken place in private and was then asked to explain, if this indeed was the situation, how the facts of the examination had reached the newspapers. Adkins replied that:

> It was the usual way, when they had been in the country, on their return to the office, to give Mr Read [Bow Street Chief Magistrate] an account of what they had done. While he was relating to Mr Read the present case, the Editor of their paper, meaning the *Hue & Cry*, was in the office; and the witness cannot account for its appearance in the papers through any other means[29]

The judge was highly critical of such behaviour, stating:

> I am extremely sorry that, when this officer made a report of what he had heard and seen of this business to Justice Read, that any editor of a newspaper should have been present, and have taken notes of what was stated by Adkins to the magistrate at Bow Street, and that partial statements should have been inserted in the public newspapers, in order to inflame the public mind; it ought to be severely punished; it has an effect on persons in some of the highest situations in this country; it poisons the minds of juries and witnesses; it is the most pernicious thing that can be done in thwarting the administration of justice; it may be turned to the very worst purposes.[30]

This appears to have been something of a running sore between Bow Street Chief Magistrates and the judiciary. Bow Street Chief Magistrate from 1821 to 1832, Sir Richard Birnie, was known to be in favour of the public reporting of police reports. The *Manchester Guardian* remarked in its edition of 3 January 1824 that:

> Sir Richard, we perceive has been sneeringly echoing – in a case where the publication of a police report has just led to the detention of a thief – the solemn twaddle of Mr Justice Park, about the mischief of publishing police reports. What a mortification it must be to the knight of the common pleas, to be so snubbed by his Bow Street brother![31]

The concern voiced by the judge in the case of the Reverend Bingham seems to have stemmed as much from his dissatisfaction at having the name of a 'gentleman' besmirched in public as from a concern about the implications of prejudicing a jury.

Bow Street officials had always utilized the press as a means of both disseminating information about crime and advertising the availability and success of the Bow Street Principal Officers:

> Whereas many thieves and robbers daily escape justice for want of immediate pursuit, it is therefore recommended to all persons, who shall henceforth be robbed on the highway or in the streets, or whose shops or houses shall be broken open, that they give immediate notice thereof, together with as accurate a description of the offenders as possible, to John Fielding, Esq., at his house in Bow Street, Covent Garden: By which means, joined to an advertisement, containing a description of the things lost (which is also taken in there) thieves and robbers will seldom escape: as most of the principal pawnbrokers taking this paper, and by the intelligence they get from it assist daily in discovering and apprehending rogues. And if they would send a special messenger on these occasion, Mr Fielding would not only pay that messenger for his trouble, but would immediately despatch a set of brave fellows in pursuit, who have been long engaged for such purposes, and are always ready to set out to any part of this town or kingdom, on a quarter of an hour's notice. It is to be hoped that the late success of this plan will make all persons for the future industrious to give the earliest notice possible of all robberies and robbers whatever.[32]

From the time of the creation of the Principal Officers the Fieldings were keen to publicize the Officers' existence in an attempt to increase the reporting and solving of crime (although, for obvious reasons, the Officers' individual identities were not widely circulated). Henry Fielding began the process with the short-lived *Covent Garden Journal*, which ran from 1752 to 1756, and his half-brother John continued with the publication of the *Public Advertiser* from late 1754, followed by the *Quarterly* and *Weekly Pursuit* in 1772.[33] On 3 December 1773 John published the first edition of Fielding's General Preventive Plan or *Public Hue & Cry*. The first edition claimed that:

> the front page of this newspaper is stuck up in the Market Place of every Corporate Town from Cornwall to Edinburgh, by order of the mayors and

chief officers of such corporations and also in some conspicuous place of the Public Road, by the Magistrates of the counties at large to which it is sent.[34]

The publication was often flagrant in the self-promotion of the Bow Street system of policing; for example, in 1809 it carried details of the robbery of the Whitehaven Bank, in which some £15,000 was stolen, remarking that the particular nature of the case 'renders it extremely difficult for any other than the Bow Street police to discover, explore and trace'.[35] The other constituents of the Bow Street police were also often praised for their effectiveness; in 1816 it referred to a case involving the Horse Patrol, 'whom scarcely any robber can escape', while in 1822 it reported that 'the Day Patrol lately established at Bow Street has already been of great service in clearing the streets of pick-pockets; the most experienced men of the Night Patrol having been appointed to this service.'[36]

The effectiveness of *Hue & Cry* was often called into question later, but the 1818 Select Committee Report mentions it favourably in the context of dissemination of information, at least with regard to more serious offences:

> Your Committee are of opinion that [. . .] the more enormous offences are at present rapidly published and circulated, by the diurnal press, the correspondence of magistrates, and the *Hue & Cry and Police Gazette*'.[37]

That the publication of serious crimes in *Hue & Cry* was still seen as a useful strategy for provincial law-enforcement bodies in 1839 is exemplified in the evidence of Mr Sadler, High Constable of Stockport, to the 1839 Select Committee on the Constabulary Force in England and Wales. He was asked what measures he usually adopted when he received notice of a serious felony and replied that he instructed local searches and investigations to be carried out, including the interviewing of all known local fences and suspects, but, if these investigations were unforthcoming, he stated that 'it may be requisite to send to the *Hue & Cry* in London, and advertise and adopt any measures that may be expedient.'[38] Sadler's evidence suggests that, even at the end of the period under discussion, advertising details of provincial felonies in *Hue & Cry* was still considered to be a worthwhile activity.

Whatever the perceived efficacy of *Hue & Cry*, it has certainly been underutilized in the subsequent study of policing history. It is of significant interest not just for the activities of the various London Police Offices but also for the considerable amount of detail that it carries about the formative years of the Metropolitan Police and the interaction between existing law-enforcement agencies and the newly created force.[39]

Ordinarys' *Accounts*, trial pamphlets and broadsides

The printing of accounts of Bingham's trial was by no means unusual and such accounts, normally cut-down versions of notes taken in shorthand, were by no means the only way in which crimes and the offenders who had perpetrated them were brought to the attention of the public. One of the most popular alternatives (at least for London-based crimes) was the Ordinarys' *Accounts*, as illustrated in the following case study.

Case study 19: Richard Brabant, forgery, 1741

On 21 March 1741 the *London Daily Post & General Advertiser* carried the following advertisement:

> This Day is published Price 6d By John Applebee, Printer in Bolt-Court, Fleet-Street;
>
> The Ordinary of Newgate's Account of the Behaviour, Confession, and Last Dying Words of the Twenty Malefactors, executed on Wednesday at Tyburn. Containing a particular Account of the Life of Daniel Jackson (condemn'd for the Murder of his Wife) who died in Newgate; of John Catt the famous smuggler (who which several others attempted to escape out of Newgate) with the various Methods taken by him to become Captain of the Gang; of Richard Brabant, for defrauding Messrs Martin and Comp. of 60 Guineas, by counterfeiting the Hand of Mr James Tipper . . .[40]

John Applebee (*c.* 1690–1750) was an enterprising printer who published a sensationalist newspaper, the *Original Weekly Journal* (renamed *Applebee's Original Weekly Journal*), between 1715 and 1737. He specialized in crime reporting, printing accounts of the exploits of Jonathan Wild and John Shepherd aka Jack Sheppard, the notorious thief and gaol-breaker (of whom more later), and was also responsible for many editions of the *Ordinary of Newgate's Accounts.*

The Ordinary of Newgate, the chaplain for Newgate Gaol, was in a privileged position with regard to access to incarcerated prisoners, many of whom were being held there pending their execution at Tyburn. A perquisite of his post was that he was allowed to interview the prisoners and publish his account of their lives and crimes. This could earn him up to £200 per year and was a valuable addition to his salary as chaplain.[41] An account of 1812 detailed the duties of the Ordinary at Newgate:

> The chaplain, or ordinary of Newgate (at present the Rev. Mr. Cotton, an able and indefatigable man) receives £265 per annum. For that sum, he reads prayers twice on Sundays, on Wednesdays and Fridays, preaches every Sunday morning, repeats private prayers with those under sentence of death, on Tuesday and Thursday, and, after the report, attends criminals twice a-day, and on the morning of execution.[42]

The earliest Ordinary's *Accounts* date to the mid-1670s and from 1684 their publication was regulated by the City of London. At the time of the above publication the Ordinary was James Guthrie, a former curate and Latin schoolmaster, who served as Ordinary from 1725 to 1746 and stepped down with an annual pension of £40.[43]

The *Accounts* of the Ordinary catered to an ever-growing appetite for literary details of malefactors and their crimes; they were part of a canon of literature designed to meet the needs of a sector of the public that craved accounts of sensational crimes as thinly veiled 'morality tales'. This interest, which had been stimulated by the rapid growth of newspapers and advances in technology that enabled publishers to rush out cheaply printed editions containing 'verbatim' trial reports, broadsheets and penny ballads, all purporting to deliver a moral message while containing lurid and graphic details of the crimes of the offender who had recently received the penalty of death,[44] can be illustrated by examining the life and crimes of the last of those twenty unfortunate individuals who met their death on Wednesday 18 March 1741 – namely Richard Brabant, who was executed for two counts of forgery.[45]

We learn from the Ordinary that Brabant, the son of a farmer, was born 'in the Year 1720, in the Parish of Mellsum [Melksham], near Sandy Lane, in the County of Wilts'. He received a limited education at a private boarding school in Bristol and became 'a good Proficient in Writing and Accompts, and acquired some small Knowledge in the Latin Tongue'.[46] After a troubled home life he travelled through the south-west of England for a short while before visiting his former schoolteacher Mr Jones at the Bristol boarding school, where he was taken on as an assistant. He remained there for six months, but became restless and set out for London, where he arrived in January 1739. He quickly fell in with disreputable company, however, and with an Irishman, John Farrell, who pretended to be a solicitor, began to fraudulently represent himself in bail cases at the King's Bench.[47]

From the ill-gotten gains that he accrued from this work he represented himself as a man of means in search of a wealthy wife. However, it was a case of the biter almost bit, as he was presented to a 'Lady of Fortune' who turned out to be Betty Jones, the keeper of a notorious coffee house in Drury Lane.[48] Disillusioned, Brabant left Farrell's company and went to work for James Tipper, a 'Gentleman of Business', who employed him as a bookkeeper and accountant. Brabant had worked in Tipper's service for four months when business required Tipper's absence and he left an order with Brabant for the remittance of £2 10s. for a relation.[49] Instead of delivering the remittance Brabant instead recognized an opportunity to profit from Tipper's trust; returning to his lodgings, he opened the order and practised forging Tipper's handwriting. The next morning he submitted a forged order made out to Thomas Noble, whom he represented himself as, to Mr Tipper's bankers, and received £52 10s. in return. Within the next couple of days he submitted another forged order for £10 10s. and was again successful in defrauding the bank. With this considerable amount of money, Brabant employed a servant and represented himself once again as a man of fortune. An acquaintance of his recommended another supposed heiress to Brabant, who stated to the Ordinary that:

I was glad of the Proposal, and desired to see her there the next Day at Dinner. After Dinner, and drinking plentifully, I was very sweet upon my new Lady, when it was agreed that she should stay with me that Night, upon Condition, of my marrying her the next Morning.[50]

This somewhat unorthodox courtship resulted in Brabant and the young lady, Elizabeth Harrison, marrying at the Two Sawyers public house, Fleet Lane, on 13 January 1741.[51] They could marry in such haste because of a legal quirk that meant that the Fleet Prison and its environs was exempt from the requirement that the prospective bride and groom could be married only in their home parish after the publication of banns or after procuring a marriage licence. Many disreputable or disgraced clergymen took advantage of this by marrying couples quickly with 'no questions asked'; at the time that Brabant and his fiancée married more than 6,000 such marriages were taking place at the Fleet each year. This situation eventually proved intolerable to both the Church of England and the government and in 1753 Lord Hardwicke's Marriage Act (26 Geo. II. c.33) banned such ceremonies, with clergymen under pain of transportation for carrying out a clandestine marriage.[52]

Brabant seems to have regretted his choice of bride almost immediately; he complained to the Ordinary that his new wife had received a diamond ring costing five guineas from him 'which I have often since repented, she never sending or bringing me any Relief since my Confinement'. She seems also to have misled him about both her prospects and her past, as he subsequently discovered that she had two young children by the acquaintance who had recommended her to Brabant. Contemporary newspapers also reminded any female readers of the dangers of marrying in haste:

> This ought to be a Caution to all Women, whom they marry, and not to be taken with an *outside Appearance*; for if this Lady had had but Patience and common Prudence, and enquired after him, she might have discovered the Trick.[53]

In fact, Brabant appears to have been generally unlucky in both love and his choice of misdeed; apart from his disastrous love-life, he was unfortunate in that his altering of Mr Tipper's order placed his offence under the remit of the recently passed Forgery Act 1733 (7 Geo. II c.22) which made it a capital one, without benefit of clergy. Brabant suspected that his newly acquired manservant had some inkling of Brabant's nefarious activities and told an acquaintance that 'if he could get my Man John pressed, I would give him 5 Guineas'.[54] His servant found out about this plan and immediately reported Brabant's whereabouts to Mr Tipper's clerk, who obtained a warrant from Bow Street Magistrate's Court; Brabant was subsequently apprehended near his lodgings. He denied the charges, but was taken into custody at Bow Street, where Colonel De Veil committed him to Newgate Gaol to await his trial at the Old Bailey.

While in custody at Newgate Brabant determined to escape and, as he could afford to be kept on the Master's side of Newgate,[55] the turnkey (gaoler) had relatively little opportunity to see and therefore recognize him. Brabant tried to bribe a fellow prisoner to cut off his irons and to sell Brabant his waistcoat and breeches for £2 5s., as was reported in the press:

> Last week the abovesaid Richard Brabant attempted his escape out of the Master's Side in Newgate, and for that purpose had sawed his irons asunder, and was about changing his clothes with another prisoner, but was discovered by the Turnkey.[56]

Unfortunately his plan was discovered by another prisoner, who informed the turnkey, and Brabant was taken in double irons to the much less salubrious Commons' side of Newgate, from where he attended his trial at the Old Bailey on 25 February 1741.[57]

Brabant was charged on two counts of forgery and appeared before the Recorder of London, Sir John Strange. The post of Recorder dates back to at least 1298 and its occupant remains a senior judge who presides over cases at the Old Bailey and whose salary is paid by the City of London.[58] It was:

> requisite that he should be a grave and learned lawyer, skilful in the customs of the city; he sits with and advises the lord mayor and aldermen, and is a judge of their court, and attends the court of common council, and when especially required, the several committees by them appointed, likewise the sessions of the peace and gaol delivery. He takes place in councils and in courts before any man that hath not been mayor, and learnedly delivers the sentences of the whole court.[59]

The proceedings of the trial were reported in several newspapers, as Brabant had become something of a minor celebrity following his attempted escape, and readers following the twists and turns of the trial read that, although Brabant was a competent copyist of Mr Tipper's signature, two witnesses swore to the documents that he had submitted to the bank being forged; one observed that there was 'a Stiffness, as if the Person was got into an unusual Course: It wants the Freedom of an Original; they are pretty well done, but there is a Heaviness which will be in all Copies.'[60] It appears that Brabant may have suffered from epilepsy, as:

> whilst Sir John Strange, the Recorder, was delivering his charge to the jury, on the trial of Brabant, the prisoner fell down in a fit, and then into convulsions, and was half an hour in them, and the Recorder obliged to stay until he was come to himself, before he went on again.[61]

The case against him was proved conclusively and the jury returned a 'guilty' verdict. The Recorder then pronounced the sentence of death by hanging. Brabant was returned to Newgate gaol to await his fate, where, according to the Ordinary, he:

> own'd the Crime for which he suffered, and that no Body was concern'd in it besides himself; he was an ingenious sober Youth, and was not addicted to

those Vices which such unfortunate People for the generality are mostly given. He professed that he believed in Christ Jesus our only Saviour, and was sincerely penitent for the many Sins of his Life, especially for the Crime for which he died, and that he forgave all Men, as he expected Forgiveness from God.[62]

On 18 March 1741 Brabant was taken to Tyburn, seated on his own coffin in the seventh of eight carts, and hanged in front of a large crowd that had gathered to watch the proceedings. A tourist guidebook, published in 1740, described the procedure:

The rope being put about his neck, he is fastened to the fatal tree when a proper time being allowed for prayer and singing a hymn, the cart is withdrawn and the penitent criminal is turned with a cap over his eyes and left hanging half an hour.[63]

It further stated that 'these executions are always well attended with so great mobbing and impertinences that you ought to be on your guard when curiosity leads you there.'

Brabant's hanging took place in the days before the invention of the so-called 'New Drop', which was not in common use until the latter decades of the eighteenth century. This method of execution involved the suspension of the condemned individual over a closed trapdoor which was opened by a lever, thereby letting the body fall. This would cause the neck of the condemned to break, leading to almost instantaneous death. The 'New Drop' is defined in an 1811 dictionary of slang as 'the scaffold used at Newgate for hanging of criminals; which dropping down, leaves them suspended. By this improvement, the use of that vulgar vehicle, a cart, is entirely left off.'[64] Before the invention of the 'New Drop' it could take many minutes for the struggling individual to die through strangulation, but the 'New Drop' method itself was not infallible; too often an insufficient drop length was given, causing the individual a painful and extended period of suspension. It was not until 1872 that a longer, scientifically calculated drop length was introduced, which significantly reduced the risk of unnecessary further suffering.

Within a week of Brabant's execution the Ordinary's *Account* of his life and death was available for the public to read. The first of these, as detailed above, had a published price of 6d. (a not inconsiderable sum of money in 1741), but later expanded editions were published by Applebee in April 1742 (as part of a four-volume set of trials from 1720) at a cost of 12s. This set proved so popular that a second edition was printed in June 1742, thus indicating the voracious appetite that the public had for details of such misdeeds.

In a similar vein, 'Hanging Notices', giving details of the date and time of the hanging, together with an often highly sensationalized potted history of the case, were hurriedly printed and fly posted outside the relevant gaol. They, along with the penny ballad sheets or broadsides, which often put the lurid and shocking details of the perpetrator's offences to the tune of a popular song of the moment, served to promote ghoulish and sensational interest among the general public. This interest was as widespread in the provinces as in London, where the most notorious hanging sites, such as Tyburn, always drew large crowds at each event; 'the country people's zest for executions was just as keen as those in London, and [. . .] they would throng into the County [town] from the outlying rural area.'[65]

Methods such as those discussed above made many criminals overnight sensations (often posthumously). Considerably fewer achieved more lasting notoriety, being commemorated in plays and songs so that their escapades passed into myth and legend; witness the supposed activities of Dick Turpin, whose name is still the first brought to mind in any discussion of highwaymen.[66] One of the best known of this 'select' band of individuals is discussed in the case study below.

Case study 20: John Shepherd (aka Jack Sheppard), larceny and burglary, 1724

John Shepherd was baptized on 5 March 1702 at St Dunstan's Church, Stepney, the son of Thomas Shepherd, carpenter of Whiterow, London, and his wife, Mary.[67] His father died while John was still a child, but his mother managed to ensure that he received a rudimentary education at a school in Bishopsgate. John was encouraged to follow his father's trade, being apprenticed to a carpenter in April 1717. He seems to have drifted into a life of petty crime while still an apprentice; most biographers state that his first known crime was in 1723, but a John Shepherd was found not guilty along with an Alice Turbot of the theft of a silver tankard at the Old Bailey in late 1717, and it is possible that this is the same individual.[68] Around 1723 he fell in with a prostitute and petty thief known as Edgeworth Bess (aka Elizabeth Lyons) and in February 1724 he committed an unsuccessful burglary with her and his elder brother Thomas (b. 1697). Thomas had already come to the attention of the authorities, having been branded on the hand in 1723 for larceny. Consequently, he faced the death penalty if found guilty of a similar crime. Arrested on 24 April 1724, he subsequently informed upon his brother John and Bess.[69]

John was arrested and placed in St Giles Roundhouse (a lock-up) awaiting trial. It took him less than two hours to escape through a hole in the roof. A few weeks later, on 19 May 1724, he was once again arrested, this time for pick-pocketing, and was sent to St Anne's Roundhouse, where he was visited by Elizabeth Lyons. Unfortunately for her, she was recognized and was also locked up. They were transferred to New Prison, Clerkenwell, where on 25 May they escaped by filing through their irons and window bars, climbing down a twenty-five-foot wall with the help of bedsheets, blankets and Lyon's petticoat, and then clambering over a twenty-two-foot wall to freedom. John Geary, the Keeper of New Prison, was so embarrassed by this breach of security that on 6 July 1724 he petitioned the county JPs of Middlesex at the Quarter Sessions:

> To the right worshipful his Majesty's Justices of the Peace for the county of Middlesex in their General Quarter Sessions Assembled.

The humble petition of John Geary, Keeper of New Prison in Clerkenwell in the said county:

That your petitioner, upon John Sheppard's breaking out of the said gaol, repaired and strengthened that part of it, but their being several other parts weak and out of repair he humbly prays your Worships will be pleased to appoint a Committee to take a view and give directions for the repair of the same.[70]

On 23 July 1724 Shepherd was once more arrested and this time confined in Newgate prison.[71] He managed his third successful escape by picking the lock on his chains, loosening the bars in his cell and being smuggled out in female clothing by accomplices on 31 August 1724. The Ordinary's *Account* of 4 September 1724 bemoans the fact that he had escaped and thereby robbed the Ordinary of the chance to include his life story in his account:

JOHN SHEPHERD, a notorious Thief and House Breaker (whose Life should have been inserted in this Paper, had he not made his narrow Escape from Death on Monday last (about six in the Evening) we think it may not be improper, but of Service to the Public to remind them that he is got loose from his Chains, by an almost impracticable and unheard of Machine and Invention; and who has often said, that there was neither Lock nor Key ever made, that he should make any difficulty to open.[72]

Shepherd briefly left the capital, but was recaptured on Finchley Common and returned to Newgate, where he was returned to the condemned hold, reputedly the strongest of the cells in the prison. However, on 16 September his cell was searched and a set of lock-picking tools was found concealed in the seat of his chair, so he was moved to a fourth-storey room where he was kept in isolation and his visitors carefully monitored. He was also placed in handcuffs and chained to the floor.

On 15 October he managed to free himself from both handcuffs and chains, broke an iron bar in the chimney of the room and then clambered onto the sixty-foot-high roof of the prison. He managed to pick or break the locks on six doors before returning to his cell to pick up a blanket, which he used to lower himself onto the roof of a neighbouring house. Despite this prodigious feat, Shepherd was soon recaptured. After committing a burglary in a Drury Lane pawnshop he was arrested while extremely drunk on 31 October.

By now his daring exploits had made him famous with the London public, who flocked to see him in his cell at Newgate, but his luck had eventually run out. On 10 November he was tried at King's Bench, where he reputedly refused to turn King's Evidence and inform on his accomplices. He was subsequently ordered for execution within the next six days. On 16 November he was taken to Tyburn amid tight security and, despite many calls for the commutation of his sentence to transportation, hanged at the gallows before a huge crowd.

Shepherd's life, though brief, quickly became the stuff of legend. The *Daily Journal* of 18 November remarked that 'nothing more at present is talked about in town than Jack Sheppard.' Newspaper editors were certainly not slow in publishing their accounts of his life and exploits; for example, less than a week after his execution the *Weekly Journal or British Gazetteer* of 21 November 1724 printed 'An Abridgement of the Life, Robberies, Escapes, and Death, of John Sheppard, who was Executed at Tyburn on Monday the 16th Instant, 1724'.

Others were also quick to jump on the bandwagon of publicity. An 'autobiographical' account of his life which, it was stated, was 'not composed of Fiction, Fable or Stories placed at York, Rome or Jamaica, but Facts done at your Doors, Facts unheard of, altogether new, Incredible, and yet Uncontestable', reportedly written by Daniel Defoe, had been quickly printed and was on sale on the day of his execution, while a play written by John Thurmond entitled *Harlequin Sheppard* (subtitled 'A night scene in grotesque characters') opened at the Theatre Royal, Drury Lane, less than two weeks after his death (and was published shortly afterwards 'with an introduction giving an account of Sheppard's life').[73] His likeness was also painted by Sir James Thornhill, court painter to King George I and II, apparently while he awaited execution, and this was subsequently published as an engraving. John Gay modelled his anti-hero Macheath in *The Beggar's Opera* (1728) on Shepherd, while in the same year another play, entitled *The Quakers Opera*, was advertised in the *Daily Post* 'with Jack Sheppard's Escapes out of Newgate' forming a central part of the plot.[74] Shepherd's exploits were still apparently well known in 1747, as William Hogarth is reputed to have based the figure of the 'Idle Apprentice' in his series of paintings 'Industry and Idleness' on him.

'Rogue' pamphlets and other forms of popular literature

As James Sharpe has stated, 'the literature which helped form popular ideas on crime must be understood largely as a popular expression of disquiet at some of the symptoms of the social disruption of the period, with morally and socially desirable remedies either prescribed or implied.'[75] From the sixteenth century onward, the development of printing led to an explosion in popular literature dealing with peoples' fear and interest in crime and criminal behaviour.

One of the earliest tracts to deal with criminals and their behaviour was the *Caveat for Common Cursitors*, written by Thomas Harman, a member of the Kentish gentry, and first published in 1566.[76]. During the eighteenth century 'rogue' pamphleteers such as Captain Alexander Smith continued to churn out material such as his *An History of the Lives of the most noted Highwaymen, Footpads, Housebreakers, Shoplifts, and other Malefactors of both sexes, which have been executed in and about London and other parts of Great Britain, for above a hundred years last past: With a whole discovery of the art and mystery of Theft; to the end all honest people may be prevented from being robbed for the future*, first published in London in 1714. In a similar vein the publication of the *Malefactor's Bloody Register* and the *Chronicle of Tyburn* in the early decades of the eighteenth century rode upon the back of the popularity of such 'rogue' pamphleteers.[77] Such publications (eventually becoming known by the generic title of *Newgate Calendars*) were compiled from the broadsides and chapbooks (bound collections of pamphlets) that in turn resulted from accounts of trials conducted at the Old Bailey (and, occasionally, other criminal courts). These calendars fed the general public's seemingly inexhaustible appetite; as Bell states, 'the notion of a widespread criminal class stealthily at work throughout the land, a furtive and nefarious mirror-image of the frightened hard-working citizen, was a very potent idea in the eighteenth-century popular imagination.'[78]

Contemporary criminological debate

In contrast to the sensationalist and often wildly inaccurate popular crime literature of the day, such as that written about Shepherd or Wild, other writers were taking a more serious and considered approach to the problems of crime and criminals. One of the first publications to argue from a more informed perspective was Henry Fielding's *An Enquiry into the Causes of the Late Increase of Robbers etc., with some Proposals for Remedying this Growing Evil*, published in London in 1751, in which he argued strongly for more systematic and effective methods of preventing and detecting the marauding gangs of highway robbers that frequented the turnpiked outskirts of London.[79] The baton was taken up following his premature death in 1754 by his half-brother, John Fielding, Chief Magistrate at Bow Street Public Office, who, in his *Plan for Preventing Robberies within Twenty Miles of London, with an Account of the Rise and Establishment of the Real Thieftakers*, published in October 1754, detailed his views on the best means of providing an effective law-enforcement body.[80] Sir John also employed a register clerk in 1756 to compile a register 'to take all Informations and Descriptions of suspicious Persons, Robbers, and things stolen' in an attempt to create a database of offending and offenders.[81]

This system was continued and refined under subsequent magistrates, with a later register clerk, Nicholas Bond, being charged with 'completing the Register of Robberies, Informations, Examinations, Convictions, suspicious Book, and Newgate Calendars'.[82] These London-based developments could perhaps be seen as the first inchoate and imperfect attempts to collate what the habitual offenders' registers of the mid-nineteenth century later also attempted to achieve for the whole of England and Wales.[83]

Further serious and semi-systematic research into criminality and its policing was published in 1796 by Patrick Colquhoun (a Glaswegian merchant, erstwhile financial backer of slaving ships, stipendiary magistrate and influential political commentator) in the form of his *Treatise on the Police of the Metropolis: containing a Detail of the Various Crimes and Misdemeanours by which Public and Private Property and Security are, at present, injured and endangered: and suggesting Remedies for their Prevention*.[84] In this treatise Colquhoun dealt with both habitual petty offenders, including prostitutes and beggars, and the more serious crimes of highway robbery and burglary. Property crime was by this time becoming the criminal activity most hotly debated among such commentators.[85]

Colquhoun was not alone in considering the problems of criminality and policing, but his *Treatise* was one of the first publications to rely on statistical 'evidence' to further its argument.[86] Colquhoun's investigations were carried out at a time when the state seems to have first shown an interest in establishing how many habitual offenders were roaming the streets of England's cities and towns. Official crime statistics were first compiled in 1805 (although it was to be another half-century before these were utilized in a recognizably modern way in the annual publication of *Judicial Statistics*). The use of such statistics in attempts to quantify the level of crime has been often questioned by later historians and criminologists, but for contemporaries they did provide at the very least a measure of perceived criminality, albeit a deeply flawed one; in 1815 Patrick Colquhoun confidently announced that around 1.3 million of Britain's total population of *c*. 10.5 million were indigent or criminal (and many contemporaries did not often differentiate between the two).[87]

In subsequent editions of his *Treatise* Colquhoun gathered information to show how many prisoners were released back into society each year from 1792 to 1799 inclusive (a total of 21,893) and lamented the fact that 'many convicts, from dire necessity, return to their old courses'.[88] He argued that many such offenders formed gangs of habitual depredators, and that:

> robbery and theft, as well in houses and on the roads, have long been reduced to a regular system. Opportunities are watched, and intelligence procured, with a degree of vigilance similar to that which marks the conduct of a skilful General'.[89]

He estimated that some £2 million per year was being stolen in one form or another from the metropolis.[90] The *Treatise* was somewhat unusual in that, far from merely being a polemic about what was wrong with the legislative and executive system with regard to habitual offenders, it offered remedies such as the creation of a central Board of Police, detailed in a letter by Colquhoun dated 3 May 1798, one of the suggestions of which was:

> To establish a correspondence with a select number of the most active and intelligent Magistrates in every part of Great Britain, for the purpose of communicating and receiving intelligence relative to criminal offences, and of detecting Offenders of all descriptions, but particularly those depraved characters who generally leave the Metropolis in the Spring, after the drawing of the Lottery, and frequent fairs with E.O. tables, counterfeit money, stolen and smuggled goods, for the purpose of cheating and defrauding the most ignorant class of the country population.[91]

Conclusion

We have seen above that the eighteenth century was a period of considerable popular interest in crime and criminals. The emergence of an increasingly literate society coincided with the rapid and exponential growth in the popularity and availability of newspapers to the middle classes, while the illustrated broadsides and penny ballads catered for another less literate but still interested audience.

While some offenders became notorious in many forms of popular literature and culture for their daring escapades, the period also saw the first tentative development of serious criminological theorizing, with the Enlightenment stimulating discussions about crime and criminals and the ways in which their increase might be prevented. These discussions led both directly and indirectly to major changes to the criminal justice system and the ways in which England was policed during the following century, a legacy that is discussed in the following chapter.

Notes

1 *Manchester Guardian*, 29 May 1830.
2 J. Black, *The English Press 1621–1861* (Stroud: Sutton, 2001), p. 9.
3 The best accounts of the development of newspapers from the early seventeenth century corantos to the broadsheets of the nineteenth century remain Black, *The English Press*; J. Black, *The English Press in the Eighteenth Century* (Beckenham: Croom Helm, 1987), and Hannah Barker, *Newspapers, Politics and Public Opinion in Late Eighteenth-Century England* (Oxford: Clarendon Press, 1998). For popular literature other than newspapers, the most important book in this field of research remains Ian Bell's *Literature and Crime*.
4 *Staffordshire Advertiser*, 18 April 1795.
5 J. Golby, 'Newspapers', in Drake, M., Finegan, R. and Eustace, J. (eds), *Sources and Methods for Family and Community History: A Handbook*, Vol. 4 (Cambridge: CUP/OU, 1997), pp. 98–102: p. 99.
6 Ibid.
7 Raymond Williams, 'The Press and Popular Culture: An Historical Perspective', in Boyce G., *et al.*, *Newspaper History from the Seventeenth Century to the Present Day* (London: Constable, 1978), pp. 41–50: p. 51.
8 Ivan Asquith, 'The Structure, Ownership and Control of the Press, 1780–1855', in Boyce, G. *et al.*, *Newspaper History from the Seventeenth Century to the Present Day* (London: Constable, 1978), pp. 98–116: p. 100.
9 Black, *The English Press*, p. 54.
10 Bell, *Literature and Crime*, p. 12.
11 Black, *The English Press*, pp. 19 and 106.
12 *Report from the Committee on the state of Police of the Metropolis*, vol. V, p. 11.
13 Esther Snell, 'Representations of Crime in the Eighteenth-century Newspaper: The Construction of Crime Reportage in the Kentish Post' (paper delivered at the European Centre for Policing Studies, Open University, Milton Keynes, March 2005). Her research was part of a PhD thesis: 'Attitudes to Violent Crime in Post-Restoration England' (unpublished thesis, Canterbury University, 2005). See also Esther Snell, 'Discourses of Criminality in the Eighteenth-century Press: The Presentation of Crime in The Kentish Post, 1717–1768', *Continuity and Change* 22.1 (2007): 13–47.
14 Shane Sullivan has recently completed a PhD thesis on the subject of informal justice ('Law and Informal Order: Informal Mechanisms of Justice in Kent, 1700–1880' [Canterbury, 2005]) and his paper 'The Newspaper Apology as a Secular Penance 1768–1820', given at the European Centre for Policing Studies, Open University in October 2005, discussed the use of newspapers for the informal settling of mainly petty disputes, suggesting that, on occasion, such a method could also be used as an alternative to a court appearance in quite serious cases such as assault.

15 *Leeds Mercury*, 20 October 1821.
16 Bingham first became curate at Maresfield in 1804 and lived in apparent harmony there with his wife and twelve children. In addition to his work as well as being a curate, he ran a small private school for farmers' children. In September 1810 he wrote a letter to the local magistrates suggesting that a Mr Goldspring, keeper of the Hare and Hounds public house in Maresfield, not have his licence granted. Later in the same month, Bingham's stables were burnt, after threatening letters were apparently received. Rewards totalling £100 were offered by Lord Sheffield of Sheffield Park (a personal friend of Bingham), the Union Fire Office (with whom Bingham had insured the stables) and Bingham. No one was traced in connection with the arson attack, but Bingham received a settlement of £187 6s. 2d. from the Union Fire Office in October 1810.
17 Anon., *The Trial of the Reverend Robert Bingham, taken in shorthand by Mr Adams, by order of the Directors of The Union Fire Office, London* (London: J. M. Richardson, 1811), p. 10. This publication was a 239-page verbatim account of the trial recorded at the behest of the Union Fire Office for their records. As the trial had aroused considerable interest with the public, this account was subsequently published.
18 Ibid., p. 16.
19 Pannage was the ancient right of grazing pigs on common land.
20 Anon., *The Trial of the Reverend Robert Bingham, taken in shorthand*, pp. 128–9.
21 Ibid., p. 159.
22 Reverend Richard Bingham later became a canon at Chichester, but in 1813 was imprisoned for six months at Winchester for fraudulently obtaining a licence for a public house in his capacity as magistrate for Hampshire. (see East Sussex Record Office: Notes on Bingham case AMS 6403 and PRO 30/45/1/11 f. 127). A Post-Captain was a captain whose name had been posted in the Royal Navy seniority lists, was usually in command of a ship and was therefore considered to be of more senior rank than a normal captain.
23 East Sussex Record Office AMS 6403.
24 Anon., *The Trial of the Reverend Robert Bingham, taken in shorthand*, p. 123.
25 Anon., *The Trial of the Reverend Robert Bingham, Curate of Maresfield, Tuesday March 26th 1811* (Lewes: Sussex Press, 1811), p. 17.
26 East Sussex Record Office: Notes on Bingham case AMS 6403.
27 W. H. Johnson, *Previous Offences: Sussex Crimes and Punishments in the Past* (Seaford: SB Publications, 1997), p. 29.
28 *Lancaster Gazette and General Advertiser*, 16 February 1811.
29 Anon., *The Trial of the Reverend Robert Bingham, Curate of Maresfield*, p. 21.
30 Anon., *The Trial of the Reverend Robert Bingham, taken in shorthand*, p. 226.
31 Justice Park was the Chief Magistrate at the Court of Common Pleas, one of the superior courts of civil law. Jeremy Black gives several examples whereby newspaper editors pronounced the value of newspaper reports in apprehending suspects and preventing crimes – see Black, *The English Press*, p. 54.
32 *Public Advertiser*, 17 October 1754.
33 The *Covent Garden Journal* was first published in January 1752 and ran until Henry's death. In October 1754 the *Public Advertiser* was introduced, continuing in various guises until 1794. The *Quarterly* and *Weekly Pursuit* were sent out free to justices of the peace on request.
34 *Hue & Cry*, 3 December 1773, Shropshire Archives QS 20/1.
35 *Hue & Cry*, 1 April 1809. In this instance, *Hue* & Cry's peroration on behalf of the superiority of Principal Officers proved justified – the perpetrators were successfully captured and tried.
36 *Hue & Cry*, 14 December 1816 and 16 November 1822.
37 Henry Goddard, *Memoirs* (4-volume manuscript, 1875–79), Vol. 1, pp. 12 and 33, and *Third Report from the Committee on the state of Police of the Metropolis (423)* (London: House of Commons, 1817), vol. VIII, p. 23.

38 *First Report of the Commissioners appointed to inquire as to the best means of estab-lishing an efficient Constabulary Force*, vol. XIX, p. 109.

39 A concise history of the development of *Hue & Cry* can be found in Les Waters, 'Paper Pursuit: A Brief Account of the History of the Police Gazette', *Journal of the Police History Society* 1 (1986): 30–41.

40 For a debate as to the contributors to *Applebee's Original Weekly Journal* see M. Novak, 'Daniel Defoe and Applebee's Original Weekly Journal: An Attempt at Re-Attribution', *Eighteenth-Century Studies* 45.4 (2012): 585–608.

41 For a discussion of the accuracy of the Accounts and the sometimes difficult work of the Ordinary, see Linebaugh, 'The Ordinary of Newgate and his Account'.

42 Taken from Samuel Leigh, *Leigh's New Picture of London* (London: W. Clowes, 1819), reproduced unpaginated at www.londonancestor.com/leighs/pri-newgate.htm.

43 Linebaugh, 'The Ordinary of Newgate and his Account', p. 249.

44 For further discussions of broadsides/broadsheets, see Fumerton, *Ballads and Broad-sides in Britain*, and for a detailed account of the development and use of broadsheets (also known as broadsides) in the nineteenth century, see Kate Bates, 'Morality for the Masses: The Social Significance of Crime and Punishment Discourse in British Broadsides, 1800–1850' (unpublished PhD thesis, Keele University, 2012). Bates argues that the broadsides served a strong moral purpose and that the information contained within them was fundamentally accurate. She argues that far from being simply cheaply produced sensationalist literature such publications fulfilled a crucial role in educating their readers (mainly the labouring classes) in the criminal justice process, and that they also did not shy away from discussing and interpreting the courts' verdicts. Good electronic collections of broadsides can be found at www. broadsides.law.harvard.edu/ and the National Library of Scotland collection of 2,000 broadsides with a searchable index (www.nls.uk/broadsides/index.html).

45 The twenty individuals comprised sixteen men and four women. The date 18 March 1741 was one of Tyburn's busiest days with regard to executions; it was to be another forty years plus before as large a number of individuals was again hanged on one day. The most infamous of those hanged on the same day as Brabant was Mary Young aka Jenny Diver.

46 OA 17410318.

47 By this time the court of King's Bench (originally deriving from the curia regis, or King's Court, which attended the king on his travels), had become one of the three law courts which had jurisdiction over common (rather than criminal) law.

48 OA 17410318.

49 OA 17410318.

50 OA 17410318.

51 TNA RG7/730 Walter Wyatt's Notebook of the Fleet marriages performed accord-ing to the rules of the Fleet, London. Brabant's occupation is recorded as 'Gentleman'. Wyatt was one of the most notorious of the Fleet parsons, and was reputed to have made over £700 per year from his work – see A. Griffiths, *The History and Romance of Crime from the Earliest Time to the Present Day* (London: Grolier, 1900), p. 69.

52 The Act did not apply in Scotland, making Gretna Green the new choice of location for eloping couples until 1856, when the law was applied throughout Great Britain.

53 *London Evening Post*, 22–24 January 1741 (original emphasis).

54 OA 17410318. 'Pressed' refers to the activity of impressment by the Royal Navy, by which men between the ages of 18 and 55 (following an Act of Parliament in 1740) could be forcibly seized by the Navy in order to serve on board a naval vessel. This was meant to apply only to vagrants or 'disreputables' who did not have an appren-ticeship and who had seafaring experience, but in practice the Navy needed a large supply of men and was not too particular about how it acquired them. Impressment continued until the mid-nineteenth century, when pensions were instigated for those

sailors who wished to make the Navy a permanent career, thereby reducing the need for the constant replenishment of 'recruits'.

55 Newgate was a notorious gaol in which a system of payments operated in order that wealthier prisoners could be more comfortably imprisoned. Katherine Frank states that 'wealthier miscreants paid 22s. 6d. a week to stay in the relatively comfortable "Masters' Side", though such luxury as it offered was expensive: an additional charge of 3s. 6d. a week for beds and a daily charge of 1s.6d. for visitors' (K. Frank, *Crusoe: Daniel Defoe, Robert Knox And The Creation Of A Myth* [London: Random House, 2011], p. 148). Conversely, the Commons' Side offered no beds or light and little ventilation.

56 *London Evening Post*, 28 February–3 March 1741.

57 'Double irons' were heavy iron chains weighing up to 14 lb (6 kg), usually fastened around the legs to impede movement and possible escape.

58 For further details of the history of the post of Recorder, see Sir Lawrence Verney's paper 'The office of recorder of the city of London', read at the Guildhall, 30 October 2000 and available online at www.guildhallhistoricalassociation.org.uk/docs/ The%20Office%20of%20Recorder%20of%20the%20City%20of%20London.pdf.

59 T. Allen, *The History and Antiquities of London, Westminster, Southwark, and Parts Adjacent*, Vol. 2 (London: Cowie & Strange, 1828), p. 281.

60 OBP t17410225–33.

61 *Weekly Miscellany*, 7 March 1741.

62 OA 17410318. This seems to have been a fairly standard penitential 'dying confession', the Ordinary probably being keen to establish a moral narrative for the prospective reader.

63 Quoted online at www.capitalpunishmentuk.org/diver.html, taken from J. Pote, *The Foreigner's Guide: or, a Necessary and Instructive Companion both for the Foreigner and Native in their Tour through the Cities of London and Westminster* (London: J. Jolliffe, 1740).

64 F. Grose *et al.*, *Lexicon Balatronicum: A Dictionary of Buckish Slang, University Wit and Pickpocket Eloquence* (London: C. Chappel, 1811).

65 David D. Cooper, *The Lesson of the Scaffold* (London: Allen Lane, 1974), p. 20.

66 See J. Sharpe, *Dick Turpin: The Myth of the English Highwayman* (London: Profile, 2004) for a discussion of the turning of a brutal robber into an iconic romantic figure.

67 *London, England, Baptisms, Marriages and Burials, 1538–1812* accessed at www. Ancestry.co.uk.

68 OBP t17170111–6.

69 He appears to have resumed his criminal career, as on 24 February 1725 he was found guilty of larceny and sentenced to transportation – see OBP t17250224–39.

70 LL LMSMPS502220096 Middlesex Sessions: Sessions Papers – Justices' Working Documents September 1724.

71 Elizabeth Lyons had, in the meantime, been recaptured the day after her escape.

72 OA 17240904.

73 Anon. (D. Defoe), *History of the Remarkable Life of John Sheppard etc* (London: J. Applebee, 1724), preamble; J. Thurmond, *Harlequin Sheppard. A Night Scene in Grotesque Characters: as it is Perform'd at the Theatre-Royal in Drury-Lane. By John Thurmond* (London: Roberts and Dodd, 1724).

74 *Daily Post*, 10 September 1728.

75 Sharpe, *Crime in Early Modern England*, p. 165.

76 No copies of this original edition survive.

77 The earliest known edition of the *Malefactor's Bloody Register* (also known as the *Tyburn Calendar*) was published by G. Swindells (*c.* 1705), while the *Chronicle of Tyburn or Villainy Display'd in all its Branches* was first published in 1720. Chapbooks were simply broadsides that were sold already made up into booklets.

78 Bell, *Literature and Crime*, p. 15.

79 For an interesting discussion of Fielding's *Enquiry*, see Bell, *Literature and Crime*, pp. 183–97.

80 John Fielding, *A Plan for Preventing Robberies within Twenty Miles of London, with an Account of the Rise and Establishment of the Real THIEFTAKERS* (London: A. Millar, 1755).

81 TNA T38/671, f. 4.

82 TNAT1/449, f. 33, no 15.

83 For a detailed look at habitual offending in the late nineteenth century, see Godfrey *et al., Serious Offenders*.

84 For details of the inspirations behind Colquhoun's reforms, see D. G. Barrie, 'Patrick Colquhoun, the Scottish Enlightenment and Police Reform in Glasgow in the Late Eighteenth Century', *Crime, Histoire et Sociétés* 12.2 (2008): 59–79.

85 Colquhoun was also instrumental in creating the Thames Marine Police Office in 1798, which was responsible for the maritime policing of the metropolis and is often regarded as the first preventive police force in England.

86 See, for example, W. Blizard, *Desultory Reflections on Police, with an Essay on the Means of Preventing Crimes and Amending Criminals* (London: Dilly, 1785). Similar criminological theories were also being developed in Europe, the best known of which was Cesare Beccaria's *Dei Delitti e delle Pene* (*On Crimes and Punishments*), published in 1764. For a discussion of eighteenth-century discourses on policing and police, see F. M. Dodsworth, 'The Idea of Police in Eighteenth-Century England: Discipline, Reformation, Superintendence, c.1780–1800', *Journal of the History of Ideas* 69.4 (2008): 583–605.

87 Patrick Colquhoun, *Treatise on the Wealth of the British Empire* (London: Joseph Mawman, 1815), pp. 111–12.

88 Patrick Colquhoun, *A Treatise on the Police of the Metropolis*, 6th edn (London: Joseph Mawman, 1800), p. 99.

89 Ibid., p. 101.

90 Ibid., p. 612.

91 E.O. refers to 'Evens and Odds', an early form of roulette popular in the eighteenth century.

8　Review and conclusion

Beyond the eighteenth century

Introduction

The eighteenth century was a period of significant socio-economic, intellectual and political developments, many of which were reflected in the criminal justice system. This concluding chapter provides a brief review of the various developments discussed in the previous chapters and suggests ways in which these, in turn, affected subsequent modifications to the English criminal justice system.

Review

It was demonstrated in Chapter 2 that during the period under discussion there was an irreversible shift from a predominantly agrarian and rural demography to a proto-industrial economy, with agglomerations of both people and crime. This in turn encouraged the demise of traditional, local, community-based opprobrium, sanctions and punishments such as 'rough music'. In their place we see a growth in more 'organized' types of justice in the form of the enhanced role and status of both the magistracy and judiciary. These additional powers led to an increased control of both public and private space manifested in, for example, the Riot Act of 1715, which attempted to limit the rights and physical movements of protesters against authority.

At the same time the eighteenth century also saw the demise of the last remnants of the medieval feudal society dominated by lord and Church. The power and influence of both church courts and manorial courts had diminished considerably by the beginning of the nineteenth century. The eighteenth century witnessed the embryonic development of the party political system and the first stirrings of democratic methods of governance; encouraged by both the American and French revolutions, radical and secular thinkers were beginning to challenge the authority of both the ruling classes and the established Church. The rise in Enlightenment ideas such as secular rationalism and the lessening of religious intolerance saw declines in trials for activities such as witchcraft and, again, lessened the authority of the Church in what were increasingly being perceived as temporal rather than spiritual misdemeanours.

Chapter 3 discussed the problems caused by rapid and unregulated population movement and growth. The fear of the unemployed and indigent poor led to the development of new legislation against the poor and displaced. Increased urbanization also led to fears about the growing numbers of those prepared to demonstrate against their lot in life; we have seen that many of the food 'riots' originated not in rural areas but rather in the newly developed and insufficiently provisioned urban centres. This chapter also dealt with changing perceptions of what exactly constituted crime; activities such as the customary taking home of perquisites were becoming increasingly criminalized and legislated against. With the incipient rise of what would later be termed the 'middle classes', the property-owning sector of society demanded increasing safeguards against the misappropriation and theft of goods and possessions, with a concomitant rise in legislation and measures to combat such behaviour. 'Social' crimes such as poaching, smuggling and plundering all came under increasing scrutiny, with often draconian laws being employed in efforts to prevent them.

The beginnings of the Industrial Revolution also saw the rapid development of new forms of technology and these led in turn to new forms of crime, such as the forging of banknotes and coining, together with an increasing number of 'white-collar' frauds. These new types of crime demanded new methods of detection and capture, and Chapter 4 discussed the impassioned debates over policing and growing dissatisfaction with the centuries-old system of law enforcement in the form of the parish constabulary. It suggested that, while the system was not as bad as many contemporary commentators believed, and while there was not a simple teleological progression from night-watchmen to professional police forces, there was an increased demand for more viable alternatives. The rise of the private thieftaker and the ensuing problems with such a system were described, while the beginnings of the first detective force in England were briefly outlined. London was far better served than the rest of the country, but there was opposition to any kind of national police force. The role of the victim and/or his/her family in the prosecution of suspects was also delineated.

Chapter 5 discussed how new incarceral forms of punishment increasingly replaced more corporeal forms of sentencing for more serious offences, while misdemeanours were often settled by non-corporeal methods. It also demonstrated that, quite apart from the economic impetus that it enabled, the growth of the Empire also provided Britain with a new and (to many contemporary minds at least) convenient way of ridding its shores of 'undesirables'. The development of the various systems of transportation to America and subsequently Australia were discussed in detail, as were the effects suffered by individuals as a result of this kind of punishment. The increasing number of offences that came to be categorized as felonies punishable by death was also described, as were the various posthumous forms of punishment available to the judiciary.

Chapter 6 turned our attention to the relationships between gender and criminal justice in the period, highlighting the vast discrepancies between male and female in the eyes of the eighteenth-century law. Despite the stimulation of increased public debate over the disadvantages suffered by women by progressive reformers such as Mary Wollstonecraft (1759–1797), in her influential *A Vindication of the Rights of Woman*, published in 1792, females remained at a considerable legal disadvantage throughout both the eighteenth and nineteenth centuries. This chapter demonstrated that they played very little part in the law-enforcement process and that much remains to be researched concerning their role as complainants and prosecutors. It also showed that females committed proportionately fewer criminal offences than men and that they were often dealt with differently by the courts in terms of punishment.

That some women could achieve lasting notoriety in both contemporary and later society was demonstrated by the case of Mary Young aka Jenny Diver. Chapter 7 expanded upon the role of popular culture and literature with regard to crime and criminals. Newspapers emerged as the most popular form of mass media, while other forms of popular contemporary culture, such as plays and broadsheets, played an often considerable part in mythologizing certain individuals. The eighteenth century was a time of great intellectual stimulus, which resulted in the bending of minds to matters of criminal justice – from the benefits of creating a professional police force to the ways in which serious or habitual offenders could be recorded.

Conclusion

What, then, is the legacy of the eighteenth century with regard to crime and criminal justice history?

Many of the developments of the period under discussion with regard to crime and criminal justice continued to resonate throughout the nineteenth century; this period cannot be seen in isolation. However, there was not a simplistic, linear development of ideas and practices from the eighteenth century onward; advances in policing and criminal justice were often piecemeal and *ad hoc*, with many blind alleys and hesitant advances.

The debate about the creation of a professional preventive police force with full-time officers began in the second half of the eighteenth century and was not satisfactorily realized until a hundred years later, with the creation of county and borough police forces throughout England and Wales. Following the creation of the Metropolitan Police in 1829 many boroughs decided to create their own forces on similar lines. However, the Municipal Corporations Act 1835 (5 & 6 Wm IV c. 76), which enabled a total of 148 listed boroughs to create their own police forces, signally failed to usher in a new era of 'modern' policing to England and Wales, and the Royal Commission on the Municipal Corporations Act 1835 found that many boroughs' police forces were still woefully inadequate:

At Bristol, a notoriously ineffective police cannot be improved, chiefly in consequence of the jealousy with which the Corporation is regarded by the inhabitants. At Hull, in consequence of the disunion between the governing body and the inhabitants, chiefly arising out of a dispute about the tolls and duties, only seven persons attended to suppress a riot, out of 5,000 who had been sworn in as special constables, and on another similar occasion none attended. At Coventry, serious riots and disturbances frequently occur, and the officers of police, being usually selected from one political party, are often active in fomenting them.[1]

The Municipal Corporations Act 1835 affected only the 148 listed boroughs; it was not until the introduction of the Rural Constabulary Act 1839 (2 & 3 Vict. c. 93) that counties and unincorporated boroughs were formally encouraged (but still not compelled) to create their own police forces, and it was not until 1856 that all towns and boroughs within England and Wales were formally required to create police forces, following the passing of the County and Borough Police Act (19 & 20 Vict. c. 69).[2]

The creation of the Metropolitan Police, as John Beattie has remarked, 'reached back to an older ideal of policing in its total dependence on the prevention of crime by surveillance', and the Commissioners were quick to realize that this style of exclusively preventive police work was neither effective nor practical. We have seen that the Bow Street model was considered successful enough to be expanded to seven other police offices, and these all continued for a decade after the creation of the Metropolitan Police in 1829. After the disbandment of the Principal Officers in 1839 it was soon realized that the lack of a detective element within the Metropolitan force was seriously hampering its ability. Consequently, a Detective Branch of the Metropolitan Police (which employed a number of ex-Principal Officers) was formed in August 1842.

Methods of detection in the middle decades of the nineteenth century became increasingly sophisticated, with basic forensics being employed more frequently.[3] However, it was not until the very end of the nineteenth century that significant improvements were made with regard to identifying particular offenders. Forensic scientists could not distinguish between animal and human blood until 1895, and the test by which this distinction was determined was not accepted in a court of law until 1902. Fingerprinting, although developed some years earlier, was not successfully used to secure a conviction until 1902.

With regard to subsequent developments in the punishment and reformation of offenders, transportation – that fundamentally eighteenth-century 'solution' to perceived rising crime levels – continued to Australia until 1853, when the sentence of transportation was replaced by 'penal servitude' overseas.[4] This, however, still involved offenders being sent to overseas colonies, such as Western Australia, Bermuda and Gibraltar. Transportation to Western Australia finally ended in 1868, with the last convict ship (the *Hougoumont*) docking at Fremantle on 9 January 1868 with its cargo of 279 transportees.[5]

The debate concerning incarceration as a punishment for serious offenders gained urgency as a result of the end of transportation; the prison-building programme was accelerated in order to accommodate the many prisoners who would previously have been sent overseas. The increase in the number of those incarcerated precipitated major debates on the usefulness and cost-effectiveness of imprisonment as a punishment, and debate about the merits or otherwise of short prison sentences in particular continue to the present day.[6]

Throughout the first decades of the nineteenth century the debate about the effectiveness and desirability of the death penalty continued, and the number of capital offences reduced markedly in the 1830s and 1840s until only a handful remained.[7] The spectacle of the gibbet ceased in 1832, while public executions were banned after 1868.[8] Posthumous punishment also declined as a result of a number of direct and indirect factors, including the aforementioned lessening of capital offences and the growth in population, which led to an increasing number of corpses being made available to anatomists.

Many of the flaws in and problems of the eighteenth-century criminal justice system continued throughout the nineteenth century and well into the twentieth. The status of women remained especially unequal in terms of both their representation in law enforcement and their social, economic and political disadvantages.[9] It was not until the early decades of the twentieth century that children's courts were created; until then, juveniles as young as nine were tried in the same courts as adults. Similarly, probation as a sentencing option for minor or young offenders began to be widely utilized only in the early twentieth century, following its hesitant introduction in the last quarter of the nineteenth century.[10]

Several of the concerns of the eighteenth-century public remain pertinent today. For example, the recent introduction and use of community punishments such as Community Payback Orders, which require an offender to perform between 40 and 300 hours of unpaid labour in his or her local area while wearing high-visibility jackets, can be seen to operate in the same tradition as 'rough music' or 'shaming', in that the punishment is carried out in full public view, leaving the offenders liable to either approbation or opprobrium.[11]

Similarly, concerns about the current all-time-high prison population (currently *c.* 86,000 prisoners) are a clear continuation of the debate around imprisonment as a punishment option that began in the eighteenth century. Plans by the former Labour Home Secretary John Reid to amalgamate England and Wales' forty-three police forces into two-dozen or so 'super' forces' were abandoned in 2008, following strong opposition from many Chief Constables, some of whom wanted to maintain their forces' independence, while others feared the financial implications of merging various county forces.[12] This has clear historical parallels with the debates and fears surrounding a national police force that were first aired in the late eighteenth and early nineteenth centuries.

The lay magistracy, which became increasingly prominent throughout the eighteenth century, continues to predominate in the criminal justice system, with over 25,000 men and women acting on an unpaid, voluntary basis as magistrates. The number of professional stipendiary magistrates (now known as District Judges) has risen sharply in the intervening period, with around 150 such judges (together with a similar number of Deputy District Judges) currently operating in large urban centres of population. Although the circumstances are in many ways clearly different, this recent rise in the number of stipendiary magistrates can be seen in some respects as an echo of the debate in the eighteenth century concerning the future of the magistracy (Chapter 2).

The eighteenth century thus casts a long shadow over subsequent developments in the criminal justice system of England, and it is hoped that this book has at least shed some light on its darker corners.

Notes

1 Reproduced from www.leeds.ac.uk/law/staff/lawdw/cyberpolice/pol0.htm.
2 For a concise account of the development of provincial policing in the early Victorian period, see Emsley, *The English Police*, pp. 32–42, and for an overview of the period from 1829 to the present day, see David S. Wall, 'The Organisation of Police 1829–2000', in Stallion, M., and Wall, D. S., *The British Police: Police Forces and Chief Officers 1829–2000* (Hook: Police History Society, 1999), pp. 1–31.
3 Scientific advances such as the development by James Marsh of a reliable test for arsenic poisoning in the mid-1830s greatly aided the detection of such offences. Bow Street Officers had previously utilized basic forensics in the investigation of many of the cases in which they were involved. For example, one of the Bow Street Officers involved in the case of Benjamin Robins' murder (Case Study 13, Chapter 5) successfully matched three lead pistol balls with both a flawed mould and the lead ball retrieved from Mr Robins' body, thereby proving that the pistol used by Howe in the murder and the hidden weapon were part of the same set. This is possibly the earliest recorded use of ballistic forensic detection in the world. For a brief history of the development of firearms forensics, see James E. Hamby, 'The History Of Firearm And Toolmark Identification', *Association of Firearm and Tool Mark Examiners Journal* 31.3 (1999): 266–84.
4 Penal Servitude Act 1853 (16 & 17 Vict. c.99).
5 Sixty-two of these transportees were Irish political prisoners (Fenians). One transportee died during the voyage. For details of the end of transportation to Western Australia, see Godfrey and Cox, 'The "Last Fleet"'.
6 See Barry Godfrey, Helen Johnston and David J. Cox, *Victorian Convicts: 100 Criminal Lives* (Barnsley: Wharncliffe, forthcoming) for details of the late Victorian debates concerning the effectiveness (both socially and economically) of the imprisonment of offenders.
7 See Gatrell, *The Hanging Tree*, Epilogue (pp. 589–612) and Appendix 2: Execution and Mercy Statistics (pp. 616–20) for further details of the decline in capital offences.
8 Gibbeting was not formally ended as a punishment until 1834 by the Abolition of Hanging in Chains Act (4 & 5 Will. IV c.26), although the last gibbetings took place in 1832. Public hanging was abolished by the Capital Punishment Amendment Act 1868 (31 & 32 Vict. c.24).
9 For example, it was not until 1991 that marital rape could be prosecuted as a criminal offence, following a judgement by the Appellate Court of the House of Lords.
10 The 1887 Probation of First Offenders Act (50 & 51 Vict. c.25) allowed courts to release minor offenders into the care of a responsible authority (normally a Church Mission Society or similar), but did not cater for the official supervision of the person under probation.
11 For further details of this scheme, see www.communitypayback.com/.
12 See www.independent.co.uk/news/uk/crime/police-forces-merger-plan-will-be-scrapped-says-chief-constable-407536.html for an account of the contemporary concerns.

Appendix

Timeline 1649–1815

1649 30 Jan	Execution of Charles I at Banqueting House, London
1671	Game Act (22 & 23 Car II c.25) redefined property qualification for the hunting of game, effectively limiting the activity to the landed gentry
1673	Old Bailey (later known as Central Criminal Court) reopened after being rebuilt following the Great Fire of London in 1666
1677	Ecclesiastical Jurisdiction Act (29 Car II c.9) abolished death by fire penalty for heresy, atheism and blasphemy
1679	Habeas Corpus Act (31 Car II c.2) strengthened and defined right of *habeas corpus* i.e. right not to be detained without trial
1682 25 Aug	Last documented hanging of women for witchcraft at Heavitree, Exeter
1685 6 Feb	Death of Charles II
1685 6 Feb	Accession of James II
1685 25 Aug	'Bloody Assizes' begin at Winchester following collapse of Monmouth Rebellion
1685 23 Sep	'Bloody Assizes' finish at Wells
1689 28 Jan	Declared forced abdication of James II by Parliament
1689	'Glorious Revolution' – Coronation of William III and Mary II and introduction of Bill of Rights (1 Wm and Mary c.2)
1691	Women allowed to claim Benefit of Clergy on same grounds as men (3 & 4 Wm and Mary c.9)
1692	Highwaymen Act (4 & 5 Wm & Mary c.8) offers a £40 statutory reward for the apprehension and conviction of highwaymen
1692	Estreats Act (4 Wm & Mary c.24) stipulated that Assize jurors were to have freehold property valued at £10 per year or the same amount in copyhold land, tenements or in rents
1693	First Association for the Prosecution of Felons created (Stafford)
1694	Death of Mary II

1695	Treason Act (7 and 8 Wm II c.3) allowed for the hiring of a defence counsel in cases of High Treason. Defendants in other types of criminal cases were not allowed by law to hire defence counsel until Trials for Felony Act 1836 (6 and 7 Wm IV c.114), although in practice, such counsels were present from the 1730s onward, often only helping the defendant on points of law, rather than conducting cross-examinations
1697	Act *for supplying some Defects in the Laws for the Relief of the Poor* (8 & 9 Will II c.30) – badging of the poor by parishes (abolished Relief of the Poor Act 1810 [50 Geo. III c.50]).
1699	Shoplifting Act (10 and 11 Wm II c.23) made shoplifting of goods valued above 5s a capital offence
1702	Death of William III and accession of Anne I
1702	Witnesses on Trial for Treason Act (1 Anne c.9) allowed the defendant in a felony trial to call witnesses who gave evidence on oath
1706	Reading test for claiming Benefit of Clergy abolished (5 Anne c.6)
1712	At the Essex Assizes, Sir Thomas Parker (Lord Chief Justice) stated that death by water ordeals would be treated as murder rather than manslaughter
1712	Invention of Newcomen steam engine (precursor to the better known Boulton & Watt engines that drove the Industrial Revolution)
1713	Publication of *The History of the Common Law of England* by Matthew Hale
1714	Vagrancy Act (12 Anne c.23) – designed to reduce the laws relating to rogues, vagabonds, sturdy beggars, and vagrants, into one Act of Parliament
1714 1 Aug	Death of Anne I and accession of George I
1715	Riot Act (1 Geo. III c.5) – if gatherings of a dozen or more people did not disperse within the hour when commanded in the King's name to so do by a lawful authority, then the offenders faced the death penalty without Benefit of Clergy
1718	Transportation Act (4 Geo. I c.11) introduced penal transportation to America with a minimum sentence of seven years
1720	South Sea Bubble stocks and shares scandal
1723	Waltham Black Act (9 Geo. I c.22) makes hunting with a blackened face a capital offence, on order to deal with 'wicked and evil-disposed men going armed in disguise'
1725 24 May	Death by hanging of Jonathan Wild (self-styled Thieftaker-General)
1727	Death of George I and accession of George II

1729	Juries Act (3 Geo. II c.25) lowered property qualification for Assize jurors and also abolished many loopholes by which men had previously avoided jury duty
1735	Witchcraft Act (9 Geo. II c.5) – witchcraft ceased to be a capital crime
1736	Plays Act (10 Geo. II c.28) – introduced censorship onto the British stage
1745	Jacobite rebellion
1748/9	Henry Fielding creates Bow Street 'Runners'
1752	Act 'for better preventing the horrid crime of Murder' (25 Geo. II c.37). It became an offence with a fine of £50 to advertise a reward with 'no questions asked'. Also verdict of death had to be carried out within 48 hours (not including Sundays). Limited recompense for prosecution expenses also introduced. Judges given discretion to deliver bodies of those executed by hanging to anatomists or to allow their bodies to be hung in chains (gibbeted)
1754	Offenders Conveyance Act (27 Geo. II c.3) allowed for the court to recompense 'poor persons' who had been bound over to give evidence for the prosecution
1765	Sir William Blackstone's *Commentaries* first published
1766	Major food riots throughout midlands and southern England
1767	First publication of English translation of Cesare Beccaria's *Of Crime and Punishments*
1775 19 Apr	American War of Independence (battles of Lexington and Concord)
1776 4 Jul	Declaration of American Independence signed and transportation to America ceased: Criminal Law Act (16 Geo. III c.43) 'to authorise . . . the punishment by hard labour' of those who were previously liable to transportation. Male non-capital offenders had their sentence of seven years' transportation replaced by sentences of between three to ten years, whilst those pardoned from a death sentence were to be detained in hulks at hard labour on the Thames for a period determined in the Royal Pardon. Women and incapable men were to be detained at hard labour in Houses of Correction
1779	Penitentiary Act (19 Geo. III c.74) allowed for the creation of penitentiaries and a regime of hard labour for those convicts on prison hulks. Branding as a punishment for those in receipt of Benefit of Clergy abolished
1783	Britain negotiates end of American War of Independence
1784	Introduction of excise duties on property-owners' and gamekeepers' certificates

1787 12 May	First fleet of transported convicts sailed for Australia (landed Jan 18 1788)
1789 14 Jul	French Revolution begins
1790	Treason Act (30 George III. c.48) abolishes death by burning at the stake
1792	Middlesex Justices Act (32 Geo. III c.53) created seven police offices in London based on the Bow Street Public Office model
1793 1 Feb	France declares war on Britain
1799	Unlawful Societies Act (39 Geo. III c.79) – 'An Act for the more effectual suppression of societies established for seditious and treasonable purposes, and for better preventing treasonable and seditious practices'
1799/1800	Combination Acts (39 Geo. III c.81 & 40 Geo. III c.106) outlaw trades unions
1800/1	Acts of Union (39 & 40 Geo. III c.67 and 40 Geo. III c.38) creates the United Kingdom of Great Britain and Ireland
1801 10 Mar	First national census held
1805	First limited attempt made at compilation of national crime statistics
1811	Luddite protests begin in English midlands
1812	America declares war on Britain
1814	Treason Act (54 Geo. III c.146) abolished hanging, drawing and quartering as a punishment for High Treason
1815	War with America ends
1815 18 Jun	Battle of Waterloo – end of Napoleonic Wars with France

Bibliography

Anon., *An Account of the Manner, Behaviour and Execution of Mary Aubry* (London: D. Mallett, 1688).

Anon. (D. Defoe), *History of the Remarkable Life of John Sheppard etc* (London: J. Applebee, 1724).

Anon., *A Collection of Pieces relative to the inhuman massacre in St George's Fields on 10th May 1768* (London: n.p., 1768).

Anon. (Canon John Brown), *Another Estimate of the Manners and Principles of the Present Times* (London: G. Kearsly, 1769).

Anon. (Sir John Fielding), *Forgery Unmasked, or, Genuine Memoirs of the Two Unfortunate Brothers, Robert and Daniel Perreau, and Mrs Rudd* (London: A. Grant, 1775).

Anon., *Remarks on the Riot Act with application to certain recent and alarming facts* (London: G. Kearsly, 1768).

Anon., *The Bow Street Opera in three Acts: written on the plan of The Beggars Opera* (London: T. Mariner *et al.*, 1773).

Anon., *The Trial of the Reverend Robert Bingham, Curate of Maresfield, Tuesday March 26th 1811* (Lewes: Sussex Press, 1811).

Anon., *The Trial of the Reverend Robert Bingham, taken in shorthand by Mr Adams, by order of the Directors of The Union Fire Office, London* (London: J. M. Richardson, 1811).

Anon., *The Trial of William Howe, alias John Wood, for the Wilful Murder of Mr. Benjamin Robins of Dunsley, near Stourbridge on the 18th of December 1813* [sic] (Stourbridge: J. Heming, 1813).

Addison, Sir William, *The Old Roads of England* (London: Batsford, 1980).

Allen, T., *The History and Antiquities of London, Westminster, Southwark, and Parts Adjacent*, vol. 2 (London: Cowie & Strange, 1828).

Amussen, S. D., 'Punishment, Discipline and Power: The Social Meanings of Violence in Early Modern England', *Journal of British Studies* 34 (1995): 1–34.

Andrew, Donna T., and Randall McGowen, *The Perreaus and Mrs. Rudd: Forgery and Betrayal in Eighteenth-Century London* (Berkeley: University of California Press, 2001).

Andrews, W., *Bygone Punishments* (London: W. Andrews, 1899).

Armitage, Gilbert, *The History of the Bow Street Runners 1729–1829* (London: Wishart & Co., 1932).

Ashworth, W. J., *Customs and Excise: Trade, Production, and Consumption in England 1640–1845* (Oxford: OUP, 2003).

Asquith, Ivan, 'The Structure, Ownership and Control of the Press, 1780–1855', in Boyce, G., et al., *Newspaper History from the Seventeenth Century to the Present Day* (London: Constable, 1978), pp. 98–116.

Atkinson, Alan, 'The Free-Born Englishman Transported: Convict Rights as a Measure of Eighteenth-Century Empire', *Past and Present* 144 (1994): 88–115.

Atkinson, E. G. (ed.), *Acts of the Privy Council of England volume 34 – 1615–1616* (London: HMSO, 1925).

Babington, Anthony, *The English Bastille: A History of Newgate Gaol and Prison Conditions in Britain 1188–1902* (London: Macdonald, 1971).

Babington, Anthony, *The Rule of Law in Britain from the Roman Occupation to the Present Day: The Only Liberty* (Chichester: Barry Rose, 1978).

Babington, Anthony, *A House in Bow Street: Crime and the Magistracy, London 1740–1881*, 2nd edn (London: Macdonald, 1999).

Bailey, N., *The Universal Etymological English Dictionary*, Vol. II (London: Bailey, 1737).

Bailyn, Bernard, *The Peopling of British North America: An Introduction* (London: I B Tauris, 1987).

Baker, Geoff, and Ann McGruer (eds), *Readers, Audiences and Coteries in Early Modern England* (Newcastle-upon-Tyne: Cambridge Scholars, 2006).

Barker, Hannah, *Newspapers, Politics and Public Opinion in Late Eighteenth-Century England* (Oxford: Clarendon Press, 1998).

Barker, Hannah, *Newspapers, Politics and English Society 1695–1855* (Harlow: Pearson Educational, 2000).

Barnsby, George J., *The Working Class Movement in the Black Country 1750 to 1867* (Wolverhampton: Integrated Publishing Services, 1977).

Barrett, A. and C. Harrison, *Crime and Punishment in England* (London: UCL Press, 1999).

Barrie, D. G., 'Patrick Colquhoun, the Scottish Enlightenment and Police Reform in Glasgow in the Late Eighteenth Century', *Crime, Histoire et Sociétés* 12.2 (2008): 59–79.

Barrie, D. G., *Police in the Age of Improvement: Police Development and the Civic Tradition in Scotland, 1775–1865* (Cullompton: Willan, 2008).

Bates, Kate, 'Morality for the Masses: The Social Significance of Crime and Punishment Discourse in British Broadsides, 1800–1850' (unpublished PhD thesis, Keele University, 2012).

Baugh, G. C. (ed.), *Victoria County History of Shropshire*, Vol. III (Oxford: OUP for the Institute of Historical Research, 1979).

Baugh, G. C., 'County Government 1714–1834', in Baugh, G. C. (ed), *Victoria County History of Shropshire*, Vol. III (Oxford: OUP for the Institute of Historical Research, 1979), pp. 115–14.

Beattie, J. M., 'Early Detection: The Bow Street Runners in Late Eighteenth-century London' (unpublished essay, n.d.).

Beattie, J. M., 'The Pattern of Crime in England 1660–1800', *Past and Present* LXII (1974): 47–95.

Beattie, J. M., *Crime and the Courts in England 1660–1800* (Oxford: OUP, 1986).

Beattie, J. M., *Policing and Punishment in London 1660–1750: Urban Crime and the Limits of Terror* (Oxford: OUP, 2001).

Beattie, J. M., *The First English Detectives: the Bow Street Runners and the Policing of London 1750–1840* (Oxford: OUP, 2012).

Beattie, John, 'The Criminality of Women in Eighteenth-Century England', *Journal of Social History* 8.4 (1975): 80–116.

Beattie, John, 'London Juries in the 1690s', in Cockburn, J. S., and Green, Thomas A. (eds), *Twelve Good Men and True: The Criminal Trial Jury in England, 1200–1800* (Princeton: PUP, 1988), pp. 214–53.

Beattie, John, 'Sir John Fielding and Public Justice: The Bow Street Magistrates' Court, 1754–1780', *Law and History Review* 25.1 (2007): 61–100.

Behre, Rainer, 'Shipwrecks and the Body: 18th and 19th Century Encounters with Death and Survival at Sea' (paper delivered at the *Controlling Bodies – the Regulation of Conduct 1650–2000 Conference*, University of Glamorgan, July 2002).

Bell, Ian A., *Literature and Crime in Augustan England* (London: Routledge, 1991).

Bertelsen, Lance, 'Committed by Justice Fielding: Judicial and Journalistic Representation in the Bow Street Magistrates Office, January 3–November 24, 1752', *Eighteenth Century Studies* 30 (1996–97): 337–63.

Birkett, Lord, *The New Newgate Calendar* (London: The Folio Society, 1960).

Black, J., *The English Press in the Eighteenth Century* (Beckenham: Croom Helm, 1987).

Black, J., *The English Press 1621–1861* (Stroud: Sutton, 2001).

Blackstone, Sir W., *Commentaries on the Laws of England*, Vol. 4 (Oxford: Clarendon Press, 1765).

Bladen, F. M. (ed.), *Historical Records of New South Wales*, Vol. 2 (Sydney: Charles Potter, 1895).

Blizard, Sir William, *Desultory Reflections on Police, with an Essay on the Means of Preventing Crimes and Amending Criminals* (London: Dilly, 1785).

Bohstedt, J., *The Politics of Provisions: Food Riots, Moral Economy and Market Transition in England c.1550–1850* (Farnham: Ashgate, 2010).

Boyce, George, *et al.* (eds), *Newspaper History from the Seventeenth Century to the Present Day* (London: Constable, 1978).

Brewer, John and John Styles (eds), *An Ungovernable People: The English and Their Law in the Seventeenth and Eighteenth Centuries* (London: Hutchinson, 1980).

Brigham, Clarence S. (ed.), 'British Royal Proclamations Relating to America, 1603–1783', *Transactions of the American Antiquarian Society* 12 (1911): 52–5.

Brodie, Allan, Jane Croom and James O. Davies, *English Prisons: An Architectural History* (Swindon: English Heritage, 2002).

Brooke, Alan, and David Brandon, *Tyburn: London's Fatal Tree* (Stroud: Sutton, 2004).

Brooke, Alan, and David Brandon, *Bound for Botany Bay: British Convict Voyages to Australia* (Kew: TNA, 2005).

Brumwell, Stephen, and W. A. Speck, *Cassell's Companion to Eighteenth-Century Britain* (London: Cassell & Co., 2001).

Budiansky, Stephen, *Her Majesty's Spymaster: Elizabeth I, Sir Francis Walsingham, and the Birth of Modern Espionage* (New York: Viking Penguin, 2005).

Burns, Richard, *Justice of the Peace and Parish Officer*, 23rd edn, ed. George Chetwynd, 5 volumes (London: Longman *et al.*, 1820).

Butler, James Davie, 'British Convicts Shipped to American Colonies', *American Historical Review* 2 (1896): 12–33.

Cameron, Alan, *Bank of Scotland 1695–1995: A Very Singular Institution* (Edinburgh: Mainstream Publishing, 1995).

Carter, Paul, *et al.* (eds), *Pardons and Punishments: Judges' Reports on Criminals, 1783 to 1830, List and Index Society*, Vol. 304 (London: List and Index Society, 2004).

Caswell, Marisha C., 'Married Women, Crime, and Questions of Liability in England 1640–1760' (unpublished PhD thesis, Queens University, Kingston, Ontario, 2012).

Charlesworth, A. (ed.), *An Atlas of Rural Protest in Britain 1548–1900* (London: Croom Helm, 1983).

Christian, Garth (ed.), *A Victorian Poacher: James Hawker's Journal* (Oxford: OUP, 1978).

Christianson, S., *With Liberty For Some: 500 Years of Imprisonment in America* (Boston: Northeastern University Press, 2000).

Cirket, Alan Frank (ed.), *Samuel Whitbread's Notebooks, 1810–11, 1813–14* (Ampthill: Publications of the Bedfordshire Historical Record Society 50, 1971).

Cockburn, J. S., *A History of English Assizes 1558–1714* (London: CUP, 1972).

Cockburn, J. S. (ed.), *Crime in England 1550–1800* (London: Methuen, 1977).

Cockburn, J. S., 'Twelve Silly Men? The Trial Jury at Assizes, 1560–1670', in Cockburn, J. S., and Green, Thomas A. (eds), *Twelve Good Men and True: The Criminal Trial Jury in England, 1200–1800* (Princeton: PUP, 1988), pp. 158–81.

Cockburn, J. S., and Green, Thomas A. (eds), *Twelve Good Men and True: the Criminal Trial Jury in England, 1200–1800* (Princeton: PUP, 1988).

Cockerell, H. A. L., and Edwin Green, *The British Insurance Business 1547–1970* (London: Heinemann Educational books, 1976).

Cohen, Stanley, and Andrew Scull (eds), *Social Control and the State: Historical and Comparative Essays* (Oxford: OUP, 1983).

Coldham, Peter Wilson, *Emigrants in Chains: A Social History of Forced Emigration to the Americas of Felons, Destitute Children, Political and Religious Non-Conformists, Vagabonds, Beggars and Other Undesirables, 1607–1776* (Baltimore MD, Geneaological Publishing, 1992).

Coldham, Peter Wilson, *The King's Passengers to Maryland and Virginia* (Westminster, MD: Heritage Books, 1997).

Colquhoun, Patrick, *A Treatise on the Police of the Metropolis*, 6th edn (London: Joseph Mawman, 1800).

Colquhoun, Patrick, *Treatise on the Wealth of the British Empire* (London: Joseph Mawman, 1815).

Constable, M., *The Law of the Other: The Mixed Jury and Changing Conceptions of Citizenship, Law and Knowledge* (Chicago: University of Chicago Press, 1994).

Cooper, David D., *The Lesson of the Scaffold* (London: Allen Lane, 1974).

Cox, D. C., 'County Government 1603–1714', in Baugh, G. C. (ed.), *Victoria County History: Shropshire*, volume III (Oxford: OUP for the Institute of Historical Research, 1979), pp. 90–114.

Cox, David J., 'Bow Street Runners in the Black Country: the arrest, trial and execution of "Lord Howe"', *The Blackcountryman* 33.1 (1999/2000): 27–31.

Cox, David J., *The Dunsley Murder of 1812: A Study in Early Nineteenth-century Crime Detection, Justice and Punishment* (Kingswinford: Dulston Press, 2003).

Cox, David J., 'Civil Unrest in the Black Country, 1766–1816', in *Family and Local History Yearbook*, 9th edn (Nether Popple: Blatchford Publishing Ltd, 2005), pp. 30–33.

Cox, David J., 'Shropshire Justices of the Peace before the 18th Century', in Cox, David J., and Godfrey, B. (eds), *Cinderellas & Packhorses: A History of the Shropshire Magistracy* (Almeley: Logaston Press, 2005), pp. 13–22.

Cox, David J., 'The Shropshire Magistracy in the Eighteenth Century', in Cox. D. J., and Godfrey, B. (eds), *Cinderellas & Packhorses: A History of the Shropshire Magistracy* (Almeley: Logaston Press, 2005), pp. 23–42.

Cox, David J., *Foul Deeds & Suspicious Deaths in Shrewsbury and around Shropshire* (Barnsley: Wharncliffe Books, 2008).

Cox, David J., ' "Trying to get a good one": Bigamy Offences in England and Wales 1850–1950', *Plymouth Law & Criminal Justice Review* 4 (2011): 1–32.

Cox, David J., ' "The wolves let loose at Wolverhampton": A Study of the South Staffordshire Election Riots, May 1835', *Law, Crime and History* 1.2 (2011): 1–31.

Cox, David J., *A Certain Share of Low Cunning: A History of the Bow Street Runners 1792–1839* (London: Routledge, 2012).

Cox, David J., and Barry Godfrey (eds), *Cinderellas & Packhorses: A History of the Shropshire Magistracy* (Almeley: Logaston Press, 2005).

Cox, David J., and Michael Pearson, *Foul Deeds & Suspicious Deaths around the Black Country* (Barnsley: Wharncliffe Books, 2006).

Cox, Joseph, *A Faithful Narrative of the most Wicked and Inhuman Transactions of the Bloody-Minded Gang of Thief-takers, alias Thief-makers Macdaniel, Berry, Salmon, Eagan alias Gahagen* (London: Mechell, 1756).

Critchley, T. A., *A History of Police in England and Wales* (London: Constable, 1978).

Crittall, Elizabeth (ed.), *The Justicing Notebook of William Hunt 1744–1749* (Devizes: Wiltshire Record Society, 1982).

Curtis, T. C., 'Explaining Crime in Early Modern England', *Criminal Justice History* 1 (1980): 117–37.

D'Cruze, S., and L. Jackson, *Women, Crime and Justice in England since 1660* (Basingstoke: Palgrave Macmillan, 2009).

Dagall, H., *Creating a Good Impression: 300 Years of the Stamp Office & Stamp Duties* (London: The Stamp Office, 1994).

Davies, K. G., *The Royal African Company* [Vol. 5 of the 7-volume series *Emergence of International Business 1200–1800*] (London: Taylor & Francis, 1999).

Davies, O., *Witchcraft, Magic and Culture 1736–1951* (Manchester: MUP, 1999).

Devereaux, S. and P. Griffiths (eds), *Penal Practice and Culture, 1500–1900: Punishing the English* (2003).

Deveraux, Simon, 'Imposing the Royal Pardon: Execution, Transportation, and Convict Resistance in London, 1789', *Law and History Review* 25.1 (2007): 101–38.

Dinsmor, A., 'Glasgow Police: The First Fifty Years' (paper delivered at the Police History Society Conference, Ripon, September 2001).

Dinsmor, A., 'Glasgow Police Pioneers', *Journal of the Police History Society* 15 (2000): 9–11.

Dinsmor, A., and R. H. J. Urquhart, 'The Origins of Modern Policing in Scotland', *Scottish Archives, the Journal of the Scottish Records Association* 7 (2001): 36–44.

Dodsworth, F. M., 'The Idea of Police in Eighteenth-Century England: Discipline, Reformation, Superintendence, c.1780–1800', *Journal of the History of Ideas* 69.4 (2008): 583–605.

Dolan, Frances, 'Battered Women, Petty Traitors, and the Legacy of Coverture', *Feminist Studies* 29.2 (2003): 249–77.

Dolan, Frances E., 'Hobry, Mary (d. 1688)', in *Oxford Dictionary of National Biography* (Oxford: OUP, 2004). Available at www.oxforddnb.com/view/article/68003

Doran, Susan, and Christopher Durston, *Princes, Pastors and People: The Church and Religion in England, 1500–1700*, 2nd edn (London: Routledge, 2003).

Dudley, D., *Metallum Martis: or Iron made with Pit-Coale, Sea-Coale, &c. And with the same Fuell to Melt and Fine Imperfect Mettals, And Refine perfect Mettals* (London: Dud Dudley, 1665).

Duman, D., *The Judicial Bench in England 1727–1875: The Reshaping of a Professional Elite* (London: Royal Historical Society, 1982).

Dunkley, Peter, *The Crisis of the Old Poor Law in England 1795–1834: An Interpretive Essay* (New York: Garland Publishing, 1982).

Durston, Christopher, *Cromwell's Major-Generals: Godly Government during the English Revolution* (Manchester: MUP, 2001).

Earle, P., *Monmouth's Rebels: The Road to Sedgemoor 1685* (London: Weidenfeld & Nicholson, 1977).

Eastwood, David, *Governing Rural England: Tradition and Transformation in Local Government 1780–1840* (Oxford: Clarendon, 1994).

Eastwood, David, *Government and Community in the English Provinces 1700–1870* (Basingstoke: Macmillan, 1997).

Ekirch, A. Roger, *Bound for America: The Transportation of British Convicts to the Colonies, 1718–1775* (Oxford: Clarendon Paperbacks, 1987).

Emsley, Clive, 'The Home Office and its Sources of Information and Investigation 1791–1801', *English Historical Review* XCIV (1979): 532–61.

Emsley, Clive, 'An Aspect of Pitt's "Terror": Prosecutions for Sedition during the 1790s', *Social History* 6.2 (1981): 155–84.

Emsley, Clive, *Policing and its Context 1750–1870* (London: Macmillan Press, 1983).

Emsley, Clive, 'Detection and Prevention: The Old English Police and the New (1750–1900)', *Historical Social Research* 37 (1986): 69–88.

Emsley, Clive, *The English Police: A Political and Social History*, 2nd edn (Harlow: Longman, 1996).

Emsley, Clive, 'The Policeman as Worker: A Comparative Survey, c.1800–1940', *International Review of Social History* 45.1 (2000): 89–110.

Emsley, Clive, *Crime and Society in England 1750–1900*, 3rd edn (London: Longman, 2005).

Emsley, Clive, *Hard Men: The English and Violence since 1750* (London: Hambledon and London, 2005).

Emsley, Clive, *Crime, Police, and Penal Policy: European Experiences 1750–1940* (Oxford: OUP, 2007).

Emsley, Clive, *The Great British Bobby: A History of British Policing from the 18th Century to the Present* (London: Quercus, 2009).

Emsley, Clive, and James Wallin (eds), *Artisans, Peasants & Proletarians 1760–1860* (London: Croom Helm, 1985).

Emsley, Clive, and Haia Shpayer-Makov (eds), *Police Detectives in History, 1750–1950* (Aldershot: Ashgate, 2005).

England, R. W., 'Investigating Homicides in Northern England, 1800–1824', *Criminal Justice History* 6 (1985): 105–24.

Ewan, E., 'Crime or Culture? Women and Daily Life in Late-Medieval Scotland', in Galloway Brown, Y., and Ferguson, R. (eds), *Twisted Sisters: Women, Crime and Deviance in Scotland Since 1400* (East Linton: Tuckwell Press, 2002), pp. 117–36.

Feeley, M., and D. Little, 'The Vanishing Female: the Decline of Women in the Criminal Process 1687–1912', *Law and Society Review* 25 (1991): 719–57.

Fido, Martin, and Keith Skinner, *The Official Encyclopedia of Scotland Yard* (London: Virgin, 1999).

Fielding, Henry, *An Enquiry into the Causes of the Late Increase of Robbers and Related Writings*, ed. Malvin R. Zirker (Oxford: Clarendon Press, 1988).

Fielding, John, *A Plan for Preventing Robberies within Twenty Miles of London, with an Account of the Rise and Establishment of the Real THIEFTAKERS* (London: A. Millar, 1755).

Fielding, Sir J. Jr, *et al.*, *The New London Spy; or a Modern Twenty-four Hour Ramble through the Great British Metropolis* (London: Alex Hogg, 1816).

First Report of the Commissioners appointed to inquire as to the best means of establishing an efficient Constabulary Force in the counties of England and Wales (169) (London: House of Commons, 1839).

Fitzgerald, P., *Chronicle of Bow Street Police Office: With an Account of the Magistrates, "Runners" and Police*, 2 volumes (London: Chapman & Hall, 1888 [reprinted as a one-volume book with an introduction by Anthony Babington and index: Montclair, NJ: Patterson Smith, 1972]).

Foss, Edward, *Biographia Juridica: A Biographical Dictionary of the Judges of England 1066–1870* (London: John Murray, 1870).

Foucault, Michel, *Discipline and Punish: the Birth of the Prison*, trans. Alan Sheridan (London: Penguin, 1991).

Frank, K., *Crusoe: Daniel Defoe, Robert Knox And The Creation Of A Myth* (London: Random House, 2011).

Friedman, David, 'Making Sense of English Law Enforcement in the Eighteenth Century', *The University of Chicago Law School Roundtable* 2.2 (1995): 475–505.

Fritz, Paul, and David Williams, *The Triumph of Culture: 18th Century Perspectives* (Toronto: A. M. Hakkert, 1972).

Frost, A., *The First Fleet – The Real Story* (Collingwood, Victoria: Blacks Inc., 2012).

Fumerton, P., *et al.* (eds) *Ballads and Broadsides in Britain, 1500–1800* (Farnham: Ashgate, 2010).

Galloway Brown, Yvonne, and Rona Ferguson (eds), *Twisted Sisters: Women, Crime and Deviance in Scotland Since 1400* (East Linton: Tuckwell Press, 2002).

Garland, David, *Punishment and Modern Society: A Study in Social Theory* (Oxford: OUP, 1997).

Gaskill, M., 'Reporting Murder: Fiction in the Archives in Early Modern England', *Social History* 23.1 (1998): 1–30.

Gaskill, Malcolm, *Crime and Mentalities in Early Modern England* (Cambridge: CUP, 2000).

Gatrell, V. A. C., *The Hanging Tree: Execution and the English People 1770–1868* (Oxford: OUP, 1996).

Gatrell, V. A. C., *et al.*, *Crime and the Law: A Social History of Crime in Western Europe since 1500* (London: Europa, 1980).

Gibson, Madge, *From Belbroughton to Botany Bay* (Belbroughton: Belbroughton History Society, 1987).

Gillet, Henry, *Guide to the Archives of the Bank of England*, 2nd edn (London: Bank of England, 2001).

Glasse, Samuel, *The Magistrates Assistant: or a Summary of those Laws which Immediately Respect the Conduct of the Justice of the Peace, by a County Magistrate* (Gloucester: R. Raikes, 1784).

Glassey, Lionel K. J., *Politics and the Appointment of Justices of the Peace, 1673–1720* (New York: OUP, 1979).

Goddard, Henry, *Memoirs* (4-volume manuscript, 1875–9).

Godfrey, Barry, and Paul Lawrence (eds), *Crime and Justice 1750–1950* (Cullompton: Willan, 2005).

Godfrey, Barry, and David J. Cox, 'The "Last Fleet": Crime, Reformation, and Punishment in Western Australia after 1868', *Australia and New Zealand Journal of Criminology* 1.2 (2008): 236–58.

Godfrey, Barry, and David J. Cox, *Policing the Factory: Theft, Private Policing and the Law in Modern England 1777–1968* (London: Bloomsbury Academic, 2013).

Godfrey, Barry, David J. Cox and Stephen Farrall, *Criminal Lives: Family Life, Employment, and Offending* (Oxford: OUP, 2007).

Godfrey, Barry, David J. Cox and Stephen Farrall, *Serious Offenders: A Historical Study of Habitual Offenders* (Oxford: OUP, 2010).

Godfrey, Barry, Helen Johnston and David J. Cox, *Victorian Convicts: 100 Criminal Lives* (Barnsley: Wharncliffe, forthcoming).

Golby, J., 'Newspapers', in Drake, M., Finegan, R. and Eustace, J. (eds), *Sources and Methods for Family and Community History: A Handbook*, Vol. 4 (Cambridge: CUP/OU, 1997), pp. 98–102.

Gowing, L., *The London Church Courts, 1572–1640* (London: University of London, 1993).

Gray, Drew, '"A well-constructed and efficient system of police?" Constables, substitutes and the watching systems in the City of London c.1750–1839' (paper given at European Centre for Policing Studies, Open University, July 2002).

Gray, Drew D., 'Summary Proceedings and Social Relations in the City of London, c.1750–1820' (unpublished PhD thesis, University of Northampton, 2007).

Gray, Drew D., 'The Regulation of Violence in the Metropolis; the Prosecution of Assault in the Summary Courts, c.1780–1820', *The London Journal* 32.1 (2007): 75–87.

Gray, Drew D., *Crime, Prosecution and Social Relations: The Summary Courts of the City of London in the Late Eighteenth Century* (Basingstoke: Palgrave Macmillan, 2009).

Green, Thomas Andrew, *Verdict According to Conscience: Perspectives of the English Criminal Trial Jury 1200–1800* (Chicago: University of Chicago Press, 1985).

Greenslade, M. W., and D. G. Stuart, *A History of Staffordshire*, 2nd edn (Chichester: Phillimore, 1998).

Gregory, Jeremy, and John Stevenson, *The Longman Companion to Britain in the Eighteenth Century* (London: Longman, 2000).

Griffin, Carl, 'Woodtaking and Customary Practice: William Hunt's Justice's Notebook 1744–49', *The Regional Historian* 13 (2005): 19–24.

Griffiths, A., *The History and Romance of Crime from the Earliest Time to the Present Day* (London: Grolier, 1900).

Grose, F., *et al.*, *Lexicon Balatronicum: A Dictionary of Buckish Slang, University Wit and Pickpocket Eloquence* (London: C. Chappel, 1811).

Gurney, J., *The trial of David Tyrie for High Treason at the Assize at Winchester on Saturday August 10 1782* (London: M. Gurney, 1782).

Guy, Kenneth (ed.), *New Letters of Robert Southey vol. 2 1811–38* (New York and London: Columbia University Press, 1965).

Haem, Mark, 'La Repression du Banditisme en Grande-Bretagne aux XVII ème et XVIII ème siècles', *Revue Du Nord* 59.234 (1977): 365–75.

Haining, Peter, *The English Highwayman: A Legend Unmasked* (London: Robert Hale, 1991).

Hair, P. (ed.), *Before the Bawdy Court: Selections from Church Court and Other Records Relating to the Correction of Moral Offences in England, Scotland and New England, 1300–1800* (New York: Barnes & Noble, 1972).

Hale, Sir Matthew, *History of the Pleas of the Crown*, 2 volumes (London: Payne, 1736).

Hall, Stuart, and Gregor McClennan, *Custom and Law: Law and Crime as Historical Processes* (Milton Keynes: Open University Press, 1981).

Hamby, James E., 'The History Of Firearm And Toolmark Identification', *Association of Firearm and Tool Mark Examiners Journal* 31.3 (1999): 266–84.

Hammond, J. L., and Barbara Hammond, *The Village Labourer 1760–1832: A Study in the Government of England before the Reform Bill*, 4th edn, 2 volumes (London: Guild Books, 1948).

Hammond, J. L., and Barbara Hammond, *The Town Labourer 1760–1832: The New Civilisation*, 2nd edn, 2 volumes (London: Guild Books, 1949).

Hammond, J. L., and Barbara Hammond, *The Skilled Labourer 1760–1832*, revised edn (London: Longman, 1979).

Harris, Andrew Todd, 'Policing the City, 1785–1838: Local Knowledge and Central Authority in the City of London (England)' (unpublished PhD thesis, Stanford University, 1997).

Hastings, R. P., 'Private Law-Enforcement Associations', *The Local Historian* 14.4 (1980): 226–31.

Hawkings, David T., *Criminal Ancestors: A Guide to Historical Criminal Records in England and Wales* (Stroud: Sutton Publishing, 1996).

Hawkings, David T., *Fire Insurance Records for Family and Local Historians 1696 to 1920* (London: Francis Boutle, 2003).

Hay, D., and F. Snyder (eds), *Policing and Prosecution in Britain, 1750–1850* (Oxford: OUP, 1989).

Hay, Douglas, 'Property, Authority and the Criminal Law', in Hay, D., *et al.*, *Albion's Fatal Tree: Crime and Society in Eighteenth-Century England* (London: Allen Lane, 1975), pp. 17–64.

Hay, Douglas, 'Crime and Justice in Eighteenth and Nineteenth Century England', *Crime and Justice: an annual review of research* 2 (1980): 45–84.

Hay, Douglas, 'War, Dearth and Theft in the Eighteenth Century: The Record of the English Courts', *Past and Present* 95 (1982): 117–60.

Hay, Douglas, 'Manufacturers and the Criminal Law in the Later Eighteenth Century: Crime and "Police" in South Staffordshire', *Past and Present Colloquium: Police and Policing* (1983), unpaginated.

Hay, Douglas, 'Dread of the Crown Office: The English Magistracy and Kings Bench 1740–1800', in Landau, N. (ed.), *Law, Crime and English Society 1660–1800* (Cambridge: CUP, 2002), pp. 19–45.

Hay, Douglas, *et al.*, *Albion's Fatal Tree: Crime and Society in Eighteenth-Century England* (London: Allen Lane, 1975).

Hayward, A. L. (ed.) *Lives Of The Most Remarkable Criminals Who have been Condemned and Executed for Murder, the Highway, Housebreaking, Street Robberies, Coining or other offences, Collected from Original Papers and Authentic Memoirs, and Published in 1735* (New York: n.p., 1927).

Hill, B., *Eighteenth-Century Women: An Anthology* (London: Allen & Unwin, 1984).

Hill, Brian, *The Early Parties and Politics in Britain, 1688–1832* (Basingstoke: Macmillan, 1996).

Hindle, Steve, *The State and Social Change in Early Modern England, c.1550–1640* (London: Macmillan, 2000).

Hippisley Coxe, Antony D., *A Book about Smuggling in the West Country 1700–1850* (Padstow: Tabb House, 1984).

Hitchcock, Tim, *Down and Out in Eighteenth-Century London* (London: Hambledon, 2004).

Hitchcock, Tim, Robert Shoemaker, Clive Emsley, Sharon Howard, Jamie McLaughlin *et al.*, *The Old Bailey Proceedings Online, 1674–1913* available at www.oldbaileyonline.org

Hitchcock, Tim, Robert Shoemaker, Sharon Howard, Jamie McLaughlin *et al.*, *London Lives, 1690–1800* available at www.londonlives.org

Holdsworth, William, *The History of English Law*, 16 vols (London: Methuen, 1903–66).

Hopkins, Harry, *The Long Affray: The Poaching Wars 1760–1914* (London: Secker & Warburg, 1985).

Hostettler, John, *A History of Criminal Justice in England and Wales* (Hook: Waterside Press, 2009).

Howell, T. J., *Howell's State Trials*, Vol. XXIV (1794) (London: Longman, 1818).

Howson, G., *Thief-taker General: Jonathan Wild and the Emergence of Crime and Corruption as a Way of Life in Eighteenth-Century England* (New Brunswick, NJ: Transaction Publishers, 1985).

Hufton, Olwen, *The Prospect Before Her: A History of Women in Western Europe, volume one 1500–1800* (London: HarperCollins, 1995).

Hughes, Robert, *The Fatal Shore* (London: Collins/Harvell, 1987).

Hunt, Joseph (ed.), 'Bombelles in Britain: The Diary kept by a French Diplomat during a Visit to Midlands England 1784', trans. L. E. Page (unpublished material, 2000).

Ingram, M., *Church Courts, Sex and Marriage in England, 1570–1640* (Cambridge: CUP, 1990).

Innes, J., 'Parliament and the Shaping of Eighteenth Century English Social Policy', *Transactions of the Royal Society* 5th series XL (1990): 63–92.

Innes, J., and J. Styles, 'The Crime Wave: Recent Writing on Crime and Criminal Justice in Eighteenth-Century England', *Journal of British Studies* 25 (1986): 380–435.

Inwood, Stephen, *A History of London* (London: Macmillan, 1998).

James, P. D., and T. Critchley, *The Maul and the Pear Tree: The Ratcliff Highway Murders 1811* (London: Faber & Faber, 2000).

Jenkins, David, and Takau Yoneyama (eds), *The History of Insurance*, 8 volumes (London: Pickering and Chatto, 2000).

Jenkins, Philip, 'From Gallows to Prison? The Execution Rate in Early Modern England', *Criminal Justice History* 7 (1986): 51–72.

Jenkins, Philip, *A History of Modern Wales 1536–1990* (London: Longman, 1992).

Jennings, Paul, 'Liquor Licensing and the Local Historian: Inns and Alehouses 1753–1828', *The Local Historian* 40.2 (2010): 136–50.

Jerrard, Bryan, 'Early Policing in Gloucestershire', *Transactions of the Bristol and Gloucestershire Archaeological Society for 1992* C (1993): 221–40.

Johnson, W. H., *Previous Offences: Sussex Crimes and Punishments in the Past* (Seaford: SB Publications, 1997).

Jones, David J. V., *Before Rebecca: Popular Protests in Wales 1793–1835* (London: Allen Lane, 1973).

Jones, D. J. V., *Crime in Nineteenth Century Wales* (Cardiff: University of Wales Press, 1992).

Jones, David J. V., 'The Poacher: A Study in Victorian Crime and Punishment', *Historical Journal* XXII (1974): 825–60.

Kent, Joan, *The English Village Constable 1580–1642: A Social and Administrative Study* (Oxford: OUP, 1986).

Kenyon, J. P., *The Stuart: A Study in English Kingship* (London: Fontana, 1970).

Kercher, Bruce, 'Perish or Prosper: The Law and Convict Transportation in the British Empire, 1700–1850', *Law and History Review* 21.3 (2003): 527–84.

Kermode, J., and G. Walker (eds), *Women, Crime and the Courts in Early Modern England* (Chapel Hill, NC: University of North Carolina, 1995).

Kilday, Anne-Marie, and David Nash (eds), *Histories of Crime: 1600–2000* (Basingstoke: Palgrave Macmillan, 2010).

King, Peter, 'Decision Makers and Decision Making in the English Criminal Law 1750–1800', *Historical Journal* XXVII (1984): 25–58.

King, Peter, 'Newspaper Reporting, Prosecution Practice and Perceptions of Urban Crime: the Colchester Crime Wave of 1765', *Continuity & Change* 2.3 (1987): 423–54.

King, Peter, 'Locating Histories of Crime: A Bibliographic Study', *British Journal of Criminology* 39.1 (1999): 161–74.

King, Peter, *Crime, Justice, and Discretion in England 1740–1820* (Oxford: OUP, 2000).

King, Peter, *Crime and Law in England, 1750–1840: Remaking Justice from the Margins* (Cambridge: CUP, 2006).

King, Peter, 'Newspaper Reporting and Attitudes to Crime and Justice in Late-Eighteenth- and Early-Nineteenth-century London', *Continuity and Change* 22.1 (2007): 73–112.

Landau, Norma, *The Justices of the Peace 1679–1760* (Berkeley: University of California, 1984).

Landau, Norma (ed.), *Law, Crime and English Society 1660–1830* (Cambridge: CUP, 2002).

Langbein, J. H., *The Origins of Adversarial Criminal Trial* (Oxford: OUP, 2003).

Langbein, John, 'Criminal Trials before the Lawyers', *University of Chicago Law Review* 45.2 (1978): 263–316.

Langbein, John, '*Albion*'s Fatal Flaws', *Past and Present* 98 (1983): 96–120.

Langbein, John, 'Shaping the Eighteenth-Century Criminal Trial: A View from the Ryder Sources', *University of Chicago Law Review* 50.1 (1983): 1–136.

Langford, P., *Public Life and the Propertied Englishman 1689–1798* (Oxford: Clarendon Press, 1994).

Lawson, P. G., 'Property Crime and Hard Times in England, 1559–1624', *Law & History Review* 4 (1986): 95–127.

Lawson, P. G., 'Lawless Juries? The Composition and Behaviour of Hertfordshire Juries, 1573–1624', in Cockburn, J. S., and Green, Thomas A. (eds), *Twelve Good Men and True: The Criminal Trial Jury in England, 1200–1800* (Princeton: PUP, 1988), pp. 117–57.

Lea, John, 'Social Crime Revisited', *Theoretical Criminology* 3.3 (1999): 307–25.

Leigh, Samuel, *Leigh's New Picture of London* (London: W. Clowes, 1819).

Lemmings, D., *Professors of the Law: Barristers and English Legal Culture in the Eighteenth Century* (Oxford: OUP, 2000).

Leslie-Melville, A. R., *The Life and Works of Sir John Fielding* (London: Lincoln & Williams, 1935).

Linebaugh, Peter, 'The Ordinary of Newgate and his Account', in Cockburn, J. S. (ed.), *Crime in England 1550–1800* (London: Methuen, 1977), pp. 246–69.

Linebaugh, Peter, *The London Hanged* (London: Allen Lane, 1991).

Linebaugh, Peter, 'A Reply to Professor Langbein', in Weiss, R. P. (ed.), *Social History of Crime, Policing and Punishment* (Aldershot: Ashgate, 1999), pp. 55–88.

Linnane, Fergus, *London's Underworld: Three Centuries of Vice and Crime* (London: Robson Books, 2003).

Linnell, C. D. (ed.), *Diary of Benjamin Rogers, Rector of Carlton 1720–1771* (Bedford: Bedfordshire Historical Record Society, 1950).

Little, Craig B., and Christopher P. Sheffield, 'Frontiers of Criminal Justice: English Private Prosecution Societies and American Vigilantism in the Eighteenth and Nineteenth Centuries', *American Sociological Review* 48 (1983): 796–808.

Livingstone, Sheila, *Confess and be Hanged: Scottish Crime & Punishment Through the Ages* (Edinburgh: Birlinn, 2000).

Lock, Joan, *Marlborough Street: The Story of a London Court* (London: Robert Hale, 1980).

Lowndes, T., *The London Directory for the Year 1780. Containing an Alphabetical List of Names and Places of Abode of the Merchants and Principal Traders of the City of London*, 15th edn (London: T. Lowndes, 1780).

McCalman, I. (ed.), *Oxford Companion to the Romantic Age: British Culture 1776–1832* (Oxford: OUP, 2001).

Macaulay, T. B., *The History of England from the Accession of James the Second in Five Volumes*, Vol. II [originally printed 1848] (New York: Cosimo, 1999).

McConville, Sean, *A History of English Prison Administration*, Vol. 1 (London: Routledge & Kegan Paul, 1981).

Macfarlane, Alan, *The Justice and the Mare's Ale: Law and Disorder in Seventeenth-century England* (Oxford: Basil Blackwell, 1981).

McGowen, Randall, 'The Bank of England and the Policing of Forgery, 1797–1821' (paper given 28 November 2003, European Centre for Policing Studies, Open University).

McGowen, Randall, 'The Bank of England and the Policing of Forgery 1797–1821', *Past and Present* 186 (2005): 81–116.

McGowen, Randall, 'Managing the Gallows: The Bank of England and the Death Penalty, 1797–1821', *Law and History Review* 25.2 (2007): 241–82.

McGowen, Randall, 'Forgery and the Twelve Judges in Eighteenth-Century England', *Law & History Review* 29.1 (2011): 221–57.

MacKay, Lynn, 'Refusing the Royal Pardon: London Capital Convicts and the Reactions of the Courts and Press, 1789', *London Journal* 28.2 (2003): 21–40.

MacKay, Peter, '"The Foundation of a Professional Police Force was Historically Inevitable"', *Police Studies* 10.2 (1987): 85–9.

MacKay, Peter, 'Class Relationships, Social Order and the Law in Eighteenth-century England', *Police Studies* 11.2 (1988): 92–7.

Mckenzie, Andrea, '"This Death Some Strong and Stout Hearted Man Doth Choose": The Practice of *Peine Forte et Dure* in Seventeenth- and Eighteenth-Century England', *Law and History Review* 23.2 (2005): 279–313.

McLynn, Frank, *Crime and Punishment in Eighteenth-century England* (London: Routledge, 1989).

McMahon, Richard (ed.), *Crime, Law and Popular Culture in Europe, 1500–1900* (Cullompton: Willan, 2008).

McMahon, Vanessa, *Murder in Shakespeare's England* (London: Hambledon & London, 2004).

McMullan, John L., 'Crime, Law and Order in Early Modern England', in *British Journal of Criminology* 27 (1987): 252–74.

McMullan, John L., 'The Political Economy of Thief-taking', *Crime, Law and Social Change* 23.2 (1995): 121–46.

Manchester, A. H., *Sources of English Legal History: Law, History and Society in England and Wales, 1750–1950* (London: Butterworth, 1984).

Mander, G. P., 'The Wolverhampton "Association"', *The Wolverhampton Antiquary* 11.1 (1934): 60–63.

Marston, Edward, *Prison: five hundred years of life behind bars* (Kew: National Archives, 2009).

Martin, Randall (ed.), *Women and Murder in Early Modern News Pamphlets and Broadside Ballads, 1573–1697* (Farnham: Ashgate, 2005).

Maxwell-Stewart, H., and R. Kippen, 'Morbidity and Mortality on Convict Voyages to Australia', available at www.hsmt.history.ox.ac.uk/ecohist/seminars/Papers2011–12/Morbidy_Mortality_atsea.pdf

Means, C., 'Pleading the Belly 1387–1931. The Phoenix of Abortional Freedom: Is a Penumbral or Ninth-Amendment Right about to Arise from the Nineteenth-century Legislative Ashes of a Fourteenth-century Common-law Liberty?', *New York Law Forum* 17 (1971): 335–410.

Midland Mining Commission: First Report South Staffordshire (508) (London: HMSO, 1843).

Moore, L., *Con Men and Cutpurses: Scenes from the Hogarthian Underworld* (Harmondsworth: Penguin, 2001).

Morgan, Gwenda, and Peter Rushton, *Rogues, Thieves and the Rule of Law: The Problem of Law Enforcement in North-east England, 1718–1800* (London: UCL Press, 1998).

Morgan, Gwenda, and Peter Rushton, 'The Magistrate, the Community and the Maintenance of an Orderly Society in Eighteenth-century England', *Historical Research* 76.191 (2003): 54–77.

Morgan, Gwenda, and Peter Rushton. 'Running Away and Returning Home: The Fate of English Convicts in the American Colonies', *Crime, Histoire & Sociétiés/Crime, History & Societies* 7.2 (2003): 61–80.

Morris, Robert M., '"Lies, Damned Lies and Criminal Statistics": Reinterpreting the Criminal Statistics in England and Wales', *Crime, Histoire & Sociétés* 5.1 (2001): 111–27.

Morrison, Kathryn, *The Workhouse: A Study of Poor-Law Buildings in England* (London: Royal Commission on the Historical Monuments of England, 1999).

Munsche, P. B., 'The Gamekeeper and English Rural Society', *Journal of British Studies* XX.2 (1981): 82–105.

Munsche, P. B., *Gentlemen and Poachers: The English Game Laws 1671–1831* (Cambridge: CUP, 1981).

Murphy, Brian, *A History of the British Economy 1740–1970* (London: Longman, 1973).

Nelson, R. R., *The Home Office 1782–1801* (Durham, NC: Duke University Press, 1969).

Newburn, Tim, and P. Neyroud (eds), *Dictionary of Policing* (Cullompton: Willan Publishing, 2008).

Newman, Gerald (ed.), *Britain in the Hanoverian Age 1714–1837* (New York and London: Garland Publishing Inc., 1997).

Norton, Rictor, *Mother Clap's Molly House: The Gay Subculture in England, 1700–1830* (Stroud: History Press, 2006).

Norton, Rictor (ed.), *Homosexuality in Eighteenth-Century England: A Sourcebook*, available at www.rictornorton.co.uk/eighteen/

Novak, M., 'Daniel Defoe and *Applebee's Original Weekly Journal*: An Attempt at Re-Attribution', *Eighteenth-Century Studies* 45.4 (2012): 585–608.

O'Connell, Sheila, *The Popular Print in England 1580–1850* (London: British Museum Press, 1999).

Oldham, James, 'Informal Lawmaking in England by the Twelve Judges in the Late Eighteenth and Early Nineteenth Centuries', in *Law & History Review* 29.1 (2011): 181–220.

Osborne, Bertram, *Justices of the Peace 1361–1848: A History of the Justices of the Peace for the Counties of England* (Shaftesbury: The Sedgehill Press, 1960).

Outhwaite, R. B., *Dearth, Public Policy and Social Disturbance in England, 1550–1800* (Cambridge: CUP, 1995).

Paley, Ruth, 'The Middlesex Justices Act of 1792: Its Origins and Effects' (unpublished PhD thesis, Reading, 1983).

Paley, Ruth, '"An Imperfect, Inadequate and Wretched System"? Policing London Before Peel', *Criminal Justice History* X (1989): 95–130.

Paley, Ruth, 'Thief-takers in London in the Age of the McDaniel Gang c.1745–1754', in Hay, D., and Snyder, F. (eds), *Policing and Prosecution in Britain, 1750–1850* (Oxford: Clarendon, 1989), pp. 301–41.

Paley, Ruth (ed.), *Justice in Eighteenth-century Hackney – The Justicing Notebook of Henry Norris and the Hackney Petty Sessions Book* (London: London Record Society, 1991).

Paley, Ruth, and Simon Fowler, *Family Skeletons: Exploring the Lives of our Disreputable Ancestors* (Kew: National Archives, 2005).

Palk, Deirdre, *Gender, Crime and Judicial Discretion 1780–1830* (Woodbridge: The Royal Historical Society/Boydell Press, 2006).

Palmer, Stanley H., *Police and Protest in England and Ireland 1780–1850* (London: Longman, 1992).

Pearce, C. J., *Cornish Wrecking, 1700–1860: Reality and Popular Myth* (Woodbridge: The Boydell Press, 2010).

Philips, David, 'Good Men to Associate and Bad Men to Conspire: Associations for the Prosecution of Felons in England 1760–1860', in Hay, D., and Snyder, F. (eds), *Policing and Prosecution in Britain, 1750–1850* (Oxford: Clarendon, 1989), pp. 113–70.

Philips, David, and Robert Storch, *Policing Provincial England 1829–1856: The Politics of Reform* (Leicester: Leicester University Press, 1999).

Phillipson, David, *Smuggling: A History 1700–1970* (Newton Abbot: David & Charles, 1973).

Pickering, Danby, *The Statutes at Large from the 23rd to the 26th Year of King George II*, Statute 26 Geo. II c.19 (London and Cambridge: Joseph Bentham, 1765).

Porter, J. H., *Common Crime, Law and Policing in the English Countryside 1600–1800* (Exeter: University of Exeter, Brookfield Papers no. 2, 1989).

Pote, J., *The Foreigner's Guide: or, a Necessary and Instructive Companion both for the Foreigner and Native in their Tour through the Cities of London and Westminster* (London: J. Jolliffe, 1740).

Pringle, Patrick, *Hue & Cry: The Birth of the British Police* (London: Museum Press, 1956).

Pringle, Patrick, *The Thief Takers* (London: Museum Press, 1958).

Quinault, R., and J. Stevenson (eds), *Popular Protest and Public Order: Six Studies in British History 1790–1920* (London: Allen and Unwin, 1974).

Radzinowicz, L., *A History of English Criminal Law and its Administration from 1750*, Vol. 1 (London: Stevens & Sons, 1948).

Radzinowicz, L., *A History of English Criminal Law and its Administration from 1750*, Vol. 2 (London: Stevens & Sons, 1956).

Radzinowicz, L., *A History of English Criminal Law and its Administration from 1750*, Vol. 3 (London: Stevens & Sons, 1956).

Randall, A., 'Peculiar Perquisites and Pernicious Practices. Embezzlement in the West of England Woollen Industry, c.1750–1840', *International Review of Social History* 35 (1992): 193–219.

Rawlings, Philip, *Crime and Power: A History of Criminal Justice* (London: Longman, 1999).

Rawlings, Philip, *Policing: A Short History* (Cullompton: Willan, 2002).

Rayner, Tony, *Female Factory Female Convicts* (Dover, Tasmania: Esperance Press, 2005).

Reay, Barry (ed.), *Popular Culture in Seventeenth-Century England* (London: Routledge, 1985).

Reay, Barry, *Popular Cultures in England 1550–1750* (London: Longman, 1998).

Reed, Mick, and Roger Wells (eds), *Class, Conflict and Protest in the English Countryside* (London: Frank Cass, 1990).

Reid, R., *The Peterloo Massacre* (London: Heinemann, 1989).

Reiner, Robert, *The Politics of the Police*, 4th edn (Oxford: OUP, 2010).

Reith, Charles, *A Short History of the British Police* (Oxford: OUP, 1948).

Report from the Committee on the state of Police of the Metropolis (510) (London: House of Commons, 1816).

Reports from Committees of the House of Commons vol. XIII Finance Reports XXIII to XXXVI 1803, containing Twenty-eighth Report from the Select Committee on Finance: Police, including Convict Establishments 1798 (London: House of Commons, 1803).

Reynolds, Elaine A., 'The Night Watch and Police Reform in Metropolitan London' (unpublished PhD thesis, Cornell University, 1991).

Reynolds, Elaine A., *Before the Bobbies: The Night Watch and Police Reform in Metropolitan London: 1720–1830* (Basingstoke: Macmillan, 1998).

Richardson, Ruth, *Death, Dissection and the Destitute* (London: Routledge & Kegan Paul, 1987).

Ritson, Joseph, *In the Office of Constable* (London: Whieldon & Butterworth, 1791).

Roberts, Randy, 'Eighteenth-Century Boxing', *Journal of Sport History* 4.3 (1977): 246–59.

Roberts, Richard, and David Kynaston (eds), *The Bank of England: Money, Power and Influence 1694–1994* (Oxford: Clarendon Press, 1995).

Roberts, Stephen K., 'Juries and the Middling Sort: Recruitment and Performance at Devon Quarter Sessions, 1649–1670', in Cockburn, J. S., and Green, Thomas A. (eds), *Twelve Good Men and True: The Criminal Trial Jury in England, 1200–1800* (Princeton: PUP, 1988), pp. 182–213.

Robinson, Cyril D., 'Ideology as History: A Look at the Way some English Police Historians look at the Police', *Police Studies* 2.2 (1979): 35–49.

Rogers, N., *Mayhem: Post-War Crime and Violence in Britain, 1748–53* (Yale: YUP, 2013).

Rudé, George, *Criminal and Victim: Crime and Society in Early Nineteenth-century England* (Oxford: Clarendon Press, 1985).

Rudé, George, *The Crowd in History: A Study of Popular Disturbances in France and England 1730–1848* (London: Serif, 1995).

Rule, John, 'Food Riots in England 1792–1818', in Quinault, R. and Stevenson, J. (ed.), *Popular Protest and Public Order: Six Studies in British History 1790–1920* (London: Allen and Unwin, 1974), pp. 37–74.

Rule, John, 'Social Crime in the Rural South in the Eighteenth and Early Nineteenth Century', *Southern History* 1 (1979): 35–53.

Rule, John, *Albion's People: English Society, 1714–1815* (London: Macmillan, 1992).

Rule, John, and Roger Wells, *Crime, Protest and Popular Politics in Southern England 1740–1850* (London: Hambledon Press, 1997).

Rumbelow, Donald, *I Spy Blue: The Police and Crime in the City of London from Elizabeth I to Victoria* (London and Basingstoke: Macmillan St Martin's Press, 1971).

Sainty, J., *The Judges of England 1272–1990: a list of judges of the superior courts* (London: Selden Soc. Supp. Series X, 1993).

Salgādo, Gāmini, *The Elizabethan Underworld* (Stroud: Sutton, 2005).

Salmon, T., *The Complete Collection of State-trials, and Proceedings for High-treason, and other Crimes and Misdemeanours: From the Reign of King Richard II to the end of the Reign of King George I*, Vol. I (London: J. Walthoe, 1730).

Samaha, J., *Law and Order in Historical Perspective. The case of Elizabethan Essex* (New York: Academic Press, 1974).

Saxon, Kirsten T., *Narratives of Women and Murder in England* (Farnham: Ashgate, 2009).

Sayer, Edward, *Observations on the Police or Civil Government of Westminster with a Proposal for Reform* (London: Debrett, 1784).

Shakesheff, Timothy, *Rural Conflict, Crime and Protest Herefordshire, 1800–1860* (Woodbridge: Boydell Press, 2003).

Sharpe, J. A., *Crime in Seventeenth-century England: A County Study* (Cambridge: CUP, 1983).

Sharpe, J. A., 'Policing the Parish in Early Modern England', *Past and Present Colloquium: Police and Policing* (1983), unpaginated.

Sharpe, J. A., *Crime in Early Modern England 1550–1750* (London: Longman, 1984).

Sharpe, J. A., *Crime and the Law in English Satirical Prints 1600–1832* (Cambridge: Chadwyck-Healey, 1986).

Sharpe, J., *Dick Turpin: The Myth of the English Highwayman* (London: Profile, 2004).

Shaw, A. G. L., *Convicts and Colonies: A Study of Penal Transportation from Great Britain and Ireland to Australia and other parts of the British Empire*, 2nd edn (London: Faber, 1971).

Sheppard, Francis, *London 1808–1870: The Infernal Wen* (London: Secker & Warburg, 1971).

Sheridan, T. (ed.), *The Works of the Rev. Dr Jonathan Swift in 17 Volumes*, Vol. 15 (London: Bathurst *et al.*, 1784).

Shoemaker, Robert B., 'The "Crime Wave" Revisited: Crime, Law Enforcement and Punishment in Britain, 1650–1900', *The Historical Journal* 34.3 (1991): 763–8.

Shoemaker, Robert B., 'The Decline of Male Honour and Public Violence in Eighteenth-Century London', *Social History* 26.2 (2001): 190–208.

Shoemaker, Robert B., 'The Taming of the Duel: Masculinity, Honour and Ritual Violence in London, 1660–1800', *The Historical Journal* 45.3 (2002): 525–45.

Shoemaker, Robert B., *The London Mob: Violence and Disorder in Eighteenth-century England* (London: Hambledon and London, 2004).

Shore, Heather, *Artful Dodgers: Youth and Crime in Early Nineteenth-century London* (London: Royal Historical Society/Boydell Press, 1999).

Shubert, Adrian, 'Private Initiative in Law Enforcement: Associations for the Prosecution of Felons, 1744–1856' in Bailey, V. (ed.), *Policing and Punishment in Nineteenth-Century Britain* (Piscataway, NJ: Rutgers University Press, 1981), pp. 25–41.

Skyrme, Thomas, *History of the Justices of the Peace*, 2nd edn (Chichester: Barry Rose Publishers, 1994).

Smith, A. E., *Colonists in Bondage: White Servitude and Convict Labor in America, 1607–1776* (New York: Norton, 1971).

Smith, Bruce P., 'English Criminal Justice Administration, 1650–1850: A Historiographic Essay', *Law and History Review* 25.1 (2007): 593–634.

Smith, William and Anon., *A History of New-York, from the First Discovery to the Year 1732: With a Continuation, from the Year 1732, to the Commencement of the Year 1814* (Albany, NY: Ryer Schermerhorn, 1814).

Snell, Esther, 'Attitudes to Violent Crime in Post-Restoration England' (unpublished thesis, Canterbury University, 2005).

Snell, Esther, 'Representations of Crime in the Eighteenth-century Newspaper: The Construction of Crime Reportage in the Kentish Post' (paper delivered at the European Centre for Policing Studies, Open University, Milton Keynes, March 2005).

Snell, Esther, 'Discourses of Criminality in the Eighteenth-century Press: The Presentation of Crime in *The Kentish Post*, 1717–1768', *Continuity and Change* 22.1 (2007): 13–47.

Soderlund, R., '"For the Protection of Manufacturer's Property": Policing the Workplace in the Yorkshire Worsted Industry in the Age of Liberal Capitalism, 1810–45' (paper given to the annual meeting of the North American Labour History Conference 1993).

Solmes, Alwyn, *The English Policeman 871–1935* (London: Allen & Unwin, 1935).

Southey, Robert, *Southey's Common Place book (Fourth Series): Original Memoranda etc.* (London: Longman, Brown, Green and Longman, 1851).

Spragg, Gillian, *Outlaws and Highwaymen: The Cult of the Robber in England from the Middle Ages to the Nineteenth Century* (London: Pimlico, 2001).

Standley, A. J., *Stafford Gaol: The Chronological Story* (Stafford: Standley, 1990).

Starkie, T., *A Treatise on Criminal Pleading: With Precedents of Indictments, Special Pleas etc.*, Vol. 2 (London: J. & W. T. Clarke, 1822).

Stephen, J. F., *A History of the Criminal Law of England*, 3 volumes (London: Macmillan, 1883).

Stevenson, John, *Popular Disturbances in England 1700–1832*, 2nd edn (London: Longman, 1992).

Stone, Lawrence, 'Interpersonal Violence in English Society, 1300–1980', *Past and Present* 101 (1983): 22–33.

Stuart, Denis, *Latin for Local and Family Historians* (Chichester: Phillimore, 1995).

Styles, John, 'An Eighteenth-Century Magistrate as Detective: Samuel Lister of Little Horton', *Bradford Antiquary* New Series XLVII (1982): 98–117.

Styles, John, 'Sir John Fielding and the Problem of Criminal Investigation in Eighteenth-century England', *Transactions of the Royal Historical Society* Fifth Series 33 (1983): 127–49.

Styles, John, 'The Emergence of the Police: Explaining Police Reform in Eighteenth and Nineteenth Century England', *British Journal of Criminology* 27.1 (1987): 15–22.

Sullivan, Shane, 'Law and Informal Order: Informal Mechanisms of Justice in Kent, 1700–1880' (unpublished PhD thesis, Canterbury, 2005).

Sullivan, Shane, 'The Newspaper Apology as a Secular Penance 1768–1820' (paper delivered at the European Centre for Policing Studies, Open University, October 2005).

Sutton, James, 'The Staffordshire Society for the Apprehension of Felons', *Staffordshire Studies* 14 (2002): 32–52.

Swift, R., 'The English Magistracy Past and Present', in Cox, David J., and Godfrey, B. (eds), *Cinderellas & Packhorses: A History of the Shropshire Magistracy* (Almeley: Logaston Press, 2005), pp. 1–12.

Swift, Roger E., 'The English Urban Magistracy and the Administration of Justice during the early nineteenth century: Wolverhampton, 1815–60', *Midland History* XVII (1992): 75–93.

Tarver, Anne, 'English Church Courts and their Records', *The Local Historian* 38.1 (2008): 4–22.

Taylor, Howard, 'Rationing Crime: The Political Economy of Criminal Statistics since the 1850s', *Economic History Review* 51.3 (1998): 569–90.

Third Report from the Committee on the state of Police of the Metropolis (423) (London: House of Commons, 1817).

Thomas, K., *Religion and the Decline of Magic: Studies in Popular Belief in Sixteenth and Seventeenth Century England* (Harmondsworth: Penguin, 2003).

Thompson, E. P., *Whigs and Hunters: The Origins of the Black Act* (London: Pantheon, 1975).

Thompson, E. P., *The Making of the English Working Class* (Harmondsworth: Penguin, 1991).

Thompson, F. M. L., *Social Agencies and Institutions*, Vol. 3, *The Cambridge Social History of Britain 1750–1950* (Cambridge: CUP, 1996).

Thornhill, Robert (ed.), *A Village Constable's Accounts (1791–1839)* (Derby: Derbyshire Archaeological and Natural History Society, 1957).

Thurmond, J., *Harlequin Sheppard. A Night Scene in Grotesque Characters: as it is Perform'd at the Theatre-Royal in Drury-Lane. By John Thurmond* (London: Roberts and Dodd, 1724).

Tilly, Charles, *Popular Contention in Great Britain 1758–1834* (Cambridge, MA: HUP, 1995).

Tilly, Charles, 'The Rise of the Public Meeting in Great Britain, 1768–1834', *Social Science History* 34.3 (2010): 291–300.

Tobias, J. J., *Crime and Police in England 1700–1900* (Dublin: Gill & Macmillan, 1979).

Treasure, Geoffrey, *Who's Who in Early Hanoverian Britain* (London: Shepheard-Walwyn, 1991).

Treasure, Geoffrey, *Who's Who in Late Hanoverian Britain* (London: Shepheard-Walwyn, 1997).

Trench, Charles Chenevix, *The Poacher and the Squire: A History of Poaching and Game Preservation in England* (London: Longmans, 1967).

Turner, David M., *Fashioning Adultery: Gender, Sex and Civility in England, 1660–1740* (Cambridge: CUP, 2002).

Turner, Michael J., *The Age of Unease: Government and Reform in Britain, 1782–1832* (Thrupp: Sutton, 2000).

Vaughan, M., and David J. Cox, *From Belbroughton to Botany Bay: The story of a Worcestershire girl's transportation to Australia on the First Fleet and her life in the new colony* (Kingswinford: Dulston Press/Belbroughton History Society, 2013).

Vaver, A., *Bound with an Iron Chain: The Untold Story of How the British Transported 50,000 Convicts to Colonial America* (Westborough, MA: Pickpocket Publishing, 2011).

Vaver, Anthony, *Convict Transportation from Great Britain to the American Colonies* (Westborough, MA: Early American Crime.com, 2009).

Verney, Sir Lawrence, 'The Office of Recorder of the City of London' (paper delivered at the Guildhall, 30 October 2000).

Vogler, Richard, *Reading the Riot Act: The Magistracy, the Police and the Army in Civil Disorder* (Milton Keynes: Open University Press, 1991).

Wade, John, *A Treatise on the Police and Crimes of the Metropolis*, introduction by J. J. Tobias (Montclair, NJ: Patterson Smith, 1972 [original published 1829]).

Walker, Garthine, *Crime, Gender and Social Order in Early Modern England* (Cambridge: CUP, 2003).

Wall, David S., 'The Organisation of Police 1829–2000', in Stallion, M., and Wall, D. S., *The British Police: Police Forces and Chief Officers 1829–2000* (Hook: Police History Society, 1999), pp. 1–31.

Waters, Les, 'Paper Pursuit: A Brief Account of the History of the Police Gazette', *Journal of the Police History Society* 1 (1986): 30–41.

Waters, Les, 'The Bow Street Runners: A Handbook of Police in London working for Bow Street and the other Middlesex Justices Act Offices 1750–1839', unpublished work for Police History Society, undated c.1992.

Waugh, Mary, *Smuggling in Kent & Sussex 1700–1840* (Newbury: Countryside Books, 1985).

Webb, S., and B. Webb, *English Poor Law Part 1 – The Old Poor Law* (London: Cass, 1963).

Webb, S., and B. Webb, *English Local Government vol. 1: The Parish and the County* (London: Frank Cass & Co., 1963).

Weiss, Robert P. (ed.), *Social History of Crime, Policing and Punishment* (Aldershot: Ashgate, 1999).

Weisser, Michael R., *Crime and Punishment in Early Modern Europe* (Hassocks: Harvester Press, 1979).

Wells, Roger, *Insurrection: The British Experience 1795–1803* (Gloucester: Alan Sutton, 1983).

Wells, Roger A. E., *Riot and Political Disaffection in Nottinghamshire in the Age of Revolutions, 1776–1803* (Nottingham: University of Nottingham, 1983).

Wheeler-Holohan, V., *The History of the King's Messengers* (London: E. P. Dutton, 1935).

Willcocks, R. M., *England's Postal History to 1840* (London: the author, 1975).

Williams, Raymond, 'The Press and Popular Culture: An Historical Perspective', in Boyce, G. *et al.*, *Newspaper History from the Seventeenth Century to the Present Day* (London: Constable, 1978), pp. 41–50.

Willis-Bund, J. W. (ed.), *Victoria County History of Worcestershire*, Vol. 4 (London: St Catherine Press, 1924).

Wilsher, Peter, *The Pound in Your Pocket 1870–1970* (London: Cassell, 1970).

Wilson, Ben, *Decency and Disorder: The Age of Cant 1789–1837* (London: Faber & Faber, 2007).

Wollstonecraft, Mary, *A Vindication of the Rights of Woman: With Strictures on Political and Moral Subjects* (Boston: Peter Edes, 1792).

Woolrych, H. W., *Lives of Eminent Serjeants-at-Law of the English Bar*, 2 volumes (London: W. Allen, 1869, reprinted Law Book Exchange, 2002).

Wright, Brian, *Insurance Fire Brigades 1680–1929: The Birth of the British Fire Service* (Stroud: Tempus, 2008).

Wrightson, Keith, *English Society 1580–1680* (London: Routledge, 1982).

Wroughton, John, *The Stuart Age, 1603–1714* (London: Routledge, 2006).

Wyatt, Irene (ed.), *Calendar of Summary Convictions at Petty Sessions 1781–1837* [Gloucestershire Record Series vol. 22] (Gloucester: Bristol and Gloucestershire Archaeological Society, 2008).

Yetter, Leigh (ed.), *Public Execution in England, 1573–1868* Part I, Vol. 3 (London: Pickering & Chatto, 2009).

Index